A Likely Lad

*The life of Norman Lesser,
Archbishop of New Zealand*

Judy Mills

Philip
Garside
Publishing Ltd.

Copyright © 2020 Judy Mills
All rights reserved.

This book or any portion thereof may not be reproduced or used in any manner whatsoever without the express written permission of the publisher except for the use of brief quotations in a book review.

Email Judy at
judymills9@gmail.com

Assistance with the publication of this book from the Diocese of Waiapu is gratefully acknowledged.

International Print edition 2020
ISBN: 978-1-98-857235-2

Philip Garside Publishing Ltd
PO Box 17160
Wellington 6147
New Zealand

bookspgpl@gmail.com — www.pgpl.co.nz

PDF, Kindle and ePub editions also available

Front cover and other photographs:
Kindly supplied by Elisabeth Paterson, Waiapu Diocesan Archives and the John Kinder Theological Library.
Author photograph by Mike Hughes.

Contents

Foreword 5
Preface 6
Acknowledgements 7
Chapter 1: England 9
Chapter 2: Kenya 26
Chapter 3: New Zealand 38
Chapter 4: Māori Matters 55
Chapter 5: Faith and Finance 74
Chapter 6: Cathedral Re-building 91
Chapter 7: Church Union 112
Chapter 8: Change in Church and Society 129
Chapter 9: The Province and Beyond 150
Chapter 10: Bishop and Man of Many Parts 171
Chapter 11: Retirement 198
References & Abbreviations 215
Appendix: Writings, Sermons & Addresses 217
    Poems and Hymns 217
    Selection of Poems published in *Hear, Here!* 1971 219
    Pastoral letters to Clergy – Excerpts 221
    Synod Addresses: Diocesan 230
    General Synod Addresses 245
    Miscellaneous Letters, Articles, Messages: 248
    The Spoken Word:
        Extracts from Sermons, Speeches, Addresses 263
    Humour 280
    Confirmation Tour: First year in New Zealand 281
Endnotes 284
Index 310

Foreword

Norman Lesser was a man for his time. A time when Anglicans held the high ground and the cultural mainstream. He understood the privilege of that position and led the church with dignity and care. It felt good to belong under his leadership, even though you held your breath when he reached for goals like a new cathedral in an era when most people had given up on them.

Those outside the church respected him as much as the insiders, probably because he was much more than a conventional bishop. Comedian, story teller, preacher who revelled in life's delights and absurdities, and above all a man with eye for the detail of pastoral ministry; the same sense of detail that he brought to his work as a craftsman.

This book is an overdue honouring of a man who led the church through two decades with great flair and enormous devotion. Judy Mills has done Waiapu and the whole church in Aotearoa a great service through her meticulous research and even handed distilling of a huge story. And only just in time. Many of the memories and anecdotes she assembles would have soon been lost for ever.

As someone who would not ever have made it to ordination without the support and encouragement of this man, and as his eventual successor, I'm personally grateful for this book. It will help all who followed him to learn just how rich a legacy he left us.

John Bluck

Preface

Norman Lesser was Bishop of Waiapu, 'a small Diocese in an out-lying Province,' for nearly 24 years and Archbishop of New Zealand, that out-lying Province, for ten of those years. During that time he filled 15 scrapbooks with items he regularly cut and pasted from a variety of sources: newspapers from home and abroad, parish newsletters, his own pastoral letters to clergy, Synod papers and Orders of Service, and general memorabilia ranging from an advertisement for the family's lost fox terrier to the menu for a State lunch with President Lyndon Johnson. A fascinating social history in themselves, the selection of material reveals something of the personality of the man behind it, and it was these scrapbooks which initially sparked my interest in Norman Lesser.

However, the scrapbooks are not just a social history. They also preserve significant original material not found elsewhere: his pastoral letters, some sermons, various articles for different readerships, and personal information about his early life. Official church records give us the bare bones of his work and achievements, but it is these scrapbooks that put the meat on those bones. While the accuracy of the many newspaper clippings included could be questioned, Lesser himself clearly read them, sometimes commenting or correcting with his red pencil, so we can assume that if he has not done this, he himself was satisfied with them.

Other Diocesan and Provincial archival material, along with personal memories, have contributed to form a picture of a man of many parts: preacher, pastor, and liturgist; wordsmith and story-teller; sportsman, miniaturist and humorist. Above all he was a man of faith who was passionate about communicating that faith.

It is impossible to read through this volume of material without recognising his huge contribution to the life of the Waiapu diocese over his long episcopate. What he certainly gave the Diocese was stability, huge amounts of energy and dedication, and high-quality pastoral care. He was a greatly loved Bishop, remembered still by many, and there are undoubtedly hundreds more stories to be told.

Preface

In every biography it is the sense of the person, rather than what he or she did, that is both the most interesting but also the most elusive to capture. Hopefully this book is not just a testimony to the impressive work of Norman Lesser but also offers an occasional glimpse into the character of the 'likely lad' from Liverpool who became the Archbishop of New Zealand.

Acknowledgements

I am greatly indebted to his daughter, Mrs Elisabeth Paterson, and to all those who responded to requests for their particular understanding of Norman Lesser, including the following: the late Archbishop Brown Turei; Bishop Peter Atkins, Bishop John Bluck; Rev's B. Allom, C.W. Bennett and Mrs Bennett, Rex Caudwell and Mrs Caudwell, A. Gardiner, R. Foster, Iritani Hankins, Tiki Raumati and Mrs Raumati, B. White, F. Wright, Mr Sam Donald, Mrs Beverley Galloway; Mrs Shirley Hosking; Mrs Y. Mawson, Mr Robin Nairn, Faith and Nancye Panapa.

I also want to acknowledge the considerable help and kindness from the Archivist at All Saints' Cathedral, Nairobi, and the Rev Sheila Hughes of St John the Evangelist church in Barrow, UK, during our visits to those places; Robin Moor at Liverpool Cathedral; and information supplied by Ridley Hall, Fitzwilliam College and Liverpool Collegiate. In addition, the John Kinder Library at St John's Theological College in Auckland, and the Waiapu Diocesan Archivists have provided invaluable help, while Michael Blow's work on the photographs is much appreciated.

Judy Mills, QSO, MA (Hons)

A Likely Lad

Albert Lesser Senior, son Albert aged c. 20, Norman c. 8 – c.1910

Chapter 1: England

"The house in which I was born was one of a long row, standing straight on to the street and backed by a small red-tiled yard which looked on to a shippon. A shippon was a cow house, and right in the midst of the city was this shippon in which cows were kept in strictly supervised conditions and provided milk for the local inhabitants."[1]

So begins Norman Lesser's own account of his early years in Liverpool. The shippon and the cows close by were not responsible, he hastens to add, for the diphtheria which nearly killed him at the age of three. "I was one of the few in the locality to survive," he writes, although the life-saving treatment of the time – a huge needle delivering copious amounts of anti-toxin three times a day – left him with a lasting horror of injections.

The third child of Albert and Eleanor Elisabeth Lesser (née Jones) he was six years younger than sister Ruby and twelve years younger than brother Albert. They were a devout Anglican family: Albert Lesser senior would have liked to enter the Church, but in his day there had been "no opportunities for assistance such as prevail now," so he served instead as a highly-committed layman, being secretary of the vestry and superintendent of a Sunday School of over 1,500, all the while maintaining his ordinary working week at the head Post Office in Liverpool. Norman's mother was also "deeply religious, had a lovely voice (she was from Wales) and an infectious laugh."[2] Perhaps it was from her that Norman inherited his remarkable speaking voice, which was to prove so useful in his preaching. It was a faith-filled household, and no doubt there was much prayer during the diphtheria attack. There was also much laughter as the family shared enjoyment of a good joke and the sharp-witted exchange, a family trait which Norman kept very much alive in his own family.

When Norman was three, they moved to Anfield, a new suburb on the edge of town, "where we took the bold step of renting one of the houses for 10 shillings a week, which stretched our limited resources considerably, in spite of the fact that my father held a responsible position in the head Post Office."[3] 15 Sunbury Road, their new home, was a terrace house

A Likely Lad

directly opposite their family church of St Simon and St Jude,[4] and Ruby lived there until her death.

The Lessers' move to this new suburb was expressive of the new spirit of the time. Liverpool would have had its fair share of the social problems of the 19th Century brought about in part by rapid industrialisation and consequent urban growth. Lack of education, poor health services,

Norman Lesser's father Albert outside their home at 15 Sunbury Road, Anfield c. 1900

England

overcrowding leading to illness (cholera hit Britain for the first time in the 1840s), exploitation of workers and a harsh penal code made life miserable for many. Norman's own father remembered as a young boy walking twelve miles six days a week to deliver newspapers for a pittance.[5]

But by the end of the century, legislative reforms in education and working conditions, arising, at least in part, from the Christian convictions of people such as Shaftesbury and Wilberforce, had done much to improve the ordinary person's life, and there was a sense of triumphant Britain, both at home and abroad. In 1902, the year of Norman's birth, Liverpool was aware of its contribution to that sense of triumph. It had grown in a hundred years from 78,000 to a city of 685,000 with a population more diverse than was generally found in Britain, and it boasted the largest port in the world.

Church as well as State had undergone reforms during the same period. Changes were made in the training and appointing of clergy, though it was still generally assumed that they would have a middle-class background and a private income of some kind, putting ordination out of reach of people like Norman Lesser's father. But Church leaders were aware of the need to relate more effectively to the alienated Alfred Dolittles of the working class and made efforts to reach out to them with the establishment of organisations such as Wilson Carlisle's Church Army in 1882.

It was also a period of the highly popular 'revival' meetings, when visiting preachers like Moody and Sankey would call for individual conversions in a powerful and effective way, leading many well-qualified men and women to exchange the comforts of Britain for the rigours of the mission field overseas. As a lad growing up in Liverpool, young Norman Lesser would undoubtedly have had such individuals held up to him as an example of a worthwhile Christian life, and while the late 19th century brought new challenges to faith from scientists like Darwin, religion, especially in the form of the very visible Church of England, remained an accepted part of everyday life.

> "By the end of the century, no-one could possibly accuse the church of irrelevance, indifference or ineffectuality. It had not solved all the problems that beset it at the beginning of the era, but it had adapted, been re-vitalized, and had managed to give a lead in many crucial areas."[6]

A Likely Lad

This then was the kind of church and social milieu into which Norman Lesser was born.

The Lesser children attended the local Council schools which they found 'very good.' Norman's school, a new one, even boasted an indoor heated swimming pool. Parents had to pay one penny a week for the Infant school, two pence for the middle school, and three pence for the 'big boys.' He then went on to Liverpool Collegiate School, "which, until I joined it, had an enviable reputation for scholarship,"[7] a typically self-deprecatory witticism. It was indeed a very good school and still maintains a proud tradition. Here he captained the cricket team and gained a 'colour' for football.[8] Lesser himself writes dryly about his time at this school:

> "I was extremely fond of soccer and cricket, and they let me play quite often: we also did lessons."

Many years later when he returned to Liverpool during the 1968 Lambeth Conference a local newspaper columnist[9] recalled his football playing in the 1920s, describing him as "a very keen sportsman who also played tennis for the Liverpool Collegiate team in addition to his footballing activities," so he was obviously good at any sport he took up. The same couldn't be said for all his school subjects, however, and in later life he enjoyed the irony of not having done well in Divinity and Woodwork, "as one became my life's work and the other my chief hobby!"[10]

But it was his membership of the church choir of St Simon and St Jude at the age of eight that was to prove a vital turning-point in his life. The vicar at the time, John Rosbotham, clearly saw the potential of young Norman, writing fondly of him years later, "We knew him so well as a St Simon's and St Jude's boy, a keen member of the choir and the Sunday School with such a happy outlook on life." Rosbotham organised a

Norman Lesser as wicket keeper c. 1920

England

scholarship for Norman to his own old Cambridge college, Fitzwilliam Hall,[11] where Norman completed a BA in Geography and History in 1923 – while also playing his favourite sports – followed by the award of an MA in 1927.[12]

Naturally, and perhaps inevitably, his "glorious Lancashire accent… was badly mutilated at Cambridge" but traces must have remained as someone many years later remarked that they loved to hear 'the twang!'[13]

After graduation he studied theology at Ridley Hall, established in 1881 to offer "supplementary theological instruction in conformity with the doctrines of the Protestant Reformed Church to graduate candidates for ordination and to afford them economical residence." It maintains today the traditions and values of the Evangelical branch of the Church of England, and according to its website, stands for "the authority of Scripture, the need for personal faith, the uniqueness of Christ and the free gift of eternal life to humankind only through Christ's death on the Cross."

The education Lesser received at these institutions was critical to his future, as his vicar John Rosbotham had foreseen, and Lesser never ceased to be grateful to him for his influence and support.

Although the loved and respected Bishop Chavasse of Liverpool had accepted Norman Lesser for ordination,[14] he retired before the appointed time so Norman was made a deacon in Liverpool Cathedral in 1925 by the then Bishop of Liverpool, Dr A.A. David and a year later on 4 July 1926, was ordained priest. The family saved hard to buy him a Home Communion set[15] as a gift to mark the occasion, and their pride, especially that of his father, can be imagined, but sadly his mother had not lived to see this significant day in the life of her son.

Norman Lesser the student

A Likely Lad

Following ordination Lesser was sent to his home parish of St Simon and St Jude, which might have seemed a rather daunting prospect, but the vicar was his old mentor John Rosbotham, who had been instrumental in getting Norman the scholarship to Cambridge. Later Lesser was to write regarding this man, "The first curacy a man serves is most important and I have been constantly grateful that I had the privilege of serving mine under the Reverend John Rosbotham, who was instrumental in my being ordained at all."[16] It was also in this parish that the young curate, who in earlier days had been a rather haphazard Scout, had his first encounter with the Boys' Brigade, becoming an officer and then Chaplain to the group. The Liverpool 10th Brigade seems to have been a strong and lively organisation[17] and Lesser continued to support the movement in New Zealand, becoming Vice-Patron.

His curacy in this parish lasted just a year, and when the vicar left to become chaplain to the largest mental hospital in England, Norman was moved to a curacy at Holy Trinity, Formby. Typically, he observes that "some friends suggested that the vicar would have had good experience from my being his curate."

Holy Trinity Formby was a relatively new parish, established in 1889 to cater for the growing Liverpool population. Under its first curate-in-charge, John Brooke Richardson, it grew rapidly and by the time Norman Lesser was appointed, it was well equipped with a good organ, a strong choir, adequate buildings and a school attached. He was there for three years, boarding privately with a family, with the Rev Canon Colin Dawson as his Vicar. Whether there is any connection between this priest and Norman Lesser's friend Ralph Dawson, also a priest, is not certain, but it does seem likely.

Norman Lesser c. 1928

One story from this period tells of how the lights failed during a service of Evensong. The curate was equal to the occasion and promptly began the prayer beginning, "Lighten our darkness we beseech Thee O Lord," which brought the service to a premature end.[18] There is no record of how the prayer was answered!

Almost forty years later Lesser re-visited this parish during the 1968 Lambeth Conference, spending a day there to watch a children's pageant depicting the Anglican church in New Zealand.[19]

His next move as 'Bishop's Pioneer' was to Norris Green in February 1929. A new suburb of Liverpool, not very far from his home in Anfield, it was a huge housing estate with a population of 30,000, designated as a Mission District within the parish of Emmanuel, Fazerkerley. The worship centre was an old army hut, affectionately called the 'Mission Hut,' dedicated in 1927. It seated only about 100 and Lesser describes how the men of the parish would carry chairs for the women to sit on inside the Hut, while standing outside themselves. About 15 homes were used for Sunday Schools and weekday Communions and it "was a moving experience to see how rooms had been prepared so that an altar, complete with flowers, could be set up."

The new development had previously been cared for by a popular lay-reader who had obviously worked hard among the people, visiting 2,000 homes and getting together a large band of volunteers for various tasks. However, Lesser was the first ordained person appointed. He left there barely a year later but by then they had a 'fine new memorial Hall' the Chavasse Memorial Hall, opened in October 1929, followed by a smaller hall, naturally called the Lesser Hall![20]

Later a 'proper' church was built, and in a 1948 history of this Mission District, parishioner J.H. Harrison writes glowingly of Norman Lesser, describing his rise to the episcopacy as "a startlingly rapid advance in the oversight of the church" which is attributed to "his superlative qualities of leadership." In this mission district he had "boundless enthusiasm for his new task", and

> "tireless energy which enabled him to get through an extraordinary amount of routine visiting of houses, hospitals, schools, youth clubs, and still left him time to carry through all the necessary work in the Mission Church, and occasionally to visit the Cathedral where he was a frequent preacher and helper."

A Likely Lad

He took a hymn practice for 30 minutes before the evening service to teach new hymns, wrote services for special occasions and compiled whole books of services for Girl Guides and the Sunday School, and according to this parishioner "was equally at home at social gatherings and picnics as in the pulpit; children idolized him, and young people accepted him on the strength of his being something of an athlete and a good footballer… Everything he touched he enriched, everyone he met became his friend, even though not a few were also his critics." The praise continues: "Apart from all these things, however, Mr Lesser possessed extraordinary charm felt by everyone who came into contact with him. This was not just the charm of a smile. It was the personality of the man, which seemed to say, 'You are just the person I want to speak to; will you do this for me; I shall be eternally grateful.'" He was also "a brilliant scholar and an eloquent preacher" with "views on the whole, very modern, sometimes disconcertingly so. He was unconventional to a degree. He was always happy in trying out new ideas," one of which was a monthly parish leaflet, the size of an ordinary newspaper, delivered free to 2,000 households, carrying such memorable headlines as, "Norris Green or Norris Glum?"[21]

One of the 'unconventional' actions referred to above may well have been to invite a woman, Mrs Dwelly, wife of the Dean of the Cathedral, to be the guest preacher on more than one occasion. Other more conventional invitations to preach went to John Rosbotham, Lesser's old vicar and the 'donor of our piano', and Charles E. Raven, a noted Cambridge Professor of Divinity who had links with Liverpool Cathedral.[22] Lesser's friend Ralph Dawson, another visiting preacher, appears in Harrison's recollections, gratefully remembered for his generosity in slipping several large coins into the collection plate at the Easter service, thereby relieving the anxiety of the parishioners who felt the offering, traditionally made to the vicar, was rather meagre.

At the end of October 1929, the Hut was closed, as by then the Chavasse Memorial Hall had been built. At the last service in the Hut, Lesser urged his hearers "to always keep the idea of pioneering fresh in our minds… never to be afraid to try new ideas and new approaches to old problems and difficulties." He also gave them a motto remembered by Harrison and used more than once by Lesser himself in later years; "Hats off to the Past! Coats off to the Future!"[23]

England

Wedding Party of Norman and Beatrice Lesser 12 July 1930

A Likely Lad

It was during this busy Norris Green year that Lesser had his first contact with Baden-Powell, whose funeral he was to take in Kenya years later. A Jamboree attended by 30,000 scouts was being held in Arrowe Park in August 1929 to celebrate 21 years of scouting, and Dean Dwelly sent Lesser to discuss the associated celebratory Cathedral service with the great man. Torrential rain had turned the park into a quagmire and Lesser recalls ploughing his way through the mud to meet him. More than a decade later, when planning for Baden-Powell's funeral, Lesser was able to include the same Bible reading and blessing as those used at this Jamboree service.[24]

Norman Lesser was at Norris Green for only one year, but perhaps one of the consistent marks of his ministry – the care of the individual parishioner – can be found in the following account:

> "Every house was visited weekly by a large team of church members, and greetings were extended by our people to all who celebrated anniversaries. One man said to me, 'Your people came round this week to wish my wife and me well on our wedding anniversary. My wife said, "It is coming to something when the church remembers, and you forget!" Do you think you could remind me next year in good time?'"[25]

In January 1930 Lesser was appointed to Liverpool Cathedral as Chaplain and Precentor, a very convenient move for him as he had become engaged on Christmas Day 1929 to Beatrice (Dorothy Beatrice Anne in full) Barnes, who worked as a secretary for Dean Dwelly at the Cathedral. Beatrice was the eldest daughter of a Yorkshire couple. Her father owned and worked in a shirt factory in Manchester before moving to Southport. Norman met her through his friend, Ralph Dawson, the curate at Southport, who knew Beatrice and her family and asked if he could bring a friend to join in a tennis game at their home.[26]

In July 1930 they were married in the Cathedral by the Archbishop of Melbourne who had been Sub-dean and Canon at Liverpool Cathedral, and for whom Beatrice had worked before his election to Melbourne.[27] The Archbishop would have come to Liverpool for the Jubilee of the Diocese of Liverpool, attended by bishops from all around the world, and the wedding ceremony on 12 July seems to have been fitted in between preparations for the very grand and elaborate service of Jubilee the next day.[28]

Their marriage was a true partnership: Beatrice's loving support and care enabled her husband to fulfil his demanding vocation; she willingly and competently accepted responsibilities that came her way, such as leadership in the women's organisations of the church, and her hospitality was legendary.

During his year at Liverpool Cathedral Lesser had some contact with the Poet Laureate John Masefield, who had close connections with both Liverpool and its Cathedral. In his account[29] of the building of his own Cathedral Lesser writes, "It had been my privilege to meet the Poet Laureate Mr John Masefield at Liverpool Cathedral when he wrote a Ballad of the Sea [30] and Martin Shaw, who was the pianist for the Liverpool Philharmonic Orchestra supplemented the great Liverpool Cathedral Organ..." It was this encounter in 1930 which prompted Lesser many years later when building his Cathedral in Napier to ask Masefield "if he could find time and was willing to write a hymn for the Laying of the Foundation Stone of the Cathedral."

Lesser's stay at Liverpool Cathedral was brief and remarkably little record of it exists, but the place embedded itself in his heart, and he often referred to it in later years, especially when his own Cathedral in Napier was being planned. The building of the Cathedral would have been the talk of Liverpool as he was growing up: it was a monumental undertaking – one of the biggest in the world – and everyone respected and loved the saintly Bishop Chavasse who had committed himself to the lengthy project. In addition, the Dean of the time had won a national reputation as a liturgist and the Cathedral was well-known for its innovative and relevant services under his leadership.[31] Dean Dwelly would have been a great mentor for Norman Lesser, who as Chaplain and Precentor was involved with formulating special services, an activity he continued to enjoy throughout his working life. The impressive three-volume collection of services, almost all from this Cathedral, which Lesser carried around the world with him, is testimony both to his interest in liturgy and the deep affection he had for this magnificent place of worship.[32]

After a year at the Cathedral, Norman was appointed to the parish of St John the Evangelist in Barrow-in-Furness, where in 1933 their daughter Elisabeth was born. The vicar of the parish served also as honorary chaplain to the shipyard of Vickers Armstrong Ltd, so Norman became acquainted with the local philanthropist Sir Charles Craven,

A Likely Lad

Managing Director of the firm, "and a very good friend and Benefactor (sic) of St John's."[33]

This parish of about 10,000 people in 90 acres of housing was hit hard by the Depression with 90% of the workforce unemployed, so the vicar quickly set up a Men's Club to cater for these men and established a Poor Fund.[34] The poverty was such that the Christmas tree – which had somehow been obtained – was decorated with scrubbing brushes and other household items instead of tinsel, and women who had nothing to give but their labour would offer to clean up the church hall.[35] It is perhaps not surprising that the curate of this impoverished parish later stood for the Sheffield City Council elections on a Communist platform, "the first time a clergyman has been endorsed as a Communist candidate for the City Council," notes the report. "My curate at Barrow-in-Furness!" in Lesser's hand is scribbled alongside the cutting.[36]

The lack of money for any teaching resources for the Sunday School meant that the vicar had to make his own. His main material in those days was matchsticks, and as he was a chain smoker, there were always plenty around! So, from necessity Norman Lesser began his lifelong hobby of creating amazing miniatures, an activity which demanded so much concentration that he could forget any problems, ecclesiastical or otherwise, as he worked.[37]

The people of this parish had the toughness of spirit which proverbially helped Britain survive the war, and although the Lessers left Barrow-in-Furness before the war started, they were told a story which illustrates that spirit. Enemy bombs were falling fast, and the man of the house was anxious to get out and into the safety of the bomb shelter, but his wife was moving very slowly. When told to hurry up, she wailed, "I can't find me teeth!" to which the husband replied, "It's bombs they're droppin', not bloomin' ham sandwiches!" Lesser concludes, "It is impossible to speak too highly of these people."[38]

They certainly showed courage and strength of purpose in building a new church in those hard years. The parish had been working towards a new building to replace a 'temporary' wooden church from about 1910, and in 1934 under Norman Lesser's leadership, "they had by their own efforts accumulated the sum of £3,800." The Diocese contributed the remainder; benefactor Sir Charles Craven laid the foundation stone in December 1934, and the church, seating 500 and filled every Sunday

England

evening according to Lesser, was consecrated in September 1935.[39] In an interesting parallel to the building of Waiapu Cathedral years later, it replaced a temporary wooden building and was one of the early concrete churches.[40] Today, the building still seems surprisingly modern, being light and having a sense of space, with wide Byzantine-style arches separating the main body from the side areas.

Thirty years after leaving this parish he returned to preach at two Sunday services while in England for the 1968 Lambeth Conference.[41]

Today, Barrow Island is still closely settled with thousands living in huge blocks of flats. The shipbuilding industry, now history, is recorded in an interesting museum at the former docks, but the church is still there and active. Instead of ships, they now build nuclear-powered submarines and receive Japanese nuclear waste to be sent on for burial at Sellafield, according to the local vicar.

The experiences gathered from working in these different English parishes, together with the foundation of his own early home life in Liverpool, were crucial to Lesser's understanding of himself. He was proud of what might be called his 'humble origins,'[42] often describing

St John the Evangelist Church, Barrow-in-Furness 2011

A Likely Lad

himself as an 'ordinary' person, who could therefore easily mix with 'ordinary' people.[43] Liverpool remained his turangawaewae and links with this part of the 'Old Country' were especially valued.

His home parish of St Simon and St Jude naturally remained dear to him through his family connections, his professional ties, and the mutual respect the vicar, John Rosbotham, and he continued to have for each other. Writing in a 1956 parish magazine celebrating the parish's 60th birthday "J.R." after recalling the "choirboy with such a happy outlook on life," writes of the adult curate:

> "A more loyal and hardworking colleague one could not have wished for. It was a joy and privilege to be his vicar. He developed a striking gift for preaching and his leadership of young people was early evidenced… and he exerted such a wonderful influence for good on the young life of the parish."[44]

He goes on to outline Lesser's later career, noting the 'building of the new and beautiful Church of St John' in Barrow-in-Furness and his experiences in Kenya, "when happily conditions out there were more settled then than they have been in recent years, in religious Broadcasting, in administration, in Missionary activity and work among his Majesty's forces, all of which proved an invaluable training for the future."

Lesser returned the respect, making Rosbotham his Commissary in one of his first acts as Bishop, and later describing the vicar who had been so influential on him as

"a young and virile man who never spared himself. He had great vision and was never content until that vision of God's purpose for the parish had been translated into

Beatrice, Elisabeth and Norman Lesser c. 1934

action. Young people were automatically inclined to him and the Sunday school of hundreds of children told its own story of the persuasive charm of the vicar's manner."[45]

Obviously, this parish having nourished his early years was proud of his 'success' and followed his career with interest. During his 1963 visit to England, gossipy snippets about him featured in the parish magazine, the first of which begins: 'When a choirboy of this church needs to be remonstrated (with) for carving his initials on the pew… it is not the background that gives promising material for such a youngster to rise to heights in the profession of the Ministry. Yet Norman Lesser, for such he was, in the hands of the Almighty Potter, was made to become the Archbishop of New Zealand.' A second little story tells how the Archbishop, unrecognized by the shop assistant, dozed in a chair, while his wife was choosing a coat. The assistant could not be blamed 'as the Archbishop of New Zealand was in mufti.'[46]

The Mission District of Norris Green was also significant for him as his first experience of being in sole charge, although he does not seem to have returned to the area during later visits to England. However, links were maintained through food parcels sent from a Waiapu parish for some years after the war[47] and a letter of thanks from their vicar to the donor parish says inter alia, "We rejoice in our links with the church in New Zealand through Bishop Lesser who did such excellent work in the pioneer days of this parish."[48] When it celebrated its 25th anniversary in May 1952 the programme for the week's events was sent to Lesser[49] along with historical articles from the parish magazines. Lesser's motto is again quoted: "When the Bishop of Waiapu (The Rt Rev N A Lesser) was appointed curate-in-charge of the District in 1929 he gave the people of Christ Church a motto which we may well make our own at this time as we set out upon the next 25 years: 'Hats off to the Past: Coats off to the Future!'"[50]

Liverpool Cathedral was a third touchstone for him, although he had worked there for only a year. It remained for him the standard for all other cathedrals and invitations to preach there in both 1963 and 1968 were welcomed and treasured.[51] He makes frequent references to it: the leaflet appealing for funds for the re-building of the Waiapu Cathedral opens with a lengthy reference to Liverpool Cathedral, and his contributions to discussions on furnishings for his new cathedral also reveal the influence of this mighty building. He wanted the windows to

A Likely Lad

come from Whitefriars as they had for Liverpool;[52] when the design of the font was under discussion the Bishop showed the subcommittee photos of fonts in English cathedrals, "and it was finally agreed that something on the lines of the font in Liverpool Cathedral would be suitable;"[53] and when problems were being experienced in communication between the organist at the console and the priest in another part of the building the Bishop described "a satisfactory system installed in Liverpool Cathedral."[54]

A final and very tangible link with Liverpool Cathedral exists with the block of gold and red sandstone on which was carved the cross of consecration for his New Zealand Cathedral. Under the headline "Link with Liverpool in Consecration Act" an article in the *Daily Telegraph* explains the connection: "The archbishop will acknowledge a link with his home city of Liverpool as he performs the act of Consecration at the Waiapu cathedral tomorrow. He will trace a cross of consecration which has been carved in a block of gold and red sandstone from Liverpool cathedral."[55] In his own account of the building of the Cathedral, Lesser writes that the "stone had special significance to me as I had had the privilege of serving from the Cathedral designed by Sir Giles Scott."[56]

It could be argued that to the end of his life, Lesser remained 'a lad from Liverpool' and an Englishman. The threads that bound him to the past and the 'Old Country' were strong. One of his last acts as Bishop was to dedicate another stone cross in the Cathedral during the 1970 Synod, this time from Canterbury Cathedral, which Lesser had requested from the Archbishop of Canterbury "as a reminder of the stump from which we grew."[57] He listed for Synod members the other reminders: "along with the cross of nails from my old friend Dick Howard of Coventry, and the cross of consecration in the north wall of the sanctuary carved in stone from Sir Giles Gilbert Scott, the architect of Liverpool cathedral, and the Holy Bible presented and inscribed by Her Majesty the Queen we have many associations which we value highly."[58] According to his own account of the building of the Cathedral, the Bible came as a result of a conversation with the Queen when he had reminded her of her parents' gift of a Bible to the Cathedral in Nairobi during his time there. A little later he "was thrilled beyond words" to learn through the Governor-General that the Queen would like to present a Bible to Waiapu Cathedral.[59]

More adaptable than many, and more anxious than most to fit in to his new life in the "glorious country of New Zealand,"[60] he was yet unmistakeably English, as many people recall. The frequent allusions to the 'Old Country,' the stories and jokes often referencing stereotypes of English literature and life, though admittedly still familiar enough at the time to resonate with his audience; a sense of 'class' even as he rejected its implications; ingrained respect for people of significance, even while valuing 'ordinary' people; the love of tradition and Royalty; the acceptance of the strange Bishop's gaiters and cutaway-coat, all marked him as someone not 'from here.' Although most of the other New Zealand Bishops at the time were not 'from here,' Waiapu had a different history. All its previous bishops had either been born here, like the two from the Williams family, or had held a position in New Zealand before their election.

Altogether it is difficult to overestimate the importance of Norman Lesser's beginnings. The strong influence of his first vicar; the example of Dean Dwelly who shared to a surprising degree a background similar to Lesser's; the model of the saintly Bishop Chavasse, who though an Evangelical was largely responsible for building Liverpool cathedral – 'a visible witness to God in the midst of a great city' – all demonstrated to him what Christian ministry was about. All were imbued with the special brand of the Evangelical tradition of the Church of England with its emphasis on the need for a personal knowledge of Christ and its belief in the power of the Gospel to change the world for the better. Their theological values and ways of being underpinned all that followed, even as he adapted to life and work in a faraway country.

Chapter 2: Kenya

After fourteen formative years of ministry in his home country, Lesser was appointed Rector and Sub-Dean, later Provost, of Nairobi's Cathedral Church in faraway Kenya. The confusing proliferation of titles seems to have arisen because the Bishop himself chose to act as Dean or Provost of the Cathedral for the first few years following Lesser's appointment.

The Lessers sold everything except personal belongings and set sail in the *Dunluce Castle* for a six-week voyage to a very different place from anything they had known. The voyage in first class was pleasant enough, though Norman, who had been requested to act as chaplain, "spent a good deal of my time outside the first-class limits and enjoyed them immensely, making some very good friends."[61]

Choosing to work in Kenya was an adventurous step, but not necessarily a 'missionary' activity in the 19th century sense, although Lesser's name, along with that of Bishop Caulton, was annually listed under the Liverpool Diocesan Missionary Council as "members of the Diocese serving overseas," at least until 1965.[62] However, his job was primarily to act as chaplain to the white settlers not just in Nairobi, but throughout the entire colony, and the Cathedral congregation was predominantly European, however much he would have liked a broader representation of the population.

The family expected to have a furlough back home within three years, but the outbreak of war prevented that and the Lessers did not leave Kenya for seven and a half years. Communication with home was limited to aerogrammes, with telegrams, always dreaded, in emergencies.

Their arrival set the pace for what was to be a very busy life. After landing at the port of Mombasa on a Saturday afternoon, they travelled overnight by train to Nairobi arriving at 9 a.m. on Sunday morning, to be told that the new arrival was to be instituted as Sub-Dean and Canon of the Cathedral at 10 a.m.![63] A further surprise came during that service when he learned from the notices being read that he was to broadcast that evening at Evensong. "The afternoon was spent in preparation," he comments dryly.

Kenya

The Cathedral to which he had been called was the second cathedral in the Diocese of Mombasa, a situation later described by Bishop Lesser as "unique in the Anglican Communion."[64] It arose because although there was already the Memorial Cathedral in Mombasa, built at the end of the 19th century, Mombasa was nearly 500 kilometres – and many hours travel – from Nairobi, so the European settlers there raised money for a permanent church, All Saints, which in 1924 became known as the Cathedral of the Highlands.[65]

In 1939, the time of Lesser's arrival, Nairobi's population of about 61,300, (which was to double during the war from the influx of troops), was a mix of Africans, Indians and Seychelles Islanders, with Europeans very much in the minority. This would have been a new experience for the Lessers but despite not knowing a single person in Kenya when they arrived, they "soon had many friends, African, Asian and European."

Unlike South Africa, there was no legal separation of the races, but considerable disadvantage existed among the African people. The Provost was keenly aware of their situation and as an Alderman tried to influence the policy-makers of the City. Every week he would tour the poorer suburbs of Nairobi and every Sunday evening he preached about the conditions in which people were living, describing eight people sleeping in one room, four in a bed, taking it in turns. As these sermons were broadcast, awareness of African hardship increased and some improvement occurred.[66] It may have been this sort of social commentary that earned him some angry anonymous letters and caused him to

Norman Lesser and daughter Elisabeth, on ship to Kenya 1939

remark later, "I spent considerable time over my broadcast sermons and they did not please everybody by any means."[67]

There was certainly no racial segregation at the Cathedral where everyone was welcome, so at the 8 a.m. service you could see the Governor kneeling at the altar rail alongside his African driver, and his wife alongside Seychelles and African women.[68] The congregation, however, was largely European, although the Provost made efforts to increase the participation of Africans in the Cathedral Chapter.[69]

It was still colonial times in 1939 with the accompanying expectations of an expatriate life-style. The Provost joined the Club, was made an honorary member of Rotary, and an Alderman on the Municipal Council, but the family had the minimal number of servants – a cook, a 'house-boy' and a gardener, "who were exceedingly well-treated,"[70] and Mrs Lesser did not have an ayah for Elisabeth, preferring to do the child-care herself. There were pockets of high class suburbs and private schools, and Elisabeth attended one of these at first, before moving to the government primary school and later Kenya Girls' High School, where most of the pupils were from expatriate families. Staffed with Cambridge and Oxford dons, it had an excellent standard of teaching, and reputedly nobody had ever failed the Oxford and Cambridge Entrance exams.[71]

Educational standards for Africans, however, were low. Lesser writes, "There were many Africans of exceptional potential but regrettably there were insufficient opportunities for their gifts to be developed. A man with whom I had been at Cambridge had the oversight of over one hundred African schools, and he was deeply disturbed by the microscopic proportion of future potential leaders who could be assimilated in the educational system at that time."[72]

Norman Lesser in Provost's dress in Kenya 1940s

Kenya

Life for the Provost was very busy. The Cathedral, with a fine organ and choir, mainly European, provided an average of 650 services a year; it also offered an active Sunday School, and had a Children's Corner, with books and models, (made by the Provost, of course!) to illustrate the life and times of Christ. Moreover, the Cathedral served not only Nairobi but was also a centre of worship for the entire expatriate English community scattered throughout the country. The Provost's broadcasts – up to five services every week including Evensong, an Epilogue at 9 p.m. on Sunday evenings, and a mid-week service from a studio – were no doubt welcomed by these isolated members of his parish, as indeed they were by many others in nearby countries. Reflecting a few years later on his experience in Kenya, Lesser praises the work of the European chaplains, "who have, like the missionaries done a magnificent job, often with huge districts to cover. My present Diocese is 15,000 square miles; in Kenya my parish was technically 20,000 square miles."

Besides this extremely full parish life, he visited three hospitals, acted as Chaplain to a prison with about 1000 inmates, taught at three schools five miles apart, visited three nursing homes and did the usual home visiting expected of clergy. But a major commitment for both the Lessers was to provide some care of the troops. With the help of the Presbyterian minister, the Rev. Robert Howison, a 'Forces' Forum' discussion group was held every Monday night and efforts were also made to provide some social life for the men. "We tried to make our home a home for any of the troops who cared to use it,"[73] he writes, and the extent of their hospitality is further suggested in a farewell article in the *Mombasa Times*, reporting that "Mrs Lesser has had an average of 1400 callers a year through her house."[74]

War brought some privations of course, including petrol-rationing. Sometimes the only outing for the Provost's family was a trip to the cemetery with him if the funeral happened to be at a suitable time! He himself tells the story of being refused extra petrol by a clerk, after he had taken an 'undue' number of funerals and had more to come. "The clerk refused my request and so I asked the clerk to present my compliments to the Controller and to advise him that there were three funerals awaiting attention, and as I could not drive to the cemetery, perhaps he would be kind enough to discharge the responsibility."[75] He got the petrol.

Such restrictions made life difficult, but there was little real threat to their safety. The proximity of Kenya to Abyssinia and the Italians was the main

A Likely Lad

cause of concern, but there was a general consensus that the mountains would keep the enemy at bay, as although enemy planes might manage to get to Kenya, they would not be able to carry the fuel needed to return to their base! Ironically, the only damage sustained in Nairobi came from a victory salvo of anti-aircraft guns which shook the Cathedral tower, and broke its windows, giving the troops the unexpected job of erecting shelter to protect worshippers from possible falling glass at the impending thanksgiving service.[76]

A particularly memorable event, recorded fully in Lesser's incomplete memoir, occurred in January 1941, when he "was asked by the Chief Secretary, Mr G.M. Rennie, a highly efficient executive, to confidentially prepare arrangements for the funeral of Baden-Powell, who was critically ill."[77] 'B.P.' lived at Nyeri, some distance from Nairobi, and no-one knew whether the funeral service would be at his home there, or in the Cathedral at Nairobi, or near his birthplace in England or indeed in Westminster Abbey, so with typical thoroughness, the Sub-Dean prepared "a complete set of arrangements for every possibility and submitted them to Mr Rennie."

In the end 'B.P.' was buried at his home in Nyeri, a long journey from Nairobi which Lesser remembers for the great heat and dust, adding to the difficulty of keeping the wreaths alive.

As the Chief World Scout, full military honours were awarded 'B.P.' and every available cleric and VIP seems to have been present, along with 50 Boy Scouts. Lesser made a point of using the reading and blessing from the 1929 Scouting service held in Liverpool Cathedral, which was fortunately included in the collection of services he had made from the Cathedral while working there.

Life in Kenya was colourful and at times adventurous, providing a great fund of stories, some second-hand, others relating to close personal encounters with dangerous wild life or memorable characters, from the gamekeeper mauled by a lion to the Governor of Kenya who confided that he attended worship at the Cathedral not merely because he represented the crown, but because, "I know full well that I could not discharge my office and do my work unless I did." There is the story of a tiny baby baptised in an incubator with the name Faith whose survival seemed a miracle, and another whose mother admitted she had made "a little mistake" and would the Rector please christen it!

These enriching real-life experiences were well-mined for later sermons and addresses, but other stories in the memoir about cannibalism and missionaries, mothers-in-law and lions, and jumping pygmies, are no longer considered quite so apt, even if they raise an involuntary laugh. However, they are certainly further testimony to Lesser's enjoyment of humour and a good story.

Work as a chaplain in the prison also provided more rich material for the story-teller, like the time a triple-murderer surprised him by asking for a Prayer Book with rice paper leaves. Why rice paper, he wondered, and found out later from the Superintendent that the leaves of the Prayer Book were intended for use as cigarette papers! However, the humorous stories he tells of his experiences do not negate his genuine desire to help the inmates. He writes: "It was my privilege to be in constant touch with the men and to endeavour to keep their wives and dependants in full knowledge of the welfare of the 'residents.'" When he was leaving Nairobi, the men "generously decided that they would like to make me a gift" but regulations forbade that. However, "they still wanted to do something as their 'tribute,' so they decided they would show me where they kept their hidden store of cigarettes. I would never have dreamed of such a skilful hiding place and their secret will die with me!"

Apart from Lesser's personal records, some information has been gleaned about this period from Church archives in Nairobi. It is rather scanty for various reasons, one being that the war limited travel, so meetings were held infrequently. The Provost was a member of the Cathedral Chapter, but it seems to have met only four times in the period 1939-45.[78] Apart from Chapter and the Board of Finance, the Provost was on a

Norman in tropical dress, Kenya

A Likely Lad

committee planning celebrations to mark the Centenary in 1944 of the first Church Missionary Society activity in Kenya, and acted as Secretary to the Council of Churches in Nairobi, and was also on a Diocesan committee considering Church Union proposals for Kenya. Sparse though the records are, they do offer some objective insights into the principles and modus operandi of Norman Lesser, and it is interesting to follow these strands in his later work in the Waiapu Diocese.

One such strand is a pragmatic approach to church management: the need for a sound financial basis to enable the Diocese to carry out its mission. As a member of the Board of Finance (which did seem to meet quite often – three times in November 1944 for example) and a Trustee of the Diocese, he was aware of the need to build up funds. As the war seemed to be coming to an end there was talk of a major Diocesan Appeal for funds, and a celebration of the Centenary of the Church Missionary Society's arrival in 1844 – postponed because of war – seemed a good opportunity to launch such an appeal. A meeting on 23 February 1945 consequently set up the "Endowment and Mission Centenary Fund" which was to be used to support the Bishop, possibly an assistant Bishop and "the extension of the life and work of the Church of the Diocese." But Lesser also strongly believed that Christian commitment should precede monetary giving: a Minute records that,

> "Canon Lesser realised the need for an endowment of the
> Bishopric,… and funds for Chaplaincy work in the Diocese.
> *He would like to see a spiritual approach made before asking for*
> *money and thought that a pastoral letter from the Bishop to be*
> *read to Congregations of the Diocese, would help considerably.*"[79]
> (Italics mine.)

All his later efforts to raise money in the Waiapu Diocese consistently reflected his belief that if people had personal faith then the financial commitment would follow.

Church building or extension is a second theme in his working life. He had already built two halls in Norris Green, and a church in Barrow-in Furness: in Nairobi he was involved in extending and completing a Cathedral. A definite – and familiar – sense of urgency pervades the discussion on this at a Chapter meeting on 22 November 1945 when he "indicated the plans he had in mind for launching an appeal for funds to complete the building of the Cathedral." The plans, he said, had the support of His Excellency the Governor. "A service was suggested for a

Sunday in January 1946 at which the appeal for a further £2500 would be launched." Although there was a mere £1700 in hand "the Cathedral Chaplaincy Council was willing to act on behalf of Chapter co-opting such persons as may be necessary for the purpose" and "it was suggested that architects be co-opted at once."[80]

As things turned out, this was not a dream that Lesser was destined to fulfil.

Another recurring theme is his support for fairer representation of the indigenous population in church governance. At the Synod of 1944 Lesser proposed five names as representatives of Synod on the Cathedral Chapter; he then went on to refer to "the desire widely expressed to make the Cathedral the centre of worship for all races, and, as a token of this, he trusted that Synod would appoint an African layman as one of its representatives on the Chapter,"[81] a proposal that was carried unanimously. This support for indigenous people, particularly for more equitable representation in church governance and fairer treatment of their clergy, continued to be an important feature of his work in his new home of Aotearoa-New Zealand, and the consecration of the first Melanesian Bishops in the Anglican Communion in 1963, and later the first Tongan bishop, would have given him great satisfaction.

The Lessers were enjoying a well-earned furlough in England in 1946 when he was summoned to London to discuss with the Archbishop of Canterbury[82] the offer of the Bishopric of Waiapu, New Zealand. The formal offer came in telegrams from the Archbishop of New Zealand, West-Watson, via the Missionary Council – presumably that of Liverpool Diocese, as the Lessers were staying in Southport. It is dated 16 December and is pasted into the very first page of Scrapbook One. It reads:

> Dean Lesser 21 Brocklebank Rd Southport, Lancs. Cable forwarded from Missionary Council from Archbishop of New Zealand to you Cable begins Necessary Provincial consent now obtained enable me notify you of your nomination by Waiapu electoral Synod to fill vacant see Stop Diocese office house with annual stipend of 1000 and travelling expenses 200 stop Diocese will also pay reasonable removal expenses to New Zealand. Stop Please cable decision of (sic) possible Archbishop of New Zealand ++ Campbell

A Likely Lad

The Archbishop of Canterbury offered his support for the move in a telegram dated 21 December, saying "God speed you. Nothing could be better," and followed up with a letter of good wishes.

So the Lessers made a return trip to Kenya to pack and leave things in order. This sea voyage was memorable for being crowded – it was the troopship *Georgic* with 150 men all together below decks, and minimal privacy for the women crowded twenty to a cabin,[83] though Lesser later described it as "a lot of fun."

Back in Kenya, one of the first tasks was to have the Bishop's 'gear' made: the Episcopal Cross, the crook and the ring. The Cross, of pure Kenyan gold, and ring set with a large amethyst, were made by a Kenyan jeweller. The Crook was also made in Kenya but was sent later to him with a friendly message attached: "From one crook to another!"

Farewells were made and many tributes paid. A newspaper report[84] covering his farewell says he "took a keen interest in the affairs of the town and it was this that led to his appointment as one of the first Aldermen on the Nairobi Municipal Council." The same report includes a farewell speech by Deputy-Mayor Woodley broadcast on the eve of the Provost's departure for New Zealand. He placed Mr Lesser as among the greatest speakers he had ever heard and said that Kenya could ill spare him. He was a "frank and outspoken speaker" with whom not everyone would agree, and tribute was paid to "his many acts of Christian kindness and his complete lack of pretence." After referring to the broadcasts which were listened to by many who never came to church, Woodley continues:

> "It is because Provost Lesser has always seemed to me to typify the broad definition of religion that I, and I believe, many others, have found in him a man to listen to, a man to trust, one to try to follow, and a friend… while a few people had not cared for his more outspoken sermons… the majority had liked and appreciated his frankness and honesty…"

Archdeacon Brocklehurst, back in Napier, received further praise for the Bishop-elect from an unnamed person who wrote, "His loss to the Kenya Colony in general and to Nairobi in particular will be severe. It will certainly be keenly felt by his large congregation at the Cathedral here and to many hundreds of his friends who regularly listen to the services broadcast from the Cathedral every Sunday evening." The writer describes Lesser as

Kenya

> "one of the most fearless, upright and loveable men I have ever had the pleasure of meeting. His light shines with a great light before all men and his love of Christ as demonstrated by his life and actions, is a sheer inspiration. He is exceedingly democratic, and his great concern has always been for the poor, the needy and the oppressed. He is a remarkable preacher and will doubtless attract large congregations in your country as he has done here."

The letter ends with congratulations on having such a man appointed (sic) to a Bishopric in New Zealand.[85]

Another unsought tribute to the Bishop-elect came by sheer chance. Bishop Frederick Bennett happened to share a cabin on the Interisland ferry with a Mr Maingay and reported the encounter in an article in *Church and People* early in 1947. Mr Maingay had known Lesser "from the time he had come to take charge of the Cathedral in Nairobi." He described him as

> "a man of small stature, with a strong, clear voice, a splendid organiser and eloquent preacher who is very straight in his talks and draws large numbers of men to his services. The Cathedral holds about 1000 and is very often filled with loudspeakers outside for those who are unable to gain admittance. Dean Lesser is a man's man and is very highly thought of by the soldiers of the district. He made a great impression as a padre during the war. He is not engaged as a missionary in the ordinary sense of the term, for his usual congregation is about 98% British. But he visits the missionary centres of the district. Dean Lesser had learnt Swahili and was able to speak to the natives in many different centres."

Bishop Bennett also met Mrs Maingay who told him "how very helpful and capable Mrs Lesser was in all the activities of the Cathedral."[86]

With such commendation, there was reason indeed to expect great things from the new Bishop.

But travel around the world at that time was greatly restricted, whoever you were, and the journey was plagued with many delays, forcing the Lessers to live out of suitcases for six months. Even getting from Nairobi to Capetown was difficult: they travelled by train to Mombasa, then by ship to Durban, and finally another two-and-a half day train journey to the Cape, where they were held up before setting sail, at last, in the

A Likely Lad

SS *Corinthic* on her maiden voyage to Australia. There they were further delayed by a strike, eventually arriving in Auckland on 7 June, bringing with them memories of the wonderful landscapes of Kenya, the wild animals free in their natural habitat, the roads of red dirt which quickly turned to mud in sudden rain, and of course the people.

Speaking in later years about his time in Kenya – "some of the best years of our lives" – Bishop Lesser generally painted a favourable picture of a country not yet embroiled in the struggle for independence amid resistance movements such as the Mau Mau. Interviewed soon after his arrival in Auckland he said Kenya was emerging successfully from wartime difficulties and was regarded abroad, like New Zealand, as a land of opportunity.

> "Three races, Indians, Africans and Europeans were merged in Kenya and while there was a racial problem, it was capable of solution."
>
> "Africans on the land have a sense of responsibility and are tackling agricultural problems, such as soil erosion, with resolve and by modern methods,"

he said.

> "There is a great desire for more education and the Church Missionary Society, with other religious bodies, is taking a hand in this. The African will make tremendous sacrifices to see that his children are educated. However, there are 3,000,000 Africans in East Africa and until there are more teachers and schools the educational problems will be acute. Moreover, the economic condition of the country has to be considered."

He said the church was growing in Kenya where there was likely to be a big increase in European settlement in the next few years,[87] and in later interviews, defended both the Church's record in the country – "The Christian church has fought evil. For instance I have in my study a slave's Certificate of Freedom dated Zanzibar 23rd August 1875" – and the integrity of African Christians, writing of the Divinity School near Nairobi where Africans were trained for Ordination…

> "They still have much to learn but so do we!" [88]

Although he preferred to emphasise the positive aspects of life in Kenya, such as the pleasant climate and equality of races under law, he was also aware of the potential for conflict. A speech to the Church of England

Men's Society in Napier in July 1947 mentions difficulties arising from the presence of three races, and the changes in the African men who had seen service during the war in Egypt, Burma and other places, who "had therefore gained an entirely new outlook on the world and the part they could play. A new national spirit was developing rapidly."

On another occasion, warnings about the negative effect of overseas service on the native soldiers are repeated. "The process of rehabilitation of returned men had been most difficult" and although he again stresses the African's desire for education, he adds,

> "But with all this education and desire for learning it was difficult to make the natives realise they could not possibly teach the great mass of the people unless they themselves trained as teachers… Most of the boys who were educated wanted to be clerks in a white collar job."

But he thought that during the war "the natives had advanced considerably" and concluded that "the future looked bright for the people of East Africa who were now looking ahead more than ever to guide their own destiny." [89]

As indeed they were.

Norman Lesser c. 1947

Chapter 3: New Zealand

After many delays, the Lesser family finally arrived in Auckland on Saturday 7 June where they were met by Auckland's Bishop Simkin and Archdeacon Brocklehurst from the Waiapu Diocese. While their arrival in New Zealand was not quite as tight in its scheduling as it had been in Nairobi, there was little time to relax before the Consecration service on 11 June, and much to do. There would also have been much to talk about with both the Archdeacon and Bishop Simkin, who had served many years in the Waiapu Diocese.

The journey to their new home ended with the long drive from Auckland in a dusty cavalcade of cars all heading to Napier for the Consecration. Much to the surprise of the locals, the Lessers were not at all intimidated by the notorious Napier-Taupo road as they had been used to much worse in Kenya! Soon after arriving, amid the suitcases and trunks they had lived out of for six months, Dean Lesser told a reporter from the local paper that he was "thrilled to the marrow to be here," and made light of the difficulties and delays they had experienced in getting to New Zealand. They had had "a lot of fun" on the crowded troopship from England to Kenya even with "150 of us together down below" and had been excited to sail on the maiden voyage of the *Corinthic* from Capetown to New Zealand. He added that they felt "overwhelmed with kindness" and he was sure that they would be happy in their new home.[90]

What did Waiapu know of Norman Lesser?

The nomination process for bishops used to be very secretive, and nothing is recorded in the minutes of the synod held on 3 December 1946 except the motion agreeing to invite Norman Lesser. However, they took their time over it – from 2 p.m. till 5.30 p.m. and then from 7.30 p.m. to 9.20 p.m. – so it was not a hasty decision.[91]

The nomination of Norman Lesser by Archdeacon Brocklehurst is intriguing. How did he know of Lesser? Brocklehurst had indeed paid an unsuccessful visit to England in 1935-6 to see if he could raise funds for the building of a new cathedral, but there was no known connection between the two men until Lesser arrived in New Zealand.[92] The person most likely to have heard of Lesser's work in England and Kenya was the New Zealand Primate, Campbell West-Watson, who had strong links with Barrow-in-Furness before coming to New Zealand,[93] and whose name along with Lesser's features in the Carlisle Diocesan Missionary Council's list of members serving overseas.[94] Clearly West-Watson would have known people in England who might recommend Lesser to him as a candidate for the Bishopric of Waiapu.

The Diocese had experienced some hard years, and at the time of Lesser's election had been without consistent 'hands-on' episcopal leadership for almost a decade. Bishop Herbert Williams, consecrated in February 1930, courageously faced the double challenges of the Depression and the enormous damage to Church property and records caused by the 1931 Hawke's Bay earthquake,[95] but in a further blow for the Diocese, had died suddenly in office in December 1937. His successor, George Vincent Gerard, consecrated in October 1938, felt called to be Chaplain to the forces and was on leave of absence from the Diocese for most of the war, returning once to chair the 1943 Synod.[96] His offer of resignation was accepted in April 1944, and an electoral synod in the following October chose George Cruickshank, the Dean of Dunedin. They had great hopes of this new Bishop, consecrated in February 1945, but sadly, he suffered a serious stroke after only 14 months, and resigned in May 1946.[97]

Another electoral synod therefore was held on 4 September 1946, but its chosen candidate turned down the invitation. Unfortunately, his name had already been leaked to the media, in defiance of the Church's protocols and the Presiding Bishop's stern injunctions for secrecy,[98] causing much anger and embarrassment.[99] So yet another electoral synod was organized for 3 December 1946. All these electoral synods – three in just over two years – along with the previous decade of war and the lack of close episcopal oversight, must have tried the resources and patience of both lay and clergy. This time however the Diocese was luckier and chose someone who was a stayer!

As Roseveare notes in his history, Lesser, the ninth Bishop of Waiapu, was the first to come directly from an overseas position, all the others having been born here or having served in a New Zealand parish for some years before becoming Bishop.[100] Waiapu was unusual in that respect, however, and most of the bishops of the time would have shared Lesser's English heritage.

Yet the New Zealand church was quite different from the one Lesser had known either in England or in Kenya, though it might look

A Likely Lad

deceptively the same. The first Bishop of New Zealand, Selwyn, had ensured that the church's constitution established a more democratic system of government than that of the Church of England, with strong lay participation in decision-making, including the election of bishops. Moreover, State and Church are separate in New Zealand, unlike the established Church of England, and the historic concept of the 'parish' to which everyone automatically belongs is foreign to this country. However, his years in Kenya would have accustomed the new Bishop to some of the other points of difference between New Zealand and England: the sparse population, poor roads, lack of public transport and an indigenous culture in a state of flux and poised for dramatic change.

But while the New Zealand church was constitutionally different from the Church of England, at first sight it would have appeared reassuringly familiar. Clergy would have looked very much the same, the hymns would be from *Hymns Ancient and Modern*, and above all, the regular services of the church were all from the same *Book of Common Prayer* in either the 1662 or revised 1928 version, so Lesser would have been able to meditate on the sometimes arcane words of the service of Consecration in the months leading up to it.

The Consecration on St Barnabas' Day was an impressive ceremony attended by eight bishops, including W.W. Sedgewick, the 90-year-old former Bishop of Waiapu, various dignitaries and hundreds of clergy and lay people. While there is not a word of Māori in the service, the Bishop of Aotearoa was one of Lesser's presenters to the Archbishop, the other being the Bishop of Nelson, P.W. Stephenson, who also preached.

An enthusiastic report of the Consecration appears in the parish magazine of St Mary's church, Waipukurau. Written by a layman it describes the occasion as "inspiring" and goes on,

> "Inspiring, too, the man himself, this small dark man with a scholarly mien, cultured voice and lively sense of humour, who in so short a time caught the imagination of his flock and filled them with admiration for his courage in shouldering with humility, dignity and purposefulness the burden of responsibility attached to his high office. Undoubtedly, we had come to regard our Bishops rather in the light of elderly fathers to be respected and loved from a distance. The power of inspiring others is a rare gift even among spiritual people. It was a wonderful and moving experience to find in the

Episcopal seat a Bishop who radiates faith hope and love of mankind, one so vital who in ringing tones of conviction proclaims the faith not merely as an accepted and necessary part of life but as an ever-glorious, joyful thing carrying with it all there is of happiness in this world."[101]

The Enthronement followed at 7.30 p.m. the next day. The new Bishop preached on the need to enthrone Christ in the "highest places of our lives" and to listen to the "still small voice of God" using apt anecdotes to illustrate his points. Both the Consecration and Enthronement services, including his sermon, were given full coverage in the local paper, which continued to have very friendly relations with the Bishop over the years. Already too the new Bishop's ease of manner and sense of humour were being appreciatively noted.

At his Civic Reception a week later in the Municipal Theatre, attended by the Mayor, the local MP, the Chairman of the County Council, Bishop Bennett, the president of the Napier Council of Churches, the local Catholic priest and other clergy, the guest of honour offered his opinion of how he came to be elected: "It seems to me that of the two evils you chose…" Again his humorous style is referred to, although he included a serious message in his reply: the public should support and encourage those who faced civic responsibilities, young people should be educated to a community spirit and civic responsibility, and "we should encourage our councillors to think more of the next generation than of the next election."[102]

The general feeling of the Diocese might be summed up by the Dean's words in the Cathedral magazine:

> "It is a great thing to be able to say again 'We have a Bishop' and we hope and pray that our bishop will be long with us to give the Church that wise leadership so urgently needed."[103]

Amongst all the ceremony and official welcomes there is a small detail revealing one of the new Bishop's most consistent characteristics: attention to detail and thorough preparation, especially for services of worship. On his copy of the order of service for his Consecration he has written his name: N.A. Lesser. In contrast, his copy of the Enthronement service on the following evening has "Norman Waiapu" on the cover. He was by then the Bishop and had taken on a new name – and he was aware of the significance of that.

A Likely Lad

The Diocese must have welcomed with some relief the arrival of a youngish, energetic bishop. Indeed, he appears to have travelled as far and as fast as was humanly possible around the Diocese in his first year, given the difficulties of travel in those days. Even today it is still challenging to get around the 42,000 sq. kms that make up the Waiapu Diocese, extending as it does from Tauranga in the North to Woodville in the South, and inland as far West as Rotorua and Taupo. In Lesser's day the roads would have been much worse, and cars much slower, less comfortable and less reliable; on the other hand, public transport was better – there were trains! – and the rural population was not yet in decline.

A survey of his first few years in the Diocese gives some idea of both the demands of his new task and the energy and dedication he brought to it. A priority was to get to know his Diocese and its people, so after spending just under a month around Napier and Hastings, he set off on his first short tour of part of his Diocese, travelling by bus to Rotorua on 12 July, "a pleasant surprise for the parish," according to the vicar. He then went on to Ruatoki for his first Māori Synod or 'Hinota' on 14 July, so it was undoubtedly a wise and tactful move to suggest that Bishop Bennett replace him as president.[104] The Hinota received reports – from the pastorates, from Miss Bargrove, the 'Mission lady', from Bishop Bennett about the revision of the Māori Bible – and discussed what could be done about the old vicarage at Ruatoki. Lesser's only task was to give the Benediction, but the Hinota would have been an early chance for him to establish helpful relationships. According to a snippet of 'Personal' news[105] he spent the night in Rotorua before returning to Napier.

Back in Napier, he chaired a meeting of Standing Committee, installed a new headmistress at Hukarere, the Māori Girls' School founded by the Williams family in Napier; gave members of the Hawke's Bay Branches of the Church of England Men's Society an 'interesting' talk on life in Kenya ("a new national spirit was developing rapidly") after challenging them to play their full part as men in the life of the church; prepared a diary of engagements for the months August-November to go to the clergy, and conducted his first Confirmation service, which included his own daughter. A State visit from Lord Montgomery provided a change of scene as the Bishop was included in the official reception and lunch for the famous soldier.[106]

In early August he began a lengthier tour of the Diocese from Gisborne to Te Kaha with Bishop Bennett as chauffeur and guide. *Church and People*

New Zealand

reported that every "daughter church and the hospital in Gisborne were visited during the Saturday and Sunday." Of course there was always more than one service on a Sunday, and this Sunday was particularly busy[107] with a Eucharist, Children's Church and "extremely well attended morning and evening services" in Holy Trinity, the main church, and another Eucharist at Wainui at 3 p.m.[108] He preached at all of these, and would have needed two, possibly three, different sermons in case of having a 'repeat' congregation.

As they travelled up the coast, they conducted services, interviewed prospective candidates for the ministry, and were welcomed by Sir Apirana Ngata at Ruatoria with a special morning tea. Then it was on to Tikitiki and Te Araroa, visiting local people on the way before finally arriving in Te Kaha on 13 August in time for a 5 p.m. start of a two-day 'interesting' Hinota. It was at a Communion service at this Hinota that Bishop Lesser asked those present to say the Lord's Prayer in their own tongue "wherein we were born" to remind themselves that they were a family and all children of God – a concept central to his theology and one to which he often returned in sermons and Synod addresses.

It was also here that he spoke of the "Maoris (sic) doing what our Lord had done: taken a towel and a basin of water and invited their friends to refresh themselves." "Our Lord was always anxious that the simple things of life should be transfigured with a divine sense." He bade his hearers "to remember Him every time they washed and ate; Baptism and Communion were not to be regarded as something exceptional, but as an integral part of life itself, indeed the meaning of a full life." [109]

At home again in Napier briefly, he preached at Evensong in the Cathedral on 17 August, then spent a few days in Wellington for a Bishops' meeting, returning to preach at Evensong in St Luke's Havelock North the following Sunday. As usual there was a supper afterwards when parishioners could meet the new Bishop socially.

September was equally busy, starting with a clergy meeting in Hastings on 1 September, followed by a second pastoral letter on 4 September, which included a short prayer he had written for the mentally afflicted, and guidance on weddings in Lent, frowned on at the time. While people should be educated, he says, to realise that weddings in Lent "are not generally appropriate," he shows a typical willingness to put pastoral needs above rules, writing, "I believe it would be indefensible to refuse to

A Likely Lad

marry a person in any circumstances in Lent." However, there were limits to his tolerance: "My own practice would be not to allow decorations, but I would not refuse appropriate music if desired." He would not allow weddings in Holy Week except Easter Eve, when consideration must be given to the ladies decorating the church, and there was to be no confetti as "it always 'blew back' in, adding unnecessarily to that day's heavy preparation." On weddings in general, he was less willing to compromise on the choice of music, being "strongly opposed to popular songs, e.g. I'll walk beside you" and wanting only "hymns from one of the recognised hymn books… or excerpts from well-known works, e.g. *Messiah,*" although he saw "no objection to a solo being sung by a competent person after due practice."[110]

The letter is a fairly rare example of Lesser giving a clear expression of his opinion and practice to his clergy in writing, though a few months after this he does give similarly detailed advice on memorial tablets in churches, suggesting that donors' names should be inscribed in a "very beautiful book hand-printed and engraved," instead of the usual tablet on the wall, adding, "It is good to get someone to give the book and a delightful carved case in which it can be permanently displayed."[111]

He attended his third Hinota, this time at Kohupatiki marae near Clive[112] where members framed an important resolution to bring to the forthcoming Synod in October, expressing dissatisfaction at the lack of free access of the Bishop of Aotearoa to all the dioceses.[113] It was a longstanding grievance which he would have already heard at the Hinota at Ruatoki and Te Kaha.

On 11 September he chaired a Mothers' Union AGM at which he gave "a most inspiring and interesting talk." What he said is indeed interesting, for it reveals the openness of mind so praised in his early days at Norris Green. He reminds the MU that "although any great union should have its laws and regulations, any Christian body must always be careful that it was not less generous than its Lord." He went on to challenge MU members further: while their first Object of "upholding the sanctity of marriage," was important "it must always be second to what was essentially the job of the MU… namely to set forth Christ, His power and His love."[114] There is quite clearly here the implication that the exclusive rules pertaining to full MU membership might need to be reconsidered in the light of Christian compassion. Rules, at least in the organizations

New Zealand

of the Church, were secondary to the main purpose of spreading the Gospel and should never be allowed to hinder that.

Later in the month he was involved with the week-long celebrations for St Matthew's Jubilee in Hastings,[115] and a Board of Missions meeting in Wellington, where he was given the job of looking after the visiting speaker Bishop Wynn-Jones from Central Tanganyika for a few days,[116] and in the company of Wynn-Jones carried out Confirmations in six parishes in Central and Southern Hawke's Bay. Typically, while in Waipukurau he found time to visit both the hospital and the Sanatorium for TB patients.[117]

He was back in Napier for a Clergy meeting on 22 September at Bishop's Court and a Confirmation at Hukarere on the 23rd, then 'down country' for more Confirmations in Dannevirke, Takapau and Ormondville. The Dannevirke visit began with a social event on the Saturday evening; he preached at St John's, the main church on Sunday morning; at Matamau, a small country church, in the afternoon, and was back in St John's to confirm 60 candidates in the evening.

After that busy month came his first Diocesan Synod in October, an important occasion for a new Bishop, when the work of the whole Diocese would be under consideration and the ever-recurring question of funding that work would inevitably be part of the debate.

A more leisurely event in those days than today's Synods, it ran from Saturday night through to Wednesday, and included separate Clergy, Māori and Laity Conferences. The first Session began at 10.45 on Sunday with the Roll Call, a service of Holy Communion and the President's Charge. On Monday morning the business sessions started, followed by the Māori Conference in the afternoon, when select committees also met, with another business session in the evening. Lesser's well-annotated Synod papers reveal both the preparation undertaken for Synod – the 'King's business' as he liked to call it – and the close attention he paid to its processes.[118]

At the Māori Conference, presided over by Bishop Lesser as Bishop of the Diocese, the lack of access of the Māori Bishop to all the dioceses of New Zealand was again raised. Lesser was able to tell them that he had brought the matter to the attention of the other Bishops at their recent meeting in September when all present had agreed that the Bishop of Aotearoa was welcome in their dioceses. Although this was purely

A Likely Lad

an informal agreement arising from mutual goodwill[119] it was some reassurance, and the Māori Conference was at least partially satisfied. Unfortunately, the Bishop of Auckland who was the one most opposed to another Bishop coming to minister to Māori in his diocese, had not been at the Bishops' meeting as he was ill.

The Māori Conference also agreed that Bishop Bennett would represent the Diocese at the 1948 Lambeth Conference,[120] and naturally strongly supported Bishop Bennett's motion before Synod that "it be a recommendation to the Cathedral Re-Building Committee to make provision for the inclusion of Māori Art and Craft into the new building design," a recommendation accepted by the Synod. [121]

By then it seems Lesser had already decided not to go to the Lambeth Conference himself, telling his 'brethren' in a pastoral letter that he "wants to consolidate the work which I have but begun here."[122] Of course, travel times were very different from those of today and going to Lambeth would have meant at least three months away from the diocese. It would, however, have been easy enough for him to justify going. It was after all an opportunity for him as a new bishop to learn a great deal, to experience the diversity of the Anglican Communion and to build important world-wide networks. Not too many would have given away the chance of the experience – not to mention a trip 'home' largely at the expense of the Diocese. Instead, in a significant collegial move, Bishop Bennett was to represent the Diocese at this important world-wide gathering, and at the first World Council of Churches Assembly in Amsterdam.

Two decisions made by his first Synod are of interest: the membership of the Diocesan Youth Council was broadened to include four laypeople as well as four clergy, a "member of the Māori race" and three appointees by the Bishop;[123] and secondly "it was agreed that the Bishop of Aotearoa's stipend be looked at by the body responsible as no revision had been made since 1943 Synod."[124] In addition, Standing Committee had agreed before the Synod to raise all Māori stipends to £300 but it was all to come from the pastorates (i.e. the Māori parishes): "there would not be the usual subsidy."[125]

Financial matters tend to occupy the minds of Synod members and this Synod was no exception. Indeed, the Sessional Finance Committee in its report drew the attention of Synod to the "continued and rising demands made on parishes for additional money. It considers that saturation point has been reached and would impress upon members of Synod to consider very carefully before bringing forward resolutions involving the raising of extra funds or any extra calls on the General Diocesan Fund."

It wanted Standing Committee to discuss with the Bishop "the whole question of Diocesan Finance,"[126] and repeated its message, with an additional note about shortage of manpower, at the 1948 Synod.[127]

Such a dire warning possibly stimulated the Bishop to write on 1 November the first of several 'begging' letters for the church. It is a letter worth reading: a masterly combination of fact ("£3,920 is needed for the General Diocesan Fund – that is just to keep the place running without any extension of work, or new buildings"), cajoling, exhortation, inspiration and a little bit of sharpness: "We will be glad of the widow's mite – but not from a millionaire's widow."[128]

The day after Synod finished he and the Diocesan Secretary travelled to Hauiti marae at Tolaga Bay for the funeral of a well-loved Māori priest, Wi Tangohau, attended by both Māori and senior pākehā clergy, encouraging the Bishop to write, "The family ideal after which we are all striving was secured."[129]

The month of November was largely taken up with a 24-day Confirmation tour of the Waiapu and Tauranga Archdeaconries. These Confirmation services were a priority for the Bishop as the 'Laying-on of Hands' in the rite of Confirmation was exclusively the act of a Bishop. It was also a significant occasion for the candidates and their families, as it gave entry to receiving the sacrament of Holy Communion. Young people, usually in their early teens, would attend classes of instruction for some months before being confirmed at what was often a very crowded service with up to 80 candidates and their families present. Following Confirmation, the newly-confirmed would make their first Communion at a parish service – usually the following Sunday – which was again a special occasion. In smaller areas, the whole community might be involved and in this secular age it is astonishing to read that a headmaster would "gladly release the younger candidates from school for the service, (i.e. a Communion for the newly confirmed), if it is decided to have it at about 10 am."[130]

A Likely Lad

So Confirmation tours were therefore planned well in advance, and though the general pattern remained the same each year, the details were carefully managed so that each parish – and any of its 'daughter' churches – got its jealously-guarded 'share' of the Bishop's attention over time. When on one occasion Lesser was able to spend a little more time than usual in a certain parish, it was noted by the vicar: "He stayed here from October 31 to Wednesday November 3 – the longest period for a good while that our Diocesan Bishop will have spent here."[131]

Clearly the Bishop's visit meant a lot to far-flung parts of the Diocese where it was hard for people to feel part of the Diocesan family and parishes would naturally arrange for other events to be associated with the Confirmation service in order to make the most of the occasion.

The November 1947 tour was typical in that it included many activities in addition to the numerous Church services, which in themselves make daunting reading. Sunday's programme in Wairoa, for example, began with services at 7.30 a.m. and 9 a.m. in the main church of St Paul, then Nuhaka for 11 a.m., and on further to Tuai at 3 p.m., ending with a Confirmation back at St Paul's at 7 p.m. When you consider the distance between these centres, and the fact that the clergy at this time carried out the entire service on their own, the demands of the day's schedule are apparent. But as well as all the services with their associated and inevitable cups of tea where people could meet the Bishop, this tour included Civic welcomes, Rose Shows, Garden Parties, parish festivals, Church Bazaars, Men's meetings, and Mothers' Union festivals. A detailed itinerary pieced together from cuttings in the first Scrapbook[132] can be found in the Appendix for those who want to know more about this tour.

It says a lot for the Bishop's resilience that checking through his papers after this journey, his eagle eye picked up and corrected, typically, a small misprint in one account of his visit, in which a vicar had described him as a "jealous" instead of (presumably) a "zealous" leader.[133]

Back home in Napier after this lengthy tour, he preached at a Mothers' Union Diocesan Festival in the Cathedral and was on hand to welcome the ladies at Bishop's Court for afternoon tea.[134] The last Sunday of the month was very full with "special thanksgiving services throughout the day," for the Jubilee of the parish of St Andrew, Ahuriri.[135]

November was also the month of the Local Body elections, so Lesser, always keen to relate to the wider community, seized the opportunity to introduce the English tradition of a churching service for the new mayor and councillors in December. He again speaks in a forthright manner to them: "There was a prevalent idea," he said, "that the Church ought not to refer to matters relating to politics. There were people who would support the Church in the provision, say, of soup kitchens, free meals and hospitals, and at the same time they would resent the Church attacking those social ills necessitating soup kitchens, free meals and hospitals."[136]

Whatever he said, it did not put off the Hastings civic leaders, who asked for a similar service in February 1948.[137]

Other opportunities to speak to the wider community arose with requests to deliver Christmas messages to Rotary[138] and the Hawke's Bay Club, and as his reputation grew over the years he was always much in demand for speeches at prizegivings, graduations, 'openings' and/or blessings of community events. He saw this as an outreach into the community and never refused an invitation if he could help it.

The Ordination of Richard Talbot in December – his first – several Christmas services and a sermon for New Year's Eve in the Cathedral brought 1947 and his first six months as Bishop to an end.

How did the Bishop get around during that time? He would have needed a car almost immediately for local travel, and seems to have had some assistance with its purchase as he thanks the Laymen's Conference of the 1948 Synod for the "magnificent cheque towards the cost of my car."[139] He also enjoyed driving – which he was reputed to do 'like a bat out of hell!' – and drove occasionally to Gisborne in later years, as Wairoa people remember him calling in on the way, sometimes accompanied by Beatrice.[140]

However, the condition of the roads and the unreliability of cars made it preferable for him to use public transport for more distant centres and longer tours[141] and he continued to do so right up to his retirement. An undated bus ticket[142] has "The Bishop of Waiapu passenger," in Lesser's writing, with the words "Napier – Rotorua – Te Puke –Tauranga – Whakatane – Opotiki – Napier" added. Using public transport had the drawback of making him very dependent on the organisation of the Archdeacon and local clergy once he got to his destination, and a typically complicated set of arrangements[143] can be viewed in the endnote. On the other hand, bus or train travel had the advantage of giving him time to think, or perhaps write some notes – and of course to engage in conversation with the bus driver!

1948 and his second six months as Bishop began with preaching engagements on the first Sunday in February[144] in both Holy Sepulchre Church and St Paul's Symonds Street, Auckland where he was to attend the Consecration of Bishop Caulton, another Liverpudlian, as Bishop of Melanesia the following day.[145]

He spent his first Good Friday and Easter as Bishop in the Cathedral and at St Matthew's, Hastings, preaching at several services, a practice he seems to have continued throughout his episcopate. Soon after Easter he was up at Gisborne attending his first Hui Topu – a three-day meeting of the three Diocesan Māori Church Boards in the Diocese, particularly important this year as Bishop Bennett was being farewelled before leaving for Lambeth and the first World Council of Churches Assembly in Amsterdam. Attendance at Hui Topu was to become an annual commitment for Bishop Lesser, but this Hui Topu, his first, was memorable for many reasons, and is dealt with fully in the chapter "Māori Matters."

The absence of Bishop Bennett and six diocesan Bishops during this year of the Lambeth Conference brought additional responsibilities for those left at home. Bishop Lesser had to care for the Māori pastorates, and spent a week in Auckland in July carrying out Confirmations for Bishop Simkin.

His reputation as a speaker was spreading beyond his own diocese, leading to an engagement at the national conference of the Church of England Men's Society in June 1948 in Whanganui. The theme of this Conference was "Christ and Industry"[146] and Lesser told the 600 men present that "Christ did not divide life into things sacred and secular;" indeed "Christianity was meaningless unless Christ was the Lord of industry as well as of Christianity." Christ was in fact "the Lord of all good living," who had given us two fundamental things by which to remember Him: one was washing and the other eating. "They remind us of Baptism and the Last Supper. Every time we wash, we can think of Him. Every time we eat, we can think of Him." This ability to relate the faith to the simple things of everyday life made his sermons very accessible to the average person in the pew and was one reason for his popularity as a preacher.

New Zealand

A further reported extract from this speech is worth quoting as it mirrors the comments made to the City Council's Churching Service in Napier at the end of 1947:

> "When I was in Nairobi, if I pointed out things that were necessary to improve living conditions, it was said that I was dabbling in politics. If I did not do so, others said I had not the guts. If one speaks on the problems of sex, one is called a dirty old man; if one does not talk of these problems it is said that one has not the courage to face up to the problems of life."[147]

His second Diocesan Synod in October 1948 was approaching, against a background of growing world tension. There were fears that the Cold War might escalate into something more lethal and the perceived threat of militant Communism was on many people's minds. Lesser used the political situation to advantage in his address to Synod, asking "What sort of a witness is our own life?" and challenging Christians to take their religion as seriously as Communists took their political values, adding,

> "We have so watered down the Gospel of Jesus that it is with a shock that we realise afresh that if we really put it into practice it would be the most revolutionary ethic the world has known."[148]

Not surprisingly, the Synod passed a motion expressing "its great appreciation of the most willing, able and friendly service given by the Bishop to every parish,"[149] a well-earned tribute to the energy and commitment he had brought to the rôle of Bishop in his first 15 months.

1949 brought further commitments outside the Diocese, in addition to his Diocesan responsibilities. He attended his first General Synod in Wellington in May, when he reported very fully as the Chair of an Advisory Commission on Māori Education. He was back there in June for the Diamond Jubilee celebrations of St Barnabas, Roseneath, who appreciated him so much that they invited him again in the following year.[150] Later in the year he again travelled to Wellington for Board of Missions meetings and the annual Bishops' meetings, and was in Auckland three times during the year for meetings of the St John's College Trust Board.

Within the Diocese, his diary for 1949 shows a lengthy tour of the East Coast as far north as Waipiro Bay over July and August, the Installation of an Archdeacon and four new Canons, the Ordination of Brown Turei and Keepa Paenga, and Institutions of vicars in Opotiki, Porangahau, Waipawa, Taradale and Whakatane.

A Likely Lad

But underpinning these special events was the continuing work of managing a Diocese. As Bishop he was expected to chair the Standing Committee, most of the various Trust Board meetings, to keep up with the work of the many Diocesan committees set up by Synod, and deal with the mountains of correspondence, which would always accumulate while he was on a Confirmation tour. Of course he had the assistance of the Diocesan Secretary, and strong clerical and lay support in each of the three Archdeaconries, but much responsibility rested with him.

In contrast to the routine office work inherent in the rôle, certain social expectations also existed. Debutante balls were good fund-raisers for parishes and it seemed necessary, even if not part of the Prayer Book requirements, for a Bishop in strange clothing to receive curtseys from dozens of virginally-clad young women in Town Halls all around the Diocese in what seems an almost surreal ceremony in today's eyes. However, Bishop Lesser saw these occasions as 'part of the job' and may well have appreciated the opportunity of meeting people not always closely associated with the Church.

By 1950 Lesser might have felt that he was ready for a slightly slower pace, but it was the beginning of an even busier period.

The first event of interest was the visit of a Japanese bishop. While today this would hardly cause a stir, in 1950 it was a small act of courage on Lesser's part, as bitter memories of Japan's part in the war were still fresh in New Zealanders' minds, and some invitations to the Bishop had been withdrawn in other places because of public pressure.[151] In Napier his visit received minimal press coverage, but nobody seems to have objected to his presence, and Lesser was enthusiastic about his quiet Christian conviction.

But there were other much more significant events to make the year memorable in Diocesan history. It was the year celebrated as Te Aute's Centennial[152] coinciding with Hukarere's 75th Jubilee; it was the year both Sir Apirana Ngata and Bishop Bennett died, the latter just weeks after the Te Aute celebrations in August; and it was the year that fund-raising for the re-building of the Cathedral commenced in earnest, a subject which is fully covered in another chapter.

Bishop Lesser's part in the Te Aute celebrations was confined to the weekend, when he shared in a service of thanksgiving, dedicated the new Assembly Hall on Saturday morning and was one of a panel of speakers on Māori education in the afternoon. On Sunday he was occupied with the Hukarere celebrations: a service in the Cathedral at 10 a.m., the laying of the foundation stone of their new chapel in the afternoon, and Evensong in the old chapel at 6.30 p.m.[153]

The death of both Sir Apirana Ngata and Bishop Bennett in this one year dealt a double blow to the Diocese. Ngata, a charismatic leading layman, had established the hugely significant Hui Topu with their emphasis on youth participation in three days of worship, cultural activities, sport, study and business. Bishop Bennett was much loved by both pākehā and Māori and the whole country went into mourning as tributes flowed from all quarters. Lesser was in Tauranga when Bishop Bennett died and could not attend the service in the Cathedral, but joined in the funeral rites at Rotorua, writing later to his clergy "that two great leaders… have quietly left their canoes on the shores of time."

Apart from his genuine sense of personal loss, Lesser was also faced with an increased workload, as he had been in 1948 with Bennett's absence at the Lambeth Conference. The Bishops did not meet until May 1951 to choose a successor to Bishop Bennett, with Wiremu Panapa being consecrated in August 1951, so for almost a year Lesser was without the help of a Suffragan Bishop. According to his pastoral letter of 27 November 1951[154] he visited every parish, parochial district and pastorate during the year, noting that "normally the Bishop of Aotearoa will conduct many of the Confirmation services." The arrival of Bishop Panapa must have been a great relief for him, even though building a new collegial relationship would also take time and energy.

"Energy" is the word that most readily comes to mind when considering these first years of Lesser's episcopate. A second word is "commitment." He did not allow himself any real holidays and it was years before his daughter realised that Monday was traditionally the clergy 'day off.' Very occasionally he would say to Beatrice, "Put your pearls on," and they would drive to Wellington, see a film, have dinner, and drive home; sometimes, daringly, the visit would even be extended to staying the night in a hotel![155]

The pattern of work as a Diocesan bishop, established in his first few years, continued in much the same way over the next twenty, becoming even more demanding as the years passed. In the 1950s he took on additional tasks for the wider Church such as chairing the Commission on Church

A Likely Lad

Union. Within the Diocese the re-building of the Cathedral with all its associated problems dominated much of his working and personal life.

By the end of this decade he had worked at a torrid pace for twelve years without any real holiday, so it is completely understandable that a slight note of weariness has crept into some jottings he has made on a programme for a forthcoming tour of the Waiapu Archdeaconry in July 1959. Along with the usual annotations and additions which he typically made in preparing for a tour are two revealing scribbles. Beside the words "Free Day" in the programme he has written: "What a Hope! I wonder what it will include?" And the last day of the programme, Monday 20 July, has the slightly despairing note scribbled alongside it: "What is left of me hopes to catch the 7.45 Railcar."[156]

However, despite the temporary weariness suggested by these comments, another decade and more lay ahead during which he continued to dedicate his skills and energy to the Waiapu Diocese, while also carrying the additional weight of the Primacy. It is a marathon episcopate few would attempt to equal.

Norman Lesser c. 1950s

Chapter 4: Māori Matters

What did Norman Lesser and Māori know about each other? And what were Māori impressions of this new Bishop coming from across the seas?

> "To us Bishop Lesser seemed a breath of fresh air. He was different from the other bishops at that time,"

according to the late Archbishop Brown Turei, who was ordained by Bishop Lesser and served in various parishes and pastorates under him.

> "The other bishops were almost gods. Lesser was down-to-earth, much easier to talk to."[157]

He was also easy to host: "easier than Bishop Frederick Bennett," said Archbishop Brown! Bishop Lesser would undertake Confirmations in the Māori pastorates up the East Coast if the Bishop of Aotearoa was unavailable, and when the Lessers came up to Whangara, where Brown was the Māori pastor, the Turei family would either tidy up a room and pass the children on to someone else, or go to the pa themselves.

The new Bishop's preaching style was also enjoyed. "The old style was to take a text and expound your three (or more) points from it, but Lesser broke it up with stories that emphasised the point he wanted to put across."[158] He had a gift for relating faith to everyday life, as he had reminded his listeners in one of his first marae visits:

> "The Māoris (sic) at their meeting house had done what our Lord had done, taken a towel and basin of water and invited their friends to refresh themselves. Our Lord was always anxious that the simple things of life should be transfigured with a divine sense."

They should remember Him every time they washed or ate: Baptism and Holy Communion were not to be regarded as something exceptional, "but as an integral part of life itself, indeed the meaning of full life."[159]

Archbishop Brown also remembered Synods as being "a lot of fun."

> "We got through the business. He was a chain smoker, so you moved into committee as often as possible."

However, Brown was not so keen on the traditional Synod Garden Party at Bishop's Court, held on the Saturday afternoon. "We would put in an appearance and then disappear out the back down to some rugby match."[160]

General Synod too became more relaxed following Lesser's presidency in 1961. Archbishop Brown remembered being chaplain at one such Synod held in Napier, and Lesser as the new Archbishop greeted the meeting with a friendly "Good Morning." Apparently, that was new as General Synod was traditionally a "very staid affair with very strict procedures."

Archbishop Brown reflecting on the rôle of archbishop thought that in some ways it would have been more demanding in Lesser's day,

> "as you were the only one. On the other hand, the dioceses were very much a law unto themselves and there was little flexibility in the rules. So long as Lesser kept to the rules and canons he would have been OK."[161]

Māori would have welcomed Lesser's enthusiasm for sport – even though he confessed he wasn't a rugby enthusiast. But he was a keen footballer and apparently demonstrated one of his skills to a schoolboy attempting to trip up a mate, telling him "Not that way. Do it like this!" whereupon the boy went around telling everyone that the Bishop had shown him how to trip up someone![162] And as an enthusiastic cricketer, he was happy not only with Te Aute's success in the field, but also their style of play:

> "It is especially pleasing to see you have done so well at cricket – and the right kind of cricket…"

> "We want people to play hard and we want none of that stuff where you are told that if you play sufficiently stubbornly, you will force a draw. I would sooner have a glorious defeat than a stubborn draw."[163]

Māori also enjoyed his sense of humour and his willingness to make jokes at his own expense. One often-told story concerns the large Māori member of Synod who gazed down on the short and slightly-built Lesser, saying:

> "They told us if we cast our nets wide, we would get a big fish. But what did we catch? A sprat!"[164]

And when Lesser – the first Waiapu Bishop to become Archbishop – was welcomed as such by his own Synod, with waiata and haka from the Māori members,[165] Bishop Panapa knew that no offence would be caused by reminding him "that he was still the lesser half!" Other writers have noted that Lesser's "great repertoire of anecdotes and jokes was invaluable in the give and take of marae debate, opening many doors and establishing long friendships."[166]

And what did Norman Lesser know about the Māori? While confessing to very little knowledge, (apparently the family had learned the song *Waiata Poi* in Kenya from an Australian!)[167] Lesser's willingness to learn and his own easy personal style did much to overcome this initial disadvantage and from the beginning he gave considerable time and energy to things Māori.

As Bishop of Waiapu it was crucial that he quickly gain understanding of the unique historic relationship between Māori and pākehā Anglicans in his Diocese, and his efforts to do so in those first few months were noted and appreciated. Bishop Bennett was able to say at the end of Lesser's first Synod, a mere four months after his arrival, "The Bishop has greatly endeared himself to the Māori people."[168]

Waiapu, with many proud and independent tribes within its boundaries,[169] had for decades supported the Māori desire to have one of their own as a Bishop for the Māori people, and when the first Bishop of Aotearoa, Frederick Bennett, was eventually consecrated in 1928, Waiapu felt privileged to hold his Chair as Suffragan Bishop in Waiapu, though his task was to care for all Māori in Aotearoa. While this arrangement was considered the best solution to a constitutional problem at the time, it was essentially a compromise, and the Bishop of Aotearoa's position in the church hierarchy and governance continued to vex Māori for many years.

Within Waiapu itself, while the personal relationships were warm between the Bishops, the perceived inferior status of the Bishop of Aotearoa as Suffragan to the Bishop of Waiapu, and the obvious discrepancy between their working conditions, were grounds for unhappiness and even resentment among some Māori, though these feelings were clearly directed towards the Church's systems rather than to Lesser or any other individual.

At the time of Lesser's arrival in 1947, Frederick Bennett had been the loved and respected Bishop of Aotearoa for 19 years and was well-established in the rôle. He was also familiar to pākehā, having confirmed many in the absence of Bishop Gerard during the War. So it was naturally he who led the new Bishop on a fortnight's conducted tour of the diocese, and it was he who attended the Lambeth Conference of 1948 instead of Bishop Lesser, who felt that he had only just arrived in Waiapu.

But though Bennett was the senior bishop by many years, Lesser as the Bishop of Waiapu felt responsible for all the Anglicans in Waiapu, both Māori and non-Māori. The pastorates (the Māori parishes) had some degree of self-governance, with their own Boards of Management and clergy, and representation at the Diocesan Synod where the important decisions were made. They also had their own Māori Conference, which met during Synod and on other occasions, but it was chaired by the Bishop of Waiapu.

> "The Māori Bishop was present – but never in charge. Looking through today's eyes it seems patronizing, but we accepted it then,"

says Archbishop Turei.[170] So although Māori were very much part of the Diocese they were generally expected to follow the pākehā way of doing things, even if impromptu speeches and waiata were a welcome diversion to the proceedings of Synod: "Without the Māori element, Synod would have been a very boring event," comments Synodsman Colin Baker.[171]

However, while the relationship over the years between pākehā and Māori bishops might have been very warm, it was not truly collegial, even in the Waiapu diocese.[172] This lack of collegiality stemmed of course from the Anglican emphasis on the bishop as a focus of unity within a diocese, so logic dictated that there could only be one. So it was therefore Bishop Lesser who dedicated the War Memorial window in St Andrew's church at Taupo, even though it was a memorial for both Māori and pākehā killed in the war. Bishop Bennett's rôle was to give the address. And when Brown Turei was ordained, Bishop Lesser was described as the "ordaining Bishop" and Bishop Bennett was listed as "also taking part in the service." Bishop Lesser dedicated the new chapel in Hukarere school, although Bishop Panapa was present on that occasion and preached.

The relationship of the Bishop of Aotearoa to the rest of New Zealand was of even greater concern to Māori. Bishop Bennett had no automatic right of entry into other dioceses to minister to his people and had to ask permission of each Diocesan Bishop to do so. This was justifiably a source of frustration and even anger to many Māori and was frequently discussed. In September 1947, Lesser heard this frustration for the third time at a Hinota at Kohupatiki near Napier, and one of his first jobs on behalf of Māori was to "raise the matter with the bench of Bishops," as this Hinota "respectfully" asked him to do.[173] Consequently at a Board of Missions meeting in Wellington Lesser got the Bishops to pass a resolution expressing a general willingness for Bishop Bennett to visit their dioceses. Although this was an informal agreement only, as this meeting had no power to change the ruling, it was met with "general satisfaction," and Turi Carroll paid a tribute in Synod on "the efforts of the Bishop and Archdeacon Brocklehurst in bringing about a better understanding of the status of the Bishop of Aotearoa in the other Dioceses of the Province."[174]

Within the Waiapu Diocese, however, there were no personal problems between the two Bishops who had a particularly close relationship. Bennett had exceptional gifts of personality and intelligence and was held in great respect by both Māori and Pākehā. For his part, Lesser must have relied initially at least on both Bennett's long experience and his profound understanding of the Māori section of his Diocese, and the value both he and the Diocese placed on Bennett's incalculable contribution is perhaps partially acknowledged in the 1947 Synod resolution that the "Bishop of Aotearoa's stipend be looked at by the body responsible as no revision had been made since 1943 Synod."[175]

The two men were also able to share a friendly joke as well as their episcopal responsibilities and Lesser felt his loss keenly when Bennett died in 1950. In a statement made from Te Puke, where he was visiting at the time, he said Bennett "had represented the Christian faith with dignity and credit and his natural courtesy and charm endeared him to Māori and pākehā alike." On a more personal note he added,

> "Bishop Bennett was officially Bishop of Aotearoa, and my colleague and trusted friend. Never should I forget the occasion when I went to wish him 'au revoir' before coming away for my tour of the archdeaconry of Tauranga. The more intimate details of the visit are not for publication, but their spiritual significance will form a hallowed treasure to me."[176]

Paying tribute to both him and Ngata, who had died earlier in the year, in a pastoral letter of 27 September 1950, he wrote "...two great leaders of thought and action in the spiritual and temporal realms have quietly left their canoes on the shores of time,"[177] and in the same letter described some of his feelings at the funeral:

> "When we were gathered at Ohinemutu for the Bishop's funeral service, there was a very wonderful spirit abroad. All of us felt that as friends we had surrounded a friend and were in turn surrounded by a Friend. 'Our Father' took on such a wonderful significance…" "Chiefly by his efforts the lovely church at Ohinemutu was erected to God's Glory, and he, who for many years, has been a corner stone in the House of God was that day laid within the Sanctuary to be again a corner stone in the house of God."

The relationship between him and the next Bishop of Aotearoa, Wiremu Panapa, may not have been so close, for a variety of reasons, although again the two could share a good story and knew that "joy was part of the Christian Gospel." Panapa was a 'man of the people' who believed in going to where the people were, whether they were Catholic, Mormon, Ratana or Anglican, or whether they were in a pub, on a marae, or in church, and Lesser found this inclusive approach to evangelism difficult to understand.[178] Nevertheless, in paying tribute to him at his funeral, Lesser spoke warmly of Panapa's "humble spirit" and "inner reserve of deep spirituality" describing him as his "trusted friend for 17 years."

Apart from assimilating the historic background to the relationship between pākehā and Māori Anglicans in the Diocese, Lesser also felt the need to learn as quickly as he could something of Māori tikanga. He was thrown in at the deep end with the Hinota already mentioned, but tangi too were opportunities to learn, and he was scrupulous in attending these, recognising their importance in Māori culture. His first tangi was that of the highly-respected and loved priest, Wi Tangohau, held "in the presence of a large number of clergy," and following it Lesser felt able to write that "the family ideal for which we are striving was secured." The second one, Lady Ngata's, was made especially memorable by huge flooding around Ruatoria,[179] but there were many more as the years passed, often involving considerable travel.[180]

Hui Topu were other significant gatherings of the Māori church that called for his support. These three-day events, first begun in 1938 by Sir Apirana Ngata to promote churchmanship among Māori youth,[181] were a mix of worship and study, business and cultural performances.

Lesser's first Hui Topu, held at Te Poho-o-Rawiri marae in Gisborne in April 1948, was a very big occasion for two reasons: first, it was an opportunity for all Māori to farewell Bishop Bennett before he left for the

Māori Matters

Lambeth Conference, and Māori leaders in both church and government from around the whole country were present. Secondly, members of the Ringatu religious movement were going to announce at this Hui that they would agree to their founder Te Kooti's remains being returned, against the wishes of some Ngati Porou, to the Gisborne district, as Te Kooti himself had requested. So representatives from both the Ringatu church and the National Council of Churches, which had helped to negotiate the agreement between the two parties, added to the numbers.

Bishop Lesser's understanding of Māori tikanga would have been greatly extended by this Hui, which included a welcoming speech to him from Sir Apirana Ngata, and much oratory in te reo, as people from all over Aotearoa presented farewell gifts to Bishop Bennett.

Ngata's speech of welcome held a note of warning when he referred to the fact that he, (i.e. Lesser), came from a far distant land and "the labours he had undertaken, (i.e. in New Zealand), held peculiar problems with which the head of a purely European diocese would have (had) no contact." However, he said, Māori had full confidence that he would acquaint himself with every part of the work of the church in his diocese and that in time he

> "would reach an understanding not only of the structure and extent of the Māori pastorate, but also of the approach of the Māori people to matters of religion."

He also warned that deliberations among Māori people involved "plain speaking and sometimes the giving and taking of hard knocks."

In his reply Bishop Lesser "struck a happy note and enlivened his speech by an occasional jocular comment upon the difficulties of a newcomer to such a diocese." He felt that "this gathering provided him with an excellent opportunity to assimilate not only the sense of the problems associated with the Māori pastorate, but the psychological background behind them."[182] Referring to Ngata's remark about "plain speaking" he issued his own subtle warning, saying,

> "Plain speaking could have a decided value so long as the discussions themselves were illuminated by a deeply spiritual feeling… Superficial discussion of church affairs could not reflect what should be in all minds and hearts – the teachings of Jesus Christ."[183]

A Likely Lad

Bishop Lesser's part in the Hui, according to the smartly-produced bi-lingual programme,[184] was to lead a quiet day for the clergy on the Saturday morning and chair the triennial meeting of the Māori Church Boards. However, everyone knew that the really meaty discussions took place at the informal open meeting on the preceding night – the Hui-a Iwi – where proposals were framed for presentation at the formal meeting next day. There was plenty to discuss, and foremost in everyone's mind was urban drift, the dramatic post-war movement of Māori to the towns, a social phenomenon affecting all aspects of Māori life. The reported lack of pastoral care for Māori who had moved to Auckland and Wellington particularly angered Ngata, who suggested that Waiapu should step in and offer assistance, asking,

> "Are we going to let Māori youth in the cities grow up as heathens just because of artificial diocesan boundaries? This is a question bigger than bishops and must be tackled,"

an example of the plain speaking he had referred to.[185] Other topics of concern were the future of the Māori bishopric – they wanted to ensure that another Māori would be appointed to follow Bishop Bennett when the time came[186] – the training of Māori clergy, the work of the Mission ladies among the Māori communities, and the need for "a definition of policy with regard to the Māori pastorate and to the spiritual guidance of the Māori people in general."[187]

Lesser would have heard these, and similar concerns, at previous church meetings, or Hīnota, and would hear them again. They arose from a legitimate sense that Māori were constantly struggling to retain their tikanga – or way of doing things – within the Church. The training of Māori clergy was one example, so this Hui proposed to re-open Te Rau Theological College in Gisborne. If that was not immediately possible, then a Māori tutor should be appointed to St John's College in the meantime – a request which had been made more than once in previous years by the Diocesan Standing Committee without success.[188]

Another big Hui Topu was held in the Tomoana showgrounds, near Hastings, in conjunction with the Te Aute near-centenary celebrations in August 1950, although sadly Sir Apirana Ngata had already died.[189] It began with an official welcome on Tuesday night; the days were filled with hockey tournaments and rugby matches, the evenings with cultural programmes and prayers, with a speaker, the Undersecretary for Māori Affairs T.T. Ropiha, on Thursday night, but Bishop Lesser was not involved until Saturday when he took part in a panel on Māori education.[190] On Sunday he transferred his attention to Hukarere, the girls' school, where he laid the foundation stone of the new chapel to mark its 75 years.[191]

With the deaths of Ngata and Bennett, and an interim of almost a year until the Consecration of Bishop Panapa in 1951, the Hui Topu seem to have temporarily faded away, although one was held in 1952 in Whakatane[192] and the 1952 Synod agreed that "the combined Hui Topu should be held once in every year."[193]

When 1954 came, a report says "the Bishop of Waiapu, seeing that it (the Hui Topu) was in danger of dying altogether has summoned the meeting at Moruea."[194] This seems to have been true enough as Lesser writes in the preface to the smart programme for the Hui:[195] "Following protracted discussions on the holding of the Hui Topu it has been decided at Synod that we should make a new venture of activity and faith…"

This Hui, held near Rotorua, was a great success with an attendance of 600-700, and Lesser was enthusiastic when preaching at the Sunday service:

> "How grand it is to see so many young people, happy, bright young people, playing their full part in the church… how important it is now that they should be strong servants of Christ."

He challenged them to discover what God intended them to do with their lives and praised the high standard of the choirs.[196]

Hui Topu continued to be held in different parts of the Diocese with varying numbers. There appears to have been one in Wairoa in 1956 as Lesser refers to it in an undated letter headed "To all Māori Clergy and Māori Lay Members of Synod." The letter is interesting for the demanding expectations it sets out for choirs taking part in the forthcoming Hui Topu in May 1957 at Ruatoki.[197] These expectations might seem highly inappropriate today, with the requirement that "all Choirs taking part in the Māori Youth Festival (sic) next year will be affiliated to the Royal School of Church Music," and items from the standard Anglican choir repertoire being chosen as test pieces,[198] but in fact Māori church choirs at the time were proud of achieving excellent standards in the Anglican choral tradition as well as in their own culture.

A Likely Lad

The Bishop's letter ends with a warning:

> "All this can be just a competition for self-glory, or it can be a discipline of heart and soul for the greater glory of Almighty God. If it is the former, then the Hui Topu is doomed. If it is the latter, then the Church of God will be stronger to do the task with which God has graciously entrusted it. May God bless you as you prepare to do His will."[199]

In 1959, the Centenary Year of the Diocese, a well-attended Hui Topu at Omahu near Hastings featured a debutante ball at which 24 young women made their curtsey to the Bishop, and an even bigger one was held in Rotorua in 1960, attracting about 4,000 from all over the North Island.[200] Lesser was Senior Bishop by then, and one young attendee from the North remembers a small authoritative man in black-rimmed glasses with a forceful voice saying something she cannot now recall, though she does recall the sense from those around her that "it was not very complimentary to Māori."[201]

A still more ambitious event occurred in the Waikato Diocese, with Canon Wi Huata's enthusiastic involvement, when a national Hui Topu in May 1962 was held at the Māori King's base at Turangawaewae, attracting an estimated 8,000. Lesser, by then Archbishop, is given credit for suggesting it, the first of its kind, but the dates clashed with a visit to Australia where he was to represent the Church at the Australian General Synod, and he returned just in time to preach at the last service on Sunday morning.[202] He was again present at the Hui Topu at Nuhaka, (between Wairoa and Gisborne), in 1963, when the diminishing rolls of Te Aute and Hukarere was a topic on the agenda.[203]

But it seems the cost of hosting the Hui Topu was a cause of some concern.[204] Even at the 1961 Hui Topu Lesser had warned that these events were very expensive to run and needed to be entered into in the right spirit. They could be

> "either a millstone that drags you down (if you were the host) or a milestone in the advance of the Māori people."[205]

Subsequently at a Māori Clergy Conference in May 1964 "The future of the Hui Topu" was an agenda item and it was decided that "Future Hui Topus (sic) to be held by the Diocese will be financed, programmed and administrated by a special board," whose members would be the Archbishop, Bishop Panapa, Canon Rangiihu as secretary, Rev Paenga

Māori Matters

and Mrs T Ormond as treasurer.[206] Perhaps this decision coming from the Māori Clergy Conference was not taken up by Standing Committee or Synod; in any case setting up the "special board" does not seem to have brought about any changes in the management of the Hui Topu.

That Lesser continued to attend these Hui Topu until his retirement, making them a priority in his busy schedule, indicates their importance to him. As Archbishop Brown Turei said:

> "He was always part of the large Hui Topu. He chaired the Māori Synod which took place during the Hui, and he stayed right to the end. He didn't have to, but he always did."[207]

In 1969 he was ill and writes to the Rev Tony Gardiner that he "was bitterly disappointed in missing my first Hui Topu in over twenty years."[208]

When he became Archbishop, attendance at the Hui must have entailed very skilful juggling of competing engagements at times, as happened in May 1970 when a visit from the Bishop of Hong Kong clashed with the Hui. Lesser arranged for the Dean to host the visiting Bishop for his first day and he himself left the Hui early in order to fulfil, at least partially, his obligation as host.[209]

Attendance at Hui Topu was just one aspect of Lesser's support of the Māori church. Practical help over time also came from him and the Diocese, notably in the matter of stipends. His first Synod, as we have seen, reported that Standing Committee had agreed to increase the stipend of Māori clergy in Pastorates to £300,[210] though at the same time the Diocesan contribution towards the stipend was removed and it was all to come from the people themselves. However, over the years the disparity between the stipends of those working in the Pastorates (mainly Māori) and those in the parishes (mainly pākehā) was reduced until they were made equal in 1957.[211] Māori representation at the Diocesan Synod also increased from 9 to 13 in 1951,[212] when it was put on the same basis as that of the pākehā parishes.

But things moved more slowly at the national level and Lesser could do little about Māori disadvantage at General Synod, where Māori did not have direct representation and the Bishop of Aotearoa could not vote. However, following a Commission set up in 1958 to investigate Māori representation, things slowly began to change and by 1964 the Bishop of Aotearoa was permitted a vote, although the system of pākehā bishops appointing the Bishop of Aotearoa continued for many years.

Education was another area where Bishop Lesser made considerable efforts to improve Māori well-being, notably in his commitment to the two Anglican Māori schools in Hawke's Bay, Te Aute for boys and Hukarere Girls' School. Again, he was thrown in at the deep end soon after arriving in New Zealand with his appointment as Chair, (replacing Archbishop West-Watson), of a 1946 Provincial Advisory Council on Māori Educational Problems. The focus was the Māori Anglican Church schools and the first task the Council set itself was to get information from the schools on pupil and staff numbers, teacher salaries, the curriculum and accommodation, and what the school offered in academic, cultural and sporting facilities.

In a seven-page report under Lesser's name to General Synod 1949[213] the Council said, "The Church as a whole feels little responsibility for the schools which have come to be regarded as Diocesan responsibilities," and made some strong recommendations:

> "Salaries of teachers should be at government standards; standards should not fall behind those of other Church schools; the Curriculum must include Science and the Arts, not just Agricultural and General subjects,"

and,

> "Māori language should be taught so thoroughly as to create a highly favourable opinion amongst students' parents and associates."

The Council proposed to open "high-level talks with the government as to the nature and extent of any assistance offered and the terms relating to any such assistance." It also approved "in principle" negotiations with government on ways to improve conditions in the schools, but as some of the Trust Boards were wary of government support, fearing loss of independence,[214] that course of action was not pursued.

The Council's hard work and forceful recommendations sadly went nowhere for a variety of reasons and its 1952 Report[215] to General Synod is brief and pessimistic. The choice was clear: if the schools were to continue there must be an increase in the Trust Boards' income, either through increased fees or by direct Government assistance towards maintenance and capital requirements. Neither of these courses of action happened in any definitive way and the schools continued to struggle. After the 1955 General Synod, the Council gave up meeting regularly although it was re-appointed "so they would be ready if need arises."

Chairing the Advisory Council was Lesser's first frustrated effort to get some national support for the Anglican Māori schools, especially Te Aute and Hukarere, but it was far from being his last and he continued to urge General Synod members to accept more responsibility.

His concern for the two Hawke's Bay schools was no doubt strengthened by his chairmanship of the Te Aute Trust Board from the time of Archdeacon Brocklehurst's retirement in 1953 until his own retirement.

As Chair of the Board he took every opportunity to promote these schools, ensuring, for example, that they, rather than those considered more prestigious in the popular mind, received the attention of important visitors such as the Archbishops of Canterbury and Governors-general Norrie and Fergusson.[216] On another occasion he was able to highlight the importance of these schools in an address at a seminar commemorating the Centennial of the Hawke's Bay Education Board in October 1959, when he pointed out that by the year 2000 there would be about 500,000 Māori in New Zealand and that currently 70% of Māori were under the age of 21.[217]

Naturally, as Chair of the Board, he would attend the Te Aute and Hukarere end-of-year concerts and prizegivings, but the carefully preserved handwritten invitations from Hukarere suggest his attendance was not merely a matter of duty, and the collection of items in the Scrapbooks telling of a bequest for Hukarere or the Te Aute boys getting their driving licences reflects his broad interest in the pupils' activities.[218]

Both schools had continuing serious financial problems, and articles about these too are recorded in the scrapbooks, along with annual reports. Their predicament, shared by other Anglican Māori schools, must have caused great anxiety and frustration to the Bishop and the Trust Board. The non-payment of fees was conceded as a factor in the situation, although the Board took "all reasonable steps to recover bad debts before writing them off," and tightened up the application process in the hope of improving the situation.[219]

In a further effort to assist the schools, the 1963 Waiapu Synod appointed a six-member Commission to "assist the Te Aute Trust Board to resolve its financial difficulties," and "to consider the school's future in general."[220] Despite a lengthy report to the Standing Committee of the Diocese, financial difficulties continued, and 1964 sees the Archbishop still trying to get the whole Province to accept what he saw as their obligations to these schools.[221] His own Diocese made reasonable efforts to help the schools over the years: in June 1964, Waiapu Diocese gave £1,250 per annum towards reducing the debt of the Te Aute Trust Board "and the other dioceses are being asked to give what they can."[222]

In 1970 he again reminded General Synod that annual contributions to the schools made in the past by the dioceses "are now virtually non-existent. I cannot speak too forcefully about this… the schools all have a wonderful history and heritage, but we cannot live on the good name of the past, we require urgent financial assistance in the present." While all schools were facing "steeply increased charges," these schools were different from some: "they cannot pass on all the increase to intending scholars for the simple reason that their parents are not in a position to meet the increased costs… I do most earnestly urge members to keep this matter constantly and prayerfully before them."[223]

In addition to his consistent support for the Hui Topu and the schools, Bishop Lesser was aware of other Māori concerns. One of these was the lack of religious services in Māori on the radio, which in those days broadcast regular services from different churches on local stations. As no time was allocated for services in Māori,[224] the Bishop and clergy decided to give one of their slots to Hukarere and the Bishop of Aotearoa, and a monthly morning devotion from the Napier station to a Māori clergyman.

Another small but helpful action was to ensure that Māori clergy were highly visible at Diocesan and other important occasions by giving them significant rôles. For example, when the Archbishop of Canterbury dedicated the memorial tablet to Bishop Bennett in St Faith's church Rotorua, a Māori lay reader, David Naera, "uniquely led the prayers and responses at the service," which was entirely in Māori;[225] the Rev J. Tamahori gave the occasional sermon at the 1949 Synod; Rev Brown Turei preached at an ordination in Gisborne in 1958 and Rev Tiki Raumati preached at the 1970 Synod.[226] The privilege of taking the first Communion service in the completed Memorial Chapel of the Cathedral was, appropriately, given to Canon Kaa and Rev T. Tuhiwai.[227] At the 1969 Synod, held in Gisborne to honour the bi-centenary of Captain Cook's landing there, Canon Rangiihu presided at the service using the New Zealand Liturgy; Bishop Manu Bennett preached, and Māori clergy processed alongside pākehā equivalents as crucifers or chaplains.

Individual Māori in difficult circumstances also received support. It would almost certainly have been the Bishop who persuaded Standing Committee to give financial help to a Māori student, a family man, studying at St John's Theological College, and later to pay off money he owed so that he could be ordained "free of debt" when the time came.[228]

In another situation, Lesser showed a sensitive awareness of the whānau demands on Harry Tangohau, the Māori vicar of Taupo parish, who had asked to be transferred back to his own people elsewhere in the Diocese because his wife's mother was sick.[229] Lesser was preparing to do this, but when Harry's mother-in-law died, his wife changed her mind, and said she would prefer to stay in Taupo where "people had been so kind to them." Lesser, who had somehow noticed Harry Tangohau's ambivalence to the move, then wrote asking him if "in his heart of hearts" he wanted to leave Taupo, adding,

> "As I am just thinking and praying about the moves which
> should be made in the Māori work of the Diocese it would be
> of the greatest help to me if you feel you can tell me exactly
> how you see your immediate future work."

Especially important, however, was the exchange made between Canon Sam Rangiihu and Rev Edward Marsden, a descendant of Samuel Marsden, who came to New Zealand with his family in 1964 for the 150th anniversary of the first Christian mission to this country. Rangiihu had several preaching engagements in England and every snippet of news about this visit which could be procured in New Zealand has been preserved in the scrapbooks.[230] Of special interest is the presentation of a historic mere to the Queen as a symbol of peace between pākehā and Māori, and a photo of Rangiihu exchanging a hongi with a female guest at a reception given by New Zealand House where he met "42 Māori and their English wives or husbands."[231]

In New Zealand, the Marsden celebrations (as they were called) held at Waitangi and Oihi were big news for both Church and State. The Queen, the Archbishop of Canterbury, and Lesser as New Zealand Archbishop sent messages which were printed in the official souvenir programme; Governor-general Sir Bernard Fergusson, five bishops and other dignitaries attended, joined by large contingents of Māori from all over New Zealand, including 120 from the Gisborne area, and many ordinary New Zealanders.

A Likely Lad

In spite of the dignitaries, a feature of the celebrations was the informality, and judging by the photograph, Lesser seems to have enjoyed the experience of having to wade ashore at Oihi with a case of robes in each hand after a failure of the floating jetty to reach dry land. A report describes him "splashing through the water with a broad grin. 'This is a great show,' he said as he turned to watch the fortunes of his bishops. 'It makes it authentic doesn't it?'"

His message in the programme typically encouraged readers to focus on God's goodness rather than man's achievements, writing in part, "The celebration… is indeed a solemn reminder that 'he, (i.e. Marsden), long dead yet speaketh.' But it is not 'a voice from the dead' to which we listen, but a voice vibrant with life, proclaiming the eternal gospel which although old as the hills, is nevertheless 'new every morning.'" He went on,

> "The essential purpose of the Celebration will be lost unless we accept for ourselves the 'tidings of great joy.' Our joy is in the Babe of Bethlehem, for God was never so great as when he became small. A worthwhile celebration will involve thanksgiving to Almighty God for the labours of His servant Samuel Marsden, and a self-dedication to the eternal gospel in our daily lives."

The celebrations had the feel of a Hui Topu about them. They began on Thursday 24 December with a marae welcome for all visitors; prayers in the evenings were followed by a concert or a dance; Holy Communion services were held each morning; at least parts of the Christmas Day service at Oihi Bay (Psalm 100 and a carol) were in te reo and a booklet of traditional carols translated into Māori was available. The historical pageant appears to have given Ruatara appropriate honour for his part in the story, and a hakari concluded the gathering in the traditional Māori way.

It seems to have been an occasion for a meeting of the two cultures in a way that had seldom happened on a national level, and the strong presence of Māori and the unusually extensive use of the language made an impression on the media. Māori language was rarely used in situations where pākehā were present, apart from ceremonial greetings, but the Governor-general himself was a fluent speaker and may have encouraged its use on this occasion.

Māori Matters

Lesser himself, although closely associated with speakers of te reo such as Canon Sam Rangiihu, and respectful of things Māori, does not seem to have attempted to learn the language even though he had more exposure to it through tangi and hui than most pākehā of the day. The only record of any use made by him is at his first Synod in 1947 when he gave a "hearty 'haere mai' to members of the Māori Conference."[232] Later in his episcopate there was occasional use of te reo in church services, though it may have been Rangiihu's influence that led to the bi-lingual Order of Service[233] for the dedication of the new vicarage for the Wairoa-Mohaka pastorate, where he was vicar.

Nor did Lesser particularly encourage the use of Māori language in public worship even at the schools. While a Māori hymn was usually included in Synod services, notably the Bishop Bennett favourite *Oti Rawa*, other special occasion services such as the installation of a new headmaster or the consecration of the Hukarere chapel, have no Māori language content except for one hymn, usually sung by the pupils, and perhaps a reading.[234] Yet at that time Māori Anglican choral music was strong, with some celebrated church choirs in the Diocese, and a Diocesan publication of 18 Māori hymns and prayers *He Karakia Mihana* was available.[235] Certainly the singing of the Māori contingent at Synods is something pākehā delegates remember with nostalgic delight.

While his language remained limited, Lesser's interest in the Māori world was extensive, going well beyond the confines of the Church. As he once remarked Christ did not divide the world into sacred and secular things, and the numerous items in the scrapbooks covering dozens of topics relating to Māori – urban drift,[236] issues in Māori education, the legend of the Pania statue in Napier; the achievements of the boxer Ike Robin[237] – all witness to his sympathetic concern for the total well-being of Māori people.

Moreover, he saw clearly that it was essential for the whole country, not just for Māori, that they should thrive, and he was ahead of his time in saying this. It is only recently that people in positions of power and authority have been blunt in stating that pākehā also benefit if Māori flourish. Lesser said publicly 60 years ago,

> "We share this glorious country and if we live separately, we shall perish together. We all do well to remember that our brethren in Christ are given to us, not chosen by us."[238]

A Likely Lad

And to the 1968 General Synod he stressed the importance of the work being done by the Commission on Trends in Māori Work, set up in 1966 from a Waiapu motion, saying, "If one suffers, we all suffer, and conversely if our Māori brethren prosper, we all benefit."[239] And he could insert thought-provoking asides on racism into addresses or sermons, with throwaway lines such as "It is a humbling thought that there was no white face at the foot of the Cross," in a 1953 sermon to young people,[240] or "How glibly we equate white with purity and black with sin!" to his 1962 Synod.

Yet, despite his extensive experience of Māori tikanga, there were still times when the cultural divide took him by surprise. As someone who himself paid punctilious attention to detail, it was unsurprising that he occasionally found the Māori way of doing things, (or perhaps it was the New Zealand way!), too casual. For example, he has been asked to keep 25 April 1954 free for the possible consecration of a Māori church at Torere, but he suspects that the church might not be finished by then and has heard tentative talk of a date in June. He writes to the Archdeacon to be "kind enough to let them know as gently as you can that they cannot just fix a date or tell us that that is the day so fixed. They must consult me before naming any date for the Dedication or consecration of the Church."[241]

Two other examples of a more fundamental lack of understanding are remarked on by Archbishop Turei: one was the Māori's ability to forget denominational differences in the interest of working together as a group. According to the Archbishop,[242] Lesser was unable to understand why Waiapu Māori would go in busloads to Hamilton to help build the Mormon Tabernacle and College. "To Lesser this seemed to show a lack of loyalty," he said, and Bishop Panapa experienced a similar lack of understanding of this cultural norm.

The other incident concerns the value placed on land by Māori, which surfaced when Synod was discussing the sale of some Māori-owned land at Te Ngae near Rotorua – an apparently good business deal for the Church. During the Synod debate, Māori said very little but when the motion was put to the vote, Bishop Panapa's "NO!" – which vetoed the motion – was very loud and clear, and obviously took Lesser by surprise.[243] This incident may well have been in the Archbishop's mind years later, when, speaking at Panapa's funeral, he described him as a man of "unflinching courage," with a "passionate concern for the Māori people."[244]

However, towards the end of his episcopate he showed that he had taken on board to some extent Ngata's hope expressed at that first Hui Topu that he would learn the Māori way. In a letter dated 1 May 1970 he explains to the vicar of Wairoa that he has been unable to acknowledge his offer of accommodation during the Hui Topu at the Wairoa Takitimu marae because he "had to consult Joe Tuhiwai as to what arrangements they proposed. That is always a necessary preliminary."[245]

Whether he did in time come to fulfil Ngata's other hope for him – to understand "the approach of the Māori people to matters of religion" – is not something a pākehā can determine. In any case, comment on the past always risks bias from the point of view of the present. What is not in doubt is that Lesser felt privileged to have closer relationships with Māori than most pākehā of the day and was a strong advocate for their future well-being. And like Māori he recognised the truth of the well-known whakataukī, "What is the greatest thing in the world? It is people; it is people; it is people."

A Likely Lad

Chapter 5: Faith and Finance

Money, or the lack of it, tends to be a recurring theme in the life of most churches, and Waiapu was no exception. The 1947 and 1948 Synods both expressed serious concern over the financial position of the Diocese with the Finance Committee in 1947 issuing dire warnings against asking the parishes for more money. "Your committee wishes to draw the attention of Synod to the continued and rising demands made on parishes for additional money. It considers that saturation point has been reached…" It asked Synod to "consider very carefully before bringing forward any resolutions involving the raising of extra funds…"[246] A similar warning to the 1948 Synod prompted a resolution asking the Bishop to set up a committee to look into "the whole question of finance and shortage of manpower,"[247] which he duly did in March 1949.[248]

Presumably as a response in part to these concerns the Bishop wrote his first letter to individuals appealing for contributions to the General Diocesan Fund on 1 November 1947. It begins with a story of a family in a "simple slum home" where the father is secretly scratching something on a small coin. It is all he can spare for the church collection that night, and it seems very little, so he has scratched a cross on it as a "way of showing in what spirit I am giving it." The letter continues,

> "We always think that LSD means pounds, shillings and
> pence… in this case, and in thousands of other cases it means
> Love, Service and Devotion."

It is only after making this point that the Bishop sets out the financial facts: the Diocese needs £3,920 for the General Diocesan Fund to do the work of Christ in Waiapu. "We need YOUR(sic) help and we are certain that we shall not ask in vain. We shall be glad of the widow's mite, but not from a millionaire's widow." He ends, "Thank you for your past help! Allow me the privilege of thanking you for a record Thanksgiving of Love, of Service and of devotion."[249]

A similar letter written after the 1948 Synod sets out the costs of running the Diocese (£4,243) which he describes as "Family Housekeeping." It begins:

> "My predecessor, Bishop Cruikshank, who was so widely and deservedly admired and appreciated, wrote a letter about the Diocesan Fund, and I have followed his example. I fully realise that there are some of our supporters and fellow worshippers who from conviction think that it is not right that the Bishop should appeal for money. What I really want to do is not so much to appeal for money as to appeal to all my friends to give **themselves** (sic) unreservedly to God's service."

He ends,

> "If God moves you will you help us not only to maintain the work but help us also to be in a position to 'launch out into the deep?' A monk asked to see the wounds of Christ; he was not shown Christ's hands with the nail prints; he was not shown Christ's feet with the nail prints; to his surprise he was shown the marks on the shoulder with carrying the cross. Thank you for your generous support in the past, and may it be your joy and pride, that, like your Lord, you may be able to show the marks of your continuing sacrifice and service."[250]

Incidentally, there is no record of any similar letter from Bishop Cruickshank, although it is quite possible that previous bishops had made a practice of appealing to known supporters especially among the rural community.

Lesser wrote again in the same vein in November 1949, citing the vast new housing programmes and the need for "more men and more buildings, and therefore more money." Similar appeals for the GDF went out in October 1951 and November 1952,[251] with the 1951 one ending,

> "Because you have given according to your means, and not according to your meanness, I am bold to ask continuance of that help."

Although he may have felt obliged by the state of the Diocesan finances to write such appeals Lesser believed profoundly that people should first be won for Christ, as he put it, and these letters illustrate that conviction. When people really became committed to Christ, problems of finance and manpower would be resolved.

He had made this point in Kenya when he expressed the desire for "a more spiritual approach" to the appeals being made for the Diocese and had acted on that same belief in his earlier parishes of Barrow-in-Furness and Norris Green. There, despite general poverty, enthusiasm

A Likely Lad

could be engendered in populations large enough to achieve great things including the building of churches.

But in Waiapu, there were differences that had to be allowed for. Here, numbers were comparatively very small, wealthy benefactors very few and the Anglican church did not have the same status as it had in England. Nevertheless, he continued to believe firmly that effective evangelism would lead people to be generous to the Church in thankfulness.

So his focus was always on evangelism. After the 1948 Synod he wrote to clergy[252] quoting words used by Archdeacon Morris at the Synod: "Our primary task and joy is evangelism,"[253] and his 1948 Christmas letter to all congregations reiterates that message.

> "As I move about the Diocese, I hear people saying that the money problem is hard, but I have never yet come across a Parish that is vitally, spiritually alive where they are unduly worried in that way. I feel myself that there is a problem behind the money problem, and that is more difficult to attack. The method of Jesus was always first to get a man to give **himself**, then the other things followed as a matter of course. Christmas is a grand time to give ourselves to Him for it was then that He gave Himself to us."[254]

He continued to press for greater personal commitment to Christ in both his clergy and people throughout 1949, writing in May to clergy: "Have you heard two people discussing some prominent person, and perhaps one will say, 'Oh I know him.' 'Do you really?' replies the other. 'Do you know him personally?' There brothers is the question that we must ever put to ourselves, do we know Him **personally.**"[255] The need for Christians to have a personal relationship with their Saviour was a constant teaching throughout his life.

He planned to have a session on evangelism at the separate Clergy and Lay conferences traditionally held during Synod, and in August 1949 he wrote to both groups, asking each to consider how they could help the other in this task. He wants to know what they think: "Shall we prepare fully for a Mission (called by whatever name we think most helpful) or shall we intensify our present methods?"[256] In his Synod address, he said he wanted the word 'evangelism' "engraven in our hearts," and stressed the need for all of those present to know Christ: "You cannot pass on what you do not possess."

Faith and Finance

That 1949 Synod must have had some memorable moments. According to a *Church and People* report, it had been arranged that the Bishop would introduce the subject of Evangelism on Tuesday night and open the meeting for discussion.

> "The Bishop spoke quietly and simply for a few minutes then stepped aside from his Chair and asked members to imagine Our Saviour there asking what they had done to bring His people closer to Him. At the conclusion of the Bishop's words an absolute silence fell upon Synod and lasted for perhaps two minutes when it was broken by one of the clergy who said, 'I never felt less like speaking in my life, but I am doing so that the Bishop may know that our silence is not because we have nothing to say but that our hearts are too full to say it.'"

No-one felt like debating and they moved into the Cathedral "where they knelt in prayer for 15 minutes before dispersing for the night."[257] The Yearbook records more drily: "The Bishop addressed Synod urging its dedication to setting forward the Supreme cause of Evangelism in the Diocese. The Bishop was followed by other speakers. Synod adjourned at 9.15 p.m., members moving to the Cathedral for prayer."

At the end of Synod members passed a motion "thanking Almighty God for the lead given by our Bishop in the urgent matter of evangelism and assures the Bishop of their loyal and loving support at all times."[258]

In November, a month after Synod, he wrote in a pastoral letter: "It became increasingly obvious that the fundamental urgency of evangelism lies deep in our hearts."[259] However, as he "has had no respite since Synod," he plans to have some rest over January and write again with "certain suggestions about possible ways of prosecuting our common desire to set forth Christ's kingdom."

Early in 1950 he reflects on that 1949 Synod, writing in another pastoral letter:[260]

> "There was no doubt that the Holy Spirit spoke to us in most unequivocal terms. After long and most serious preparation of what God wanted me to say at the evening session, I discovered subsequently that little of what had been so painstakingly prepared, had been delivered. For me at all events it was clearly an instance of being told, 'in that hour, what ye shall speak.'"

A Likely Lad

Although still focused on evangelism, the letter is strangely lacking in any specifics. He repeats some of the suggestions he has made at Synod, such as parish groups meeting for prayer and discussion on evangelism to "see what God gives us as His purpose for us all." He asks Archdeaconries to hold meetings "where evangelism has pride of place," and that issuing from these clergy meetings "there should be regular meetings of each Vestry for the sole purpose of considering this same subject." He wants the laymen included as they "complain that they are too little considered in things spiritual," and asks Archdeacons or their representatives to let him know "what transpires in these groups of thinking praying Christian people…" However, there does not seem to be any record of such meetings, or if they did meet, what transpired from them.

Perhaps because of this lack of response, Lesser again wrote to his clergy in September 1950 on the subject so dear to his heart saying:

> "At Synod this year I am very anxious to say something again on the Tuesday evening about our prime concern, winning souls for Jesus Christ. If we are not doing that the rest of Synod's deliberations are, at best, a waste of time, and at the worst sheer hypocrisy."[261]

As a result of what he said on the Tuesday night the 1950 Synod asked the Bishop, in typical Synod fashion, to appoint a committee on evangelism "to further consider the approaches to Evangelism, to co-ordinate suggestions and to give effect to the evident desire of Synod that Prayer shall issue in Action."[262]

The committee's four recommendations to the 1951 Synod included one which involved quite large sums of money, as it suggested forming "a school of evangelism conducted by a missioner from England, Australia or America," who would address archdeaconry groups and visit parishes. The Bishop was asked to make enquiries as soon as possible about a suitable missioner, but the enquiries were not productive.[263] In his address to this Synod, Lesser refers to the committee's report and says, "The committee's findings have given us a lead on this matter and we ought not lightly to dismiss the suggestions… made after much prayerful consideration… The suggestions have much merit and they do represent action."[264]

If he felt there was a lack of passion in the Committee's report, he made up for it by ending his Synod address with an emotional plea for greater

Faith and Finance

commitment to Christ: "If Jesus Christ came to New Zealand in the flesh," he said,

> "He would of course be feted – we might add that he would probably be fated also. He would be welcomed by crowds of people and many who never took the slightest trouble to hear about his message in any of the appointed ways of His choice would throng Him and sing lustily 'For He's a jolly good fellow!' Of course, He would be taken to a really large sheep station and he would turn to the crowds of hangers-on and ask, 'How do you care for the sheep of my pasture? Do you feed my lambs?' He would be shown the great state forest plantings and be invited to admire. He would turn to the crowds now thinning a little because of the last question and say, 'Yes I know a little about trees. I was a carpenter for about 15 years. I once had a wooden sceptre in My hand. I had a wooden cross and I reigned from a tree.' Many people would feel embarrassed and walk with him no more, but the few that were left would take Him to the great hydro-electric works and invite his admiration of the grandeur of their conception and the power that they would generate. He would say, 'Water is power, the waters of baptism can lead to the power of God unto salvation.' And then in loneliness He would find his own way to the side of the Lake and talk again to the prostitutes and sinners, and the lost sheep would be found, and the Water of Life would flow in its cleansing power. And there would be peace at Eventide, the peace of God in the souls made in His own image and hitherto marred by sin. This Presence can be with us at all times and in all ways. Let us boldly claim it that our Synod may reflect something of God's purpose for a world that so sorely needs Him."[265]

He picked up the theme again in February 1953, reminding clergy in a pastoral letter[266] that "for a long time we have been discussing the vital question of bringing other people to Christ, or evangelism. The clergy decided that the first step was that for a certainty they themselves should be in the closest possible touch with our Lord." The most recent meeting of the Committee on Evangelism "had decided that a meeting of the clergy would be of greatest value provided that it was a 'refresher' on practical pastoral work." The well-known Archdeacon Jim Young was invited to lead the two-day event with four local clergy taking sessions, and it was to be a "point of honour" to attend.

A Likely Lad

It was probably a very useful day for the clergy, but it sounds rather more low-key than the Bishop might have liked. Reading between the lines it seems that the Bishop's fervent desire for organised home-grown evangelistic endeavour or a full-scale campaign from a 'Missioner' was not matched by many of the Synod members, nor indeed by all the clergy. And any venture that implied an increase in Diocesan expenditure clearly held no appeal for Synod.

Synod was indeed facing a plethora of financial demands. Apart from the re-building of the Cathedral, there was a strong call to provide Homes for the Aged; in addition, the rapidly-growing towns and suburbs all cried out for new buildings and staff. Because of these many – and rather confusing – demands, it was decided that all appeals would be combined under the title of the "Bishop's Fighting Fund" with the aim of getting £100,000 over a period of 5 years.[267] The re-building of the Cathedral would get £60,000, Church Extension £20,000 and Homes for the Aged £20,000, and an organiser would be employed at £500 per year.

The Bishop wrote to clergy, vestrymen and synodsmen in June 1952 specifically explaining the Bishop's Fighting Fund, and a similar letter to all Anglicans was read out at services on 6 July 1952. In part it says, "We have set ourselves to raise £100,000 in five years. That may sound an enormous sum for some of us but let us remember it is £20,000 per year for 5 years." He wisely takes care to break it down into manageable and personal figures:

> "If every Anglican gave £1 per year for 5 years, we would have £70,000 per year or £350,000 in five years. £1 per person would mean about 5d or five cigarettes a week."

He stresses

> "that this effort is not intended to rob the person's parish of its rightful dues."[268]

Despite the establishment of the Bishop's Fighting Fund Lesser still wrote to individuals appealing for the General Diocesan Fund as he had done in previous years. His 1953 letter refers to the contemporary problem of high inflation: "When you sign a cheque for the normal running of the home, if you cast your mind back a few years, you will readily recall that such a cheque would have served you for twice the length of time…" "The cost is tremendously increased but THE WORK MUST GO ON!" (sic)[269]

Faith and Finance

The Bishop's Fighting Fund was a highly-organised campaign. Parishioners promised to give an annual amount for five years, and official collectors would call on homes for the promised donation if these were not brought in.[270] What is more, the amounts given by each parish were regularly published in the Diocesan news sent to *Church and People*.[271]

Lesser oversaw the appointment of the Co-ordinators,[272] and was active in promoting it at every opportunity. To a Gisborne audience in 1955 he said,

> "If every professing Anglican in the Diocese was to give £1 per year for the five years of the appeal, plus their contributions to their own church, you could have a cathedral, you could have 21 church halls in all, and five old people's homes. Sounds so easy doesn't it, and that is what we could do. It would cost every man four cigarettes a week. It would cost every woman four cigarettes a week, or one ice-cream. Would it not be simply ghastly if we were to look into the face of Christ on His Cross and say, 'I am so sorry, I could not help you', and he would say, 'What, was the price too high? Four cigarettes a week, one ice-cream, my church extended, my old friends cared for, the cathedral re-built – was the price too high?'"

He continued, "We want to put love into the lives of those who have given richly to this country and let them have their declining years with a loving care," ending with the challenge,

> "Twelve men sat round a table and the church saw its beginning. Hundreds of years later 25 men sat around a table and the Church Missionary Society was born. Tonight, there are hundreds of us sitting around a table. What is going to be born tonight?"

He appears to have also written to individuals about the Fund, as the following undated example of a letter to "My Dear Friend" suggests:

> "We, as Christians, and Members of the Anglican Church, work for and support our Parish Church in varying degrees, depending on our personal enthusiasm but do we really make sacrifices to advance God's work outside of our own District? God's Church is universal and must progress and expand or it will die. With our rapidly increasing population, His work cannot stand still, but must go on steadily and as quickly as possible, and there can be no apathy on our part if we are

Christians... It is with these thoughts in mind that I would ask you give your earnest consideration to the accompanying letter. It is only with the support of all Members of our Church in every parish that we shall be able to BUILD TO THE GLORY OF GOD, the buildings necessary for His Work in this Diocese."[273]

He also added lively messages to information leaflets[274] and the *Collectors' Handbook*, a useful little publication which helped collectors to answer all the likely questions.[275] His 1956 introduction warns, "We have two years to complete our £100,000 appeal and it would be disappointing to a degree if we were not to realise this modest goal. Let us therefore make such an advance this year that we can joyously contemplate the happy fruition of our combined endeavour next year."[276]

A year later he wrote more urgently in the *Handbook*:

"The Bishop's Fighting Fund was designed to raise £100,000 in five years – a modest objective... This is the last opportunity afforded to achieve our target within the time we all agreed to specify. Let it not be said of us that we were weary of our well-doing. 'Now is the Hour,' is not only a farewell; it is a challenge to substantial giving. We have raised £55,000 as I write on 31st March and there is still £45,000 to be raised if we are going to arrive at our goal. The need is more pressing daily, and I sincerely trust that the Diocese will permit me to report to Synod that what we aimed at we have performed. 'No man having set his hand to the plough and turning back is fit for the kingdom.' Remember Lot's wife and keep moving –FORWARD."[277]

A similar letter to all parishes also went out, ending "The saddest thing of all would be that we should be content to resolve something for God and then not to be gravely disturbed by our actions not matching our highest thoughts."

Although the Bishop's Fighting Fund did not, in the end, raise the amount desired, enough money came in to make a start on the new Cathedral and the other main objective, Waiapu House, a Home for the Aged in Havelock North.

The laying of the Foundation Stone for the new Cathedral in October 1955 was a momentous occasion and an ideal time to call for greater commitment. Quoting Bishop Chavasse's words at the same ceremony

Faith and Finance

for Liverpool Cathedral, Bishop Lesser reminded the large congregation that "the only sure foundation is Jesus Christ. We need to add to our contributions at the Service of laying the Foundation Stone 'the gift Christ desires of us most of all – ourselves, our souls, and bodies to be a living sacrifice.'"

One of the reasons that the Bishop's Fighting Fund had run out of steam was the rise of the successful stewardship campaigns run by the Wells organisation which some parishes had independently adopted after seeing their success elsewhere. As early as 1955, halfway through the BFF appeal, the Synod asked the Bishop to make inquiries about this organisation; in 1956 Synod went further and wanted a speaker from Wells to be invited.[278] After some initial caution – he was anxious that the wider needs of the Diocese, not just those of the parish, were remembered[279] – Lesser became quite supportive of the Wells programme, happy that the promoters "constantly emphasised the importance of the spiritual approach to giving."[280]

By 1957 it was clear that the Bishop's Fighting Fund was not going to achieve its target. To the Synod, Bishop Lesser said "…At the end of this year the Five Year Plan of the Bishop's Fighting Fund comes to its appointed end. The figures speak for themselves, and whilst they are far short of our appointed target, there is nevertheless enshrined in them some very real sacrifice on the part of many people, but unfortunately, the many were too few." But he was quick to reassure those who feared a large-scale fund-raising programme:

> "There are many who say that the parishes will be bull-dozed into a parish canvass. That is plainly untrue. The parish will be requested to make a sacrificial gift to the Diocese and through the Diocese to assist those obeying Christ's command to go into all the world with the everlasting gospel. **How the parish obtains the money to make what they deem a worthy offering for God's work is their concern…** (sic) …there is not and will not be any compulsion. We are talking of gifts to God, not a mercenary levy."[281]

He went on to plead most urgently for attendance at the forthcoming Loyalty Dinner, which would launch the Diocesan-wide Wells programme.

> "In the ten years that I have tried to give such gifts as I may possess to this Diocese which I love, I have never asked all

> my brethren to attend a function apart from the Foundation Stone ceremony. It is from my heart that I ask you to attend this Diocesan Loyalty Dinner. I urge you with all the power at my command and the love in my heart… to come together in this way. It was when they were all together of one heart and one mind in one place that there was a great outpouring of the Holy Spirit…Will you please do me the great favour of being with me at this common meal of fellowship for the Diocesan Family and fortify yourselves first by partaking of the Divine Meal of Fellowship."[282]

The Loyalty Dinner was a great success, and the Wells programme helped to put the Diocese on a sounder financial footing, but there was still a great deal of money needed if the Cathedral were to be completed.

Aware of this, Lesser spoke powerfully at the Loyalty Dinner, saying God had been living in a "transit camp" long enough, and it was time He was given a home. Further memorable one-liners are quoted in the newspaper report of the event: "Some people say they will give till it hurts. All I can say is that some of them are very sensitive to pain," and "There is no room for model Christians. What is wanted are working models." The report ends, "The Bishop added that when people were making sacrificial gifts, they should compare them with the gift made to mankind by Christ upon the Cross,"[283] a thought never far from his preaching and writing.

Following the Loyalty Dinner, a Diocesan survey was carried out by the Wells organisation and the substantial brochure accompanying the survey carries messages from the two Bishops, the Dean, the Diocesan Chancellor and leading laymen. Bishop Lesser's message begins:

> "This is not a begging appeal: you do not beg from your family." The title 'Father in God' is not one he has ever presumed to use for himself, "because I know myself," but he is willing to be thought of as the 'under shepherd to the Great Shepherd,' and asks for the privilege of leading his readers "into the paths that belong to your peace. The peace of Easter was bought by the bloody sacrifice of Good Friday. I challenge you, as I challenge myself, to deepen that life which gives, and so outlives… Take your courage in both hands and God grant you enough to fill them."[284]

Faith and Finance

The Diocese responded positively to the Wells programme and the years following it saw churches, halls and vicarages rising mushroom-like around the Diocese.

But the Bishop was not going to allow himself or anyone else to accept that enough had been done. If a new vicarage or church was built, it was not an occasion for a pat on the back for the local congregation, but a challenge to increase or renew commitment to Christ. It was one thing to build new churches: "It is a more difficult task to fill these places with men and women whose hearts God has touched… and whose lives are built up in Christ."[285] When 750 young people crammed into the newly-dedicated first section of the Cathedral in 1960 they were told, "It is not enough to dedicate a Cathedral. People must be dedicated to a life of service, always remembering that the only worthwhile goal is Christ himself."[286] And as the Cathedral rose over the decade, there was every opportunity to remind people that building a church or Cathedral "must be matched by the spiritual building up in the lives of men."[287]

While parishes might have flourished, there seems to have been a kind of 'donation fatigue' towards the re-building of the Cathedral and other Diocesan projects after the erection of the first section of the Cathedral in 1960. It is possible people felt that enough had been accomplished, but Lesser did not agree. In a letter to be read to all parishes on 1 April 1962, he wrote:

> "Jesus gave Himself absolutely and utterly, and we are His faithful followers, (not just admirers) when we walk in those steps which lead to a throne, but only through a cross. If we desire His work to continue, we must be willing to try to match His sacrifice. At our last Synod, the Diocesan representatives, including your own, set a budget of £37,500 to do God's work

Archbishop Norman Lesser in 1960s

> in this Diocese... Of this sum, .as I write, only £13,834 has been contributed and the financial year ends on 30 June... All vestries have received a letter signed by me, asking them to regard this question as one of urgency and deep significance for our whole future work... For myself it will prove to be a miserable Easter, and much of its joy will disappear, if I have to face my risen Lord knowing that you and I together have not risen to His needs. Today is Mothering Sunday, and I appeal to you with all my love and strength, to give the word reality, and see that Mother Church is provided for her 'housekeeping.'"[288]

Later in 1962, he similarly urged his Synod to greater commitment in a typical address melding exhortation, inspiration, and humour. He begins by urging them to complete the Cathedral: "Our Mother Church is slowly coming to completion. There remains much to do and I know... that having set our hands to the plough we will not turn back. I only hope we will not engage in too many smokos!" "...May God grant that a resurrected Cathedral will be matched by us, fired with a resurrection spirit."

He appeals for a spirit of heroism, such as Scott showed in the Antarctic, culminating in a word picture of Christ on the Cross.

> "I think of a young man of thirty-three with the sweat blinding his eyes, with hair clotted with blood, catching awkwardly at his open cuts as he rolled a little from side to side to try to get some relief from the agony of the tearing nails in his hands and feet. I think of his eyes filling with tears as he sees those he has trained and trusted forsake him and flee, and I hear that triumphant pealing voice with its resurgent echo down the corridors of time, 'It is finished!' ...I think of all this majesty and courage, and then I creep into a corner and I ask myself, 'What is my church doing NOW for Jesus Christ... and those who have followed so faithfully and so bravely and so humbly in his steps?'"

He then throws in his own scathing version of *Onward Christian Soldiers*:

> "We sing vociferously *Onward Christian Soldiers* but at times I wonder if we ought not to sing another version:
>
> 'Onward Christian soldiers
> Not so fast in front
> With the Cross of Jesus
> Suffering much affront.

> Christ the Royal Master
> Leads against the foe
> Forward into battle
> Follow but go slow.
> Onward Christian soldiers
> Follow if you will
> Let the Cross of Jesus
> Suffer every ill.'

He concludes:

> "A new birth in an outlying part of an outlying province brought hope to the world on Christmas Day. Pray God that a new birth in a small diocese in an outlying province, may, some two thousand years afterwards, bring fresh hope to a world hiding itself behind iron curtains of fear and death. Men draw curtains to mark death, let us raise them to mark a new life." [289]

But whatever commitment a person might have, it was unlikely to fully satisfy Lesser who felt so keenly the debt owed by the whole world to Christ's suffering and redeeming love. He longed for his clergy – and indeed all who called themselves Christian – to have the same passion as he had for bringing others to Christ, and he often reminded Synods that the Church was not making the advances it should.

> "We should remind ourselves with shame that there are more people in the world today who have never heard the name of Christ than there were on the day of Pentecost."

> "The trouble is that Jesus Christ has too many disciples – of poor quality. I know that to be true in myself."

The quality of Christ's disciples in Waiapu might not have been up to Lesser's ideal standard, but much was achieved by hard work and real sacrificial giving from clergy and laity. Unhappily, however, financial constraints continued to place limits on the vision he had for the church and its work.

One of these constraints for Waiapu, as for most other New Zealand dioceses, was a lack of endowments such as often accompanied churches in countries with a long-established Anglican tradition.

This fact was highlighted in an article written for the *Church Times* in 1962 where Lesser contrasts the position of the New Zealand church with that of the Church of England:

"The Church in New Zealand is not an established church. It has no ancient buildings, and the vast majority of church buildings are small by English standards but the hundreds of church buildings in New Zealand have been built by the free-will offerings of the ordinary members. The financial problems which arise in a church which has virtually no endowments have been tackled, though by no means solved as yet, by a considerable measure of education in the stewardship of time, talents and money."

He gives credit to the Wells organisation for a new standard of giving being established, and concludes:

"There are not enough clergy; there are not the financial resources for all we would like to do; but we have the full conviction that God has called us to do His work here and that when He calls He will provide the means to answer that call fully. We are a small province in a 'distant' part, but we recall that it was in a small province in a 'distant part' that our Saviour was born in humble circumstances. Our prayer is therefore that 'we may be worthy of our privileges and equal to our opportunities.'"[290]

Following the Toronto Congress in 1963, Anglicans world-wide were called to consider the question of sharing resources more equitably and were encouraged to understand stewardship as a responsible commitment of one's time, talents, and energy, as well as money. This fitted well with Lesser's thinking. He reminded General Synod in 1964 that "The first thing we must give is ourselves; other gifts will then follow naturally,"[291] and told his own Synod that the Toronto document *Mutual Responsibility and Interdependence in the Body of Christ* was "a completely new evaluation of our discipleship as we kneel at the foot of the Cross."[292]

This understanding of the broader nature of stewardship was not entirely new to Waiapu and an organised stewardship campaign for the Diocese had first been proposed at the 1959 Synod,[293] although a paid Director of Stewardship was not appointed until 1963.[294] Over the next few years, each parish prepared a brochure carrying a message of its particular needs along with the needs of the Diocese and the wider Church, with an accompanying introduction from the Archbishop.

In these introductions, Lesser's belief in the essential link between personal commitment to Christ and the giving to the Church of time, energy, talents and money is again clear. One introduction, under the heading "The Open Door", begins:

> "It is my hope and prayer that this forward move in full stewardship will result in the opening of 'doors' which will in turn lead us forward to a deeper acknowledgement of Christ… Look at your possessions, mental, physical, spiritual, material, and ask yourself if you are content with what you can contribute in each 'department' to the work of God. I feel sure that an honest assessment will result in action, and action will result in a great access of strength in your parish…"

> He ends, "I pray to God to bless your labours of love, and I pray you to give Him cause for joy." [295]

A similar brochure for another parish carries a front-page message from the Archbishop, wishing them "every blessing and success," because,

> "I firmly believe that we need humbly to ask God's blessing in our labours and earnestly strive to be as worthy as is humanly possible of His ever-ready blessing. With the Father's blessing our work is assured of success. This does not mean that unlimited financial resources will be available to us, but it does mean that those who kneel at the foot of the Cross and look into the piercing, loving eyes of Christ, will desire to lay at His feet their generous gifts as did the wise men of old. Wise men still lay their gifts at His feet. God bless you all. As ever affectionately…"

The message to a third parish's brochure reads: "Stewardship then is an exciting adventure of a complete dedication of self to a cause, and not only to a cause, but to a person."[296]

The Cathedral parish received a pat on the back in their brochure, along with a challenge to maintain their high spiritual standards, when he wrote in 1969,

> "Here in this Stewardship campaign a further opportunity is afforded for the exhibition of those characteristics of generosity and enthusiasm which have marked the Cathedral Parish's life, to become evident yet again.

> Increasingly in the Diocese we have fostered the ideal of 'belonging,' belonging to God and therefore to each other. It is this high sense of responsibility which is of such signal value in the corporate life of our Church, and St John's can have the

A Likely Lad

> privilege of leading the way. Stewardship is not just giving money, it is an attitude of mind, an attitude reflected in our relationship with God and our fellow man.
>
> May I wish you every rich success in your venture. Wise men laid their gifts at the feet of Jesus. Wise men still do the same."[297]

The Diocesan Stewardship Campaign did much to relieve the Bishop of financial concerns but the illness of the Director John Bennett towards the end of the decade slowed the momentum of what seems to have been a very effective programme. In 1967 a Commission to Assess the Needs of the Diocese was set up,[298] but the 1969 Synod still faced budget constraints, and Lesser's comments on the Commission's report were succinct:

> "The needs of the Diocese will be drawn acutely to our attention and it is obvious *that they are an increasing love of God, more people committed to evangelization in its widest connotation*, and a modern concept of the way we go about our business so that it does not degenerate into mere busyness." (Italics mine)

He then moves on to the budget figures for the coming year and the challenge facing the parishes:

> "If the amount which the parishes are prepared and able to contribute falls short of this figure, then there are only two alternatives to adopt. The first is to prune the budget to meet the promised amount, and then we are faced with the urgent task of assessing priorities. The other course is to accept the budget figure and hope for the best. This seems to me to be most undesirable."[299]

"An increasing love of God and more people committed to evangelization," were the touchstones of Bishop Lesser's life and work, believing as he did that "the rest should follow naturally." His fundamental message remained the same: as he said himself, his first sermon and his last were on the love of God and our need to respond to that. But clearly budget constraints were continuing to plague the Waiapu Diocese. Perhaps different packaging of that central Christian message was needed to make it attractive to the changed world of 1969.

Chapter 6: Cathedral Re-building

The new Bishop had hardly tried out his Chair for size before a former Bishop of Waiapu, 90-year-old William Walmsley Sedgewick, was urging the building of a new cathedral as a "permanent witness to the Holy Trinity," adding the hope that "the new Bishop would live to see the fruition of such an ideal."[300]

There was a long history of dreaming behind this ideal. The 1888 brick Cathedral had been destroyed in the 1931 earthquake, and although a temporary wooden pro-Cathedral was erected within months, building a 'proper' Cathedral was impossible at that time of Depression without financial aid from outside the diocese. Despite efforts made by Dean Brocklehurst who travelled to England in the 1930s for this very purpose, no assistance had been forthcoming.[301]

The sudden death of Bishop Williams in 1937 and the outbreak of the Second World War in 1939 again put a halt to any talk of re-building the Mother Church of the Diocese. With the end of the war and a supportive Bishop Cruickshank at the helm it was once more possible for the Diocese to contemplate such a major undertaking, but sadly the illness and consequent resignation of the Bishop in May 1946 again caused any initial planning to be laid aside. However, the Re-building committee was reappointed under Dean Gibson and met for the first time on 6 May 1947, just a month before Lesser's arrival.[302]

Naturally there was little for Dean Gibson to report to the Synod in October 1947 except that the committee had met with the Diocesan Architect, Kingwell Malcolm, for discussion on design. As there was already an on-going Diocesan appeal for another major effort, the Bishopric Endowment Trust, the Dean was careful to reassure Synod that no special appeal was intended at present, but "the people of the Diocese should be made familiar with the whole principle and spiritual value which lies behind a Cathedral as the devotional centre of the Diocese."[303]

Not much more had been achieved by the 1948 Synod. The design was obviously proving somewhat contentious as the Dean warned Synod that "one's conceptions of the design will be coloured by the designs of

A Likely Lad

the past. It must be remembered, however, that the Waiapu Cathedral will be built in concrete and must be designed accordingly."[304]

The other problem of course was money – or the lack of it: there was only £1,200 in hand.[305] The Dean's proposals for fund-raising – which included an insurance scheme and re-starting the Friends of the Cathedral society – were accepted after much debate. The sums involved were quite terrifying, and perhaps it was this which prompted Archdeacon Brocklehurst, a former Dean, to set the cat among the pigeons by unexpectedly proposing that instead of re-building in Napier, St Matthew's church in Hastings could be developed as the Cathedral. After several hours of what the newspaper described as "vigorous debate" starting on Monday night and continuing into Tuesday afternoon and Wednesday morning, Brocklehurst's motion was lost.[306]

The Bishop declared his support for the Napier site, saying inter alia "It has been my... dream... that on the site of this crucifixion should stand a Cathedral of the Resurrection..." After enumerating some of the changes that would be needed to make St Matthew's a cathedral, he contrasted the result with what a new building could do:

> *"Whereas I believe we have a glorious opportunity of creating a wholly new idea in church building in line with the best architectural conceptions of our day..."* (My italics.)

He shrewdly added, "If the intention of the suggestion... be to stimulate the people of Napier to greater efforts to erect the Cathedral in their midst, I think that object has been achieved," and the matter ended. The "vigorous debate" did arouse some interest in the general public, resulting in a donation of £100 and offers to take out an insurance policy.[307]

A fund-raising leaflet with the evocative Biblical phrases "The stones... cry out" and "Let us rise up and build," appeared in the following months. It included a short prayer, a subscription form to sign and a long message from the Bishop beginning with a quote from John Masefield about another Cathedral, Liverpool Cathedral: "This cathedral, the greatest of all modern cathedrals, is a church of the Resurrection..." The Bishop then sets out several reasons for building a splendid new Cathedral:

> "We should build the noblest pile for the highest good. It must be better than the buildings dedicated to government or commerce. It must do more than challenge the indifference of the casual passer-by. It is a focus for ecclesiastical activities

Cathedral Re-building

beyond the parish, a centre for the worshipping family of the Diocese, a visible statement of the unity of the Diocesan family, where the family may worship amidst the best that music and art can provide."

He reassures people that "building a cathedral will not impoverish the parishes. In Liverpool the reverse was true," but acknowledges that "generous and systematic giving," will be needed. However, he believes that "...if people see the necessity for a course of action they will give **themselves** (sic) to the cause. If they give themselves then the rest will automatically follow." He challenges those who "may think the present building is 'big enough' but 'big enough' for what? It is not just a question of building something big, but something worthy, and with a sense of awe… a building which of itself will command a sense of worship and be in itself a poem in architectural form." He ends:

> "…the new building will not be of brick; it must be able to withstand earthquake shock. Let us hope that the only earthquake will be in the lives and hearts of men and women, that they may be shaken out of themselves and as living stones, be builded, and build, to the greater glory of Him who was known as the head Cornerstone."[308]

The Diocese was in a 'chicken and egg' situation. With no realistic sums of money around, it was difficult to proceed with planning; and until people could see some progress in the planning, it was hard to get their enthusiasm. Synod was clearly reluctant to ask for more money, was very aware of other needs within the Diocese, and was not as wholehearted about the project as Dean Gibson might have wished. Many years later he wrote about the situation to the current Dean: "We had to 'sell' the idea of a Mother Church of the Diocese to a largely uninterested diocese…We started with very little money, we met with indifference and opposition."[309] Archbishop Brown Turei's memory was that "Parishes thought the Cathedral was on the other side of those hills and they had their own concerns."[310]

The Bishop himself was fully committed to re-building from the start although neither of his Synod addresses in 1948 or 1949 mentions it. Instead the focus is on evangelism. This is consistent with his belief that people should first be brought to faith before being asked for money to build a cathedral. Nevertheless, there was some good Evangelical authority for such an undertaking, as the saintly Bishop Chavasse had

A Likely Lad

been largely responsible for the building of Lesser's beloved Liverpool Cathedral, and as time went on, Bishop Lesser became very much the public face of the re-building project, although his influence was also strongly felt behind the scenes. Unable to attend all the meetings of the Re-building Committee, he nevertheless contributed to decisions on the many facets of the demanding project: the site, the design, and as time went on, the interior furnishings, such as the style of the font and the stained-glass windows, for which he sought advice and examples from English cathedrals, particularly Liverpool. However, it was his efforts at fund-raising that led to his name being so closely associated in the public mind with the re-building of the Cathedral.

One of his first efforts was highly successful and produced very useful media coverage. Early in 1950 the committee and the newly-appointed organiser, Lieutenant-Colonel W.S. Darby, cleverly decided that a "Cathedral Day of Giving" should accompany the week of celebrations to mark Napier attaining city status, with the clear implication that a new city needed a 'proper' Cathedral.[311]

The focus of this Day of Giving was the Bishop, who sat for eight hours in his purple cassock on the Cathedral site, receiving donations from the public. Beside him was a brass-bound wooden Cathedral Chest to hold the donations, and nearby a model of the presumed Cathedral. A steady stream of people from all sections of society paused to contribute, and the memorable photo in the local newspaper of a little girl putting in her coins generated more public interest. £1,911 was received, bringing the total up to £10,000. Typically, Bishop Lesser stressed that the creation of goodwill and sense of ownership of the project was as important as the money raised.[312]

Darby lasted just a year in the job and a curious item[313] may explain why he left. A telegram from BuckinghamPlace(sic)London reads,

> "February 27th Stop. In reply to your telegram please get in touch with the GovernorGeneral (sic)as the King's representative in New Zealand ++ Private Secretary++."

Lesser has written across the top of the telegram "Telegram sent by Darby organiser without my knowledge or approval," and signed it "NAL 1950." Darby's enthusiasm for his task seems to have gone beyond the bounds of common sense or etiquette, and he had presumably sent a begging telegram to the King. However, he kept his job, even though his

Cathedral Re-building

contract had a three months' notice of termination, and didn't resign till 22 February 1951.[314]

That "Day of Giving" was a good start but Bishop Lesser also made many less public appeals to selected groups and to individuals whom he hoped might contribute. One such letter to individual sheep farmers in August 1951 begins in a jocular tone:

> "You may think, when you see the address, 'a begging letter to be sure!' As a matter of fact, I have never been any good at begging and therefore have never practised it. It has however, been my privilege to place certain facts before people, and leave it to their own consciences whether they feel what I say is true."

He goes on,

> "All I want to do is to ask you to be so kind as to consider as to whether you would care to make an offering towards the re-building of the Cathedral in Napier. We had, through the generosity and sacrifice of your forebears, a very beautiful Cathedral..."

and ends,

> "You are a sheep farmer and you know the vital importance of looking after the lambs... Help us therefore to look after the 'lambs', the sheep and the 'black sheep' too. It will be the best sheepfold that you have ever helped to build."[315]

In the following year a similar targeted appeal went out asking specifically for donations towards the cost of extra land for the Cathedral site, which had finally become available.

He also sought funding from outside the Diocese at this early stage, writing to bishops 'at home' for help. A reply from the Bishop of Coventry promised the Cross of Nails and £50 towards the Bennett Memorial Chapel, but the Bishop of Bristol's reply (26 February 1951) setting out the problems the Church of England itself was facing at the time was probably more typical: "...I shall have to ask the diocese for twice what they have given...," he wrote despairingly. Lesser seems to have got a total of £74, one shilling and sixpence, £12 of which was described as "personal gifts" from the bishops involved.[316]

The lack of funds was only one of the problems facing the Re-building Committee in 1950. Before an architect could start on a design, the site needed to be enlarged, a saga in itself. For years Lesser joined in

A Likely Lad

deputations and letter-writing in vain efforts to buy an adjoining piece of government-owned land so that the Cathedral could have a "worthy site."[317] Frustratingly he received the standard reply, "The matter will be given consideration," year after year.

However, he went a step further in July 1951 writing personally to remind Prime Minister Holland of an alleged promise by the previous PM Peter Fraser that he would recommend to cabinet that the Diocese should not only have the whole area, but also that it should be a donation, as reconstruction after an earthquake was a national responsibility.[318] Holland acknowledged the letter and said he would discuss the matter with the Minister of Works, again giving the standard reply "The matter will have to be given consideration."

A year later Lesser wrote yet again to PM Holland (July 1952) asking that the land should be a "gift from the people of New Zealand," putting added pressure on the PM with the sentence "We were indeed happy when you affirmed that it was the intention of the government that you lead with distinction, to honour any undertaking entered into by your predecessor in office."[319] But his efforts remained unrewarded.

Eventually, in August 1952 the way was cleared for the Diocese to purchase the land, but it was not going to be a gift from the people of New Zealand. In an effort to raise the necessary £9,000 Lesser again wrote personal letters to rural landowners in November 1952, asking specifically for donations towards this extra cost, cleverly appealing to a farmer's instinct to buy a "good paddock" when he saw one.[320] He tells them that he will be sitting outside the Cathedral site from 9 a.m. to 5 p.m. on Friday 14 November in order to receive gifts for this purpose – a repeat of his effort in 1950. Unhappily the day was wet, and only £1,550 was subscribed, £1,000 of which came from the generous benefactor Henry Charles, who had already contributed £1,000. But it all helped and apparently the effort made the English *Church Times!*[321]

Years later Lesser, ever hopeful, picked up his pen to write to Walter Nash, the Prime Minister of the day, asking if the money paid for the land could be re-funded, on the grounds that Peter Fraser had intimated that it should be a gift to the people of Napier. Lesser and the then Diocesan Secretary, Les Nash, met the PM – who just happened to be Les's father! – en route to another appointment at the Napier aerodrome.

Cathedral Re-building

Unfortunately for the Re-building Committee, Nash had documents to show the promise had never been made.[322]

The acquisition of the site and lack of money were two major problems faced by Lesser and the Re-building Committee in the early days of the project. Yet another was the question of architect and design. Richard Harman, a noted church architect from Christchurch, had been appointed by the Re-building Committee but his sudden and premature death in 1953 caused further delay to decisions on the design.

Lesser's view that the Diocese had the opportunity to build "a wholly new idea in church building in line with the best architectural concepts of our day," strongly suggests a desire for an exciting design, and he was heard to say he would have liked something along the lines of the modern St James' church in Lower Hutt.[323] Certainly the church he built in the 1930s in Barrow-in-Furness still feels modern, being light-filled and Byzantine in style.

This thesis is backed up by a long and detailed letter from a Rev Farrer Middlebrook in November 1954 in reply to Lesser's request for comment or advice. Middlebrook, who clearly had some interest and expertise in Church interior design, bemoans the restrictions placed upon the design by the site, writing,

> "What a great pity that most of us are only conversant with the Victorian traditions on church planning! It would take a great deal of convincing to dislodge our minds from this rut and to get away from the idea of the distant elevated altar terminating in a vista and the celebrant hardly audible to those a little hard of hearing."

He wonders,

> "if the altar and chair could be differently placed,"

and with some prescience writes,

> "…it is only a question of time before altar, choir and pews will be more advantageously placed. No doubt the arguments in favour of the Victorian Cathedral will impress those who do not want change, and who do not realise that some of the changes in the past have been unwise,"

and ends,

A Likely Lad

> "The question arises What are we bequeathing to future generations?"

but concludes resignedly,

> "If however, the present scheme with its obvious defects persists, the only thing is to make the best of the situation. I would regret the missing of a worthwhile opportunity."[324]

It is unlikely that Middlebrook would have written in such a way if he did not believe that Lesser shared at least some of his views, and might also be regretting "the missing of a worthwhile opportunity," and Lesser's tribute to Middlebrook at his 1968 Synod,[325] credits him with "considerable assistance in advice concerning… church furnishings and matters of architectural concern."

While Lesser may not have concurred with all of the opinions expressed in Middlebrook's letter, he clearly favoured a modern style of building, claiming that the few visitors who expressed disappointment with the new Cathedral were those who "wanted a Gothic church with a sombre interior."[326] However, the site remained a limiting factor on the design and in the end everyone, including the newly-appointed architect Kingwell Malcolm, had to "make the best of the situation."

As the design neared finality and the funds grew in the early 1950s, it became feasible to plan for the first big step of the process, the laying of the foundation stone. Bishop Lesser was hopeful that the young Queen might do this during her forthcoming tour of New Zealand in 1953, although it had been made clear that she would lay only one foundation stone, that of Wellington Cathedral. Nevertheless, he wrote in November 1952 to Prime Minister Holland, in England at the time precisely to plan that tour.

> "If there should be any hope of relaxation of this decision, we would be inordinately happy if you felt yourself able to suggest to Her Majesty the Queen that she should consider the possibility of laying the foundation stone of the Waiapu Cathedral in Napier also. If the idea should prove practicable it would be of absorbing interest to many. Her Majesty's grandfather graced the Consecration of Liverpool Cathedral, and Her Majesty's father and mother sent me the first Gift for Nairobi cathedral whilst I was there, namely an exquisite Bible in two volumes, containing inscriptions and signatures."

Cathedral Re-building

Holland replied (11 December 1952) saying it "was under discussion," and he would write on his return to New Zealand. Undeterred and unwilling to wait for the promised reply, Lesser wrote again early in February 1953, but Holland confirmed the decision that the only foundation stone the Queen would lay was that of Wellington Cathedral, as her father had promised to do that. So, the disappointing decision had to be accepted[327] and in due course the Governor-general Sir Willoughby Norrie substituted for the Queen.

Norman Lesser and Governor-general Sir Willoughby Norrie at the Laying of the Foundation Stone of Waiapu Cathedral in Napier 1955

Norrie, in a friendly exchange of letters detailing arrangements for the service, asked Bishop Lesser for some help "as regards the substance of the address. You know your own diocese and its history,…" but in the end used little of a full speech Lesser sent him except for the information about the Diocese, the phrase "We rejoice with you that you are not content merely to record history, but to make it," and replaced Lesser's reference to Liverpool Cathedral with one to Canterbury Cathedral![328]

As the ceremony of the Laying of the Foundation Stone in October 1955 drew near, fund-raising efforts were intensified. Lesser wrote a letter yet again on behalf of the Re-building Committee, aimed at a broader audience, particularly referring to a recent promise by the generous Henry Charles to subsidise any donations in the months leading up to the Laying of the Foundation Stone. The Cathedral, he claims, is important not just to Anglicans:

> "As an expression of Christian faith and civic pride (it) must appeal to a much wider public."
>
> "…The first section is expected to cost £46,000 of which sum approximately £32,000 is in hand. We intend to proceed with faith, believing that the remaining £14,000 will be subscribed before it is needed. One parishioner, Mr H. A. Charles, who has already given generously, has stated that he will subsidise all contributions made before October 15th by 5%."

The letter acknowledges the "many calls on us these days and the question arises, 'How much shall we give?'" "…It would be impertinent for us to advise you on this point," but as the Cathedral is a symbol of our Christian beliefs our giving should be "a real sacrifice to us rather than just a token that we will not miss. We earnestly request your practical help in this great undertaking. If you have already contributed in the past, perhaps you will, in view of Mr Charles' offer, make an effort to do so again."[329]

Whether the "remaining £14,000" was subscribed or not, arrangements for the Laying of the Foundation Stone went ahead, and all Anglicans in the Diocese were invited to attend the ceremony, at the same time being reminded that money was still needed:

> "It is my hope that every Parish will bring or send an offering for the Mother Church. I know full well the demands that are constantly made upon the same people, but I do earnestly ask you to send an offering, even if it has to be but a token, that we may feel that the whole Diocese is as one."[330]

Cathedral Re-building

Preaching to the huge crowd gathered to witness this first significant step in the re-building of the Cathedral, the Bishop said,

> "The foundation stone is a promise to God; it is a promise to ourselves and to generations yet unborn. In this process of re-building, today marks a climax. No longer is the city without the promise of a cathedral, no longer is the frame to be without a picture. We hope to be able to press forward with the first section of the cathedral, and it is public munificence that will determine how soon the entire structure may nobly bear witness to our common faith and heritage. Many people who leave religion till the eleventh hour die at 10.45. Be thoughtful. Be generous. It is later than you think. Don't count your days – weigh them."[331]

But the Bishop understood this event, however significant, was only a beginning, and warned Synod [332] that building the Cathedral would be demanding:

> "1. The effort must be great.
>
> 2. The effort must be united… the Cathedral belongs to all,
>
> 3. The effort must be sustained and
>
> 4. The effort must be made with unceasing prayer."

He went on to quote words of Bishop Chavasse of Liverpool, spoken in 1901 at the same ceremony for Liverpool Cathedral.

> "My Brethren in the Lord, it is no small honour that we should be called by God to build to His glory a cathedral which shall witness for Him, long after we are dead, in the midst of a community where the temptation is so great to make gold our god… To us, as to the builders of old, comes the message of God's prophet, 'Be strong, all ye people of the land, and work, for I am with you saith the Lord of Hosts.' Let us reply as they did, 'The God of heaven, he will prosper us, therefore we His servants will arise and build.'
>
> What those words have come to mean to Liverpool Cathedral, may they now mean to this new cathedral of a new world, built upon the ageless Foundation in the strength of Him whose love is as old as the hills and yet new every morning. So be it. Amen!"

As the first stage of the building proceeded, Lesser may well have thought of the seventy or so years it had taken to complete Liverpool Cathedral, for that famous building was much in his mind as his own Cathedral on

A Likely Lad

the other side of the world was taking shape. Although he had worked in Liverpool Cathedral for only a year, he had watched its early years of construction, had been ordained and married in it and had a lifelong reverence for it as a model of all that a Cathedral could offer to the community in terms of art and culture as well as in worship.

His time at Liverpool Cathedral in 1930 had coincided with a major musical event involving the Poet Laureate John Masefield who had strong links with the Cathedral. He had even met Masefield while working there, according to his own account of the building of Waiapu Cathedral,[333] kindling a lifelong interest in the poet.[334]

So it was not totally surprising that he should think of approaching the aging poet for a special hymn to mark the Laying of the Foundation Stone. The initial request from Lesser is not on record, but the sequence of letters from then on is almost complete, forming a correspondence that is both charming and revealing.[335]

The first one from John Masefield, dated 28 June 1955, agrees to "gladly try to make some lines for you," and asks for some description of the Cathedral and the city. Lesser's response of 6 July 1955 begins "Your most gracious letter which I received this morning thrilled me beyond words..." Well it would, wouldn't it! Today the tone seems overly-ingratiating, but Masefield responded in kindly and modest fashion and further letters went between them.

Lesser sent him some information about Napier and "lines" came back on 18 July with the comment that "Napier had been so generous to the memory of poets," (he had obviously noted the many streets in Napier honouring poets), that it would "be a happiness to try again for her," should the lines be "impossible and unsingable."

Indeed, the lines themselves might have been singable, but sadly, the Poet Laureate had specifically referred to St John the Baptist instead of St John the Evangelist, so Lesser had to write, "I feel desolated to think after your extreme kindness, I am to ask you to alter at least one verse." Masefield replied on 5 August "I am grieved to read of my stupid mistake but will at once re-write the lines." They arrived on 17 August with a note suggesting Lesser could make any necessary alterations. Lesser was full of gratitude and suitably horrified that he could improve on the poet's words: "Your very modest implication that I might presume to suggest any alteration leaves me aghast! I could not conceive of any improvement." So those

Cathedral Re-building

"lines" became a hymn for the service of the Laying of the Foundation Stone in October 1955.

In 1957 there was further correspondence between them. Lesser must have written early in January asking for another hymn to mark the approaching Dedication of the first section of the Cathedral, as a letter from Masefield postmarked 25 February 1957 agrees. "If I be still alive and able to write, and you should still want some verses from me when your Cathedral comes to be consecrated, (sic) I feel sure that I should be glad and proud to try, but it would be a testing task."

A set of lines in a letter dated 3 January 1959 arrived with the comment "There is still time to try again," and as they were not very metrical or singable Lesser must have anguished over how to deal with them. In July he wrote: "The lines… were just glorious and I am very thrilled with them." However, they were able to be sung to only one or two very unfamiliar tunes and Lesser wanted "the whole congregation to have the privilege of singing the hymn." Masefield replied (23 August) "The task you set is not easy," but he had suggestions as to how to alter the last lines to make them more singable. So that was done, and the words were used for the Dedication of the first section of the Cathedral on 24 February 1960.

As the final section of the Cathedral neared completion, Lesser wrote again in May 1964 reminding the Poet Laureate of past kindness and enquiring whether we "might trespass on your generosity to make us some lines for the congregation to sing," when the Cathedral was completed. And could they please be ready by the beginning of October? Masefield does not seem to have answered this, and a second much briefer letter from Lesser dated 6 August 1964 says: "The burden of my letter is just to enquire whether we are to have the inestimable privilege of a hymn of your composition to be included in the Dedication Service of our completed Cathedral." Masefield wrote back: "I fear that in some way I have failed to answer a letter from you." He had not been well and said, "I am afraid that I cannot hope to write a hymn for your new Cathedral. But if you will be so very kind as to let me know when you must have the lines, I will make an effort."

Lesser's answer expresses regret at Masefield's illness and reluctance to worry him but is still hopeful, writing, "I would be intensely grateful to have the lines you make by the beginning of December." Masefield promised "to try all through October to make you some verses," suggesting Francis Thompson's quatrains as a model "which should be easy to set to music and sing aloud: at least I, who cannot sing, nor make music, suppose so."

In the event the ageing poet did send the lines by September and Lesser thanked him for the words of the hymn "which we will be privileged to use in the form of Service for the Dedication of our completed Cathedral." So these words, the third set written for a Cathedral on the other side of the world, were used at the Dedication of the completed Cathedral in 1965.

However, again the words did not easily fit the regular metre required for a hymn: strange as it seems for a poet, Masefield was not being falsely modest when he claimed he "could not sing nor make music," but a tune was found. Lesser was possibly hopeful of having yet another hymn written for the Consecration service in October 1967 and may have written again, according to the 1986 history of the Cathedral[336] but Masefield was by then too frail to comply and in fact died in May 1967, so Lesser himself wrote a special hymn and poem for the occasion.

So ended a remarkable sequence of letters and "lines" linking the Poet Laureate and Liverpool Cathedral with Bishop Lesser and Waiapu Cathedral.

The Dedication Service in 1960, using Masefield's second hymn, marked the end of the first stage of re-building, and there may well have been people who hoped for some respite from the building programme. But there was to be none. There were some determined to carry on and Bishop Lesser led the charge.

Reading between the lines, it seems he dared to hope from the very beginning that the Cathedral would be completed in his lifetime. Even before the Foundation Stone was laid, an article he wrote for the *Daily Telegraph* on the proposed Cathedral ended with the words,

> "The building, we trust, will begin almost at once, *and if there is enough faith and prayer and practical support, we need not contemplate leaving the second portion of the building to posterity. We could, if we desired, build it all, and leave our children to be blessed by its witness, and in their witness to be a blessing.*"[337] (Italics mine)

Cathedral Re-building

He threw down the same challenge to the 1957 Synod saying,

> "We still need about £20,000 to pay for this first section of the Cathedral, apart from such items as organ re-building, furnishings, windows. Are we going to build this part, and then sit down and say, 'The next generation can finish it, let our children do it. Does a parent so speak?' 'Let us, having put our hands to the plough, turn not back.' Let us carry on with the task and the joy, so that Mother Church can welcome all her children to worship within her walls… I would hang my head in shame if I were to hear that when New Zealand enjoyed her greatest prosperity, we who claim that we worship God, who gives us all things, gave Him less than half a Home to dwell in."[338]

It was the 1959 Synod which had to make the critical decision on completion. Knowing that there was not enough money in hand, Bishop Lesser again went for help outside the Diocese in the months preceding the Synod, appealing to old friends in Kenya in a long letter:

> "The first section of the building is completed… at a cost of £79,778. The second essay in re-building should be complete by mid-November… this will cost approximately £49,400. The forthcoming Synod will decide whether to proceed or not. They have about £35,000 in hand and have just had a firm offer of £1,500 if we decide to proceed."

This letter seems to have gone to nine people he considered friends, as he says,

> "if you cannot, or do not wish to assist, please do not trouble to reply, and I shall perfectly understand your decision *and it will not make one iota of difference to our personal relationship.*[339] (Italics mine.)

A reply from Kenya dated 2 October 1959 acknowledges Lesser's "letter of 25 last," and says,

> "When are you coming back to Kenya? You can't possibly like New Zealand better than us! …Never have we had anyone to follow those imaginative Graces you used to give us at Rotary."

However, no donations seem to have arrived from the overseas friends.

Despite the lack of any help from outside the Diocese, the 1959 Synod was persuaded to complete the Cathedral, due in no small part to Lesser's passionate and eloquent address. "An incomplete task can please no one, least of all God," he said, and powerfully compared the amount needed with the effort of the Mormons who were building a chapel at the cost of £60,000, and the local Racing Club, building a stand for £430,000. He asked,

> "Are we going to leave it to others 20 years or so hence, to finish what we have so magnificently begun? ...A cathedral is simply a church in which is the Bishop's seat or chair. How dearly I long that all my friends will allow me to sit down there!
>
> With all reverence, our dear Lord had to die before men took Him seriously, and then they built for Him. Is our building always to be of a memorial nature? Can we never learn to give people flowers while they can still smell them? If I were to die today would my many friends, knowing my earnest desire to see this cathedral completed, say that they felt impelled to complete it as an act of friendship? I do not know, but if they do feel that way, will they rise up NOW and say, 'the bricks are fallen down, but we will build!'"[340]

After a long debate, Synod bravely made the decision to go ahead in faith and hope, but "the financial situation at the time and for some time afterwards was unfavourable and the work was delayed," according to a 1963 report in *Church and People*,[341] while a *Daily Telegraph* editorial wrote of the "two years that the Napier Cathedral had stood incomplete."

Although the Diocese had promised in 1960 not to ask for further money for the Cathedral, and Bishop Lesser wanted to be "scrupulously honest," in keeping that promise, he persisted in efforts to raise the necessary funds, writing to clergy:

> "There must still be people in every parish who have only recently come to live in the Diocese, who have not yet made a contribution, and others who have not yet supported either their own parish or the cathedral. In addition to these people there are those who have made substantial provision for their parish's work and yet feel that they would desire to give something extra to enable the Diocese to have its Mother Church completed. I will be most grateful to you if you feel that you can make the need known to such people, without adversely affecting your own needs and commitments.
> We make no appeal: all we do is to state the need and the opportunity."[342]

Cathedral Re-building

Not only did he write dozens of letters of this kind, but Lesser was also punctilious in gratefully acknowledging any gifts. Typical examples are a letter in October 1959 to Henry Charles, a major benefactor, thanking him for contributing £3,000 and hoping he is recovering from a fall;[343] another to the editor of the *Daily Telegraph* in October 1959 thanks him for the "excellent support and encouragement which you have given to the Cathedral re-building project."[344] While both local newspapers were supportive, the *Daily Telegraph* adopted the project with great enthusiasm, enlisting the support of the wider community with editorials,[345] giving frequent and generous space to the building's progress and even publishing lists of donors regularly till 1966, when a final entry is headed "Only £5,000 needed." [346]

In 1962 Henry Charles died, and in his address at the funeral, Lesser reminded the congregation of Charles' gifts and his "desire to see our Cathedral completed." "It may be that those who admired and respected Mr Charles will take the opportunity of seeing that his wish is gratified, for this would prove to be a tangible mark of esteem and regard." In addition to his generosity while alive, Henry Charles left half of his estate, estimated to be £13,500, to the Cathedral re-building Fund.

The impending visit of the Queen in February 1963 gave another spur to completion. In fact, the Napier mayor was quoted as saying, "Although we have no details, we hope that Her Majesty may be able to attend service in the Cathedral, which of course must now be completed for this occasion." Church leaders were more circumspect. Archbishop Lesser pointed out that,

> "it depends on whether the public response to the final appeal to get the Cathedral completed in time is sufficient or not, and whether a visit to Napier is included. Until the appeal position is more clear we cannot say whether or not it would be possible to consecrate the Cathedral while the Queen is in New Zealand. If it is not paid for it cannot be consecrated, although a service of dedication could be held."[347]

Indeed, the Queen did come on a Sunday to Napier, sailing in and out in the *Britannia* but she chose to worship in St Paul's Presbyterian church!

The financial position improved to the point where in May 1964 Lesser was able to write to the people of Waiapu,

"I have much pleasure in announcing that Standing Committee has instructed the architect to accept the tender of Messrs. A.B. Davis and Sons to complete the building of our Waiapu Cathedral. I am most gratified at this decision and am confident that there will be ample endorsement of the decision, demonstrated by many people making donations… It is anticipated that the contract can be completed in about six months' time and our Diocese and friends will humbly rejoice in a noble task conceived and steadily attempted. The dedication of our Cathedral will be a memorable day in the history of our Diocese for we will be the only Diocese in New Zealand unfortunately to have been compelled to build our Cathedral twice."[348]

The Cathedral was completed in 1965, though still with a debt of £32,000. It was to be dedicated in March 1965, and the Archbishop of Canterbury was going to preach. A last-minute appeal went out: if that debt could be extinguished before the Dedication Service the Archbishop could consecrate the Cathedral. It seemed too good an opportunity to miss. An article by Dean Gibson[349] in the press states that "vicars have been asked to draw the attention of their parishioners to the visit of the Archbishop and the desire to have a debt free building, …to make the

Waiapu Cathedral of Saint John the Evangelist – c.1968

Cathedral Re-building

service on March 9 a memorable occasion." And in a letter sent to all clergy and synodsmen Archbishop Lesser writes: "People had expressed a desire for an opportunity towards extinguishing the existing debt on our Cathedral." He realised the heavy commitments already entered into in most parishes – monies for the Cathedral must be in addition, not instead of. "It is certainly not our intention of depriving any parish of rightful support."[350]

So the first newsletter for the year, in any parish well-organised enough, included a letter from Archbishop Lesser and an attractive A5 poster inviting parishioners to the Dedication on 9 March when the Archbishop of Canterbury would be the preacher and asking for "your thankful prayers, continued interest in the first NZ completed Cathedral, and for your continued financial support. £32,000 would make the cathedral DEBT FREE. (sic)"[351]

The necessary amount did not come in, but the Dedication of the building in March 1965 was again a huge occasion, with the Prime Minister and other dignitaries present. The Archbishop of Canterbury preached and Lesser himself carried out the Dedication.

A mere two years later in October 1967 he was able to consecrate the building. In a full-page article in the *Daily Telegraph* outlining the history of the re-build, including the costs, he comments that £12,000 had come in during the five weeks preceding the service of Consecration.[352]

The service of Consecration was yet another magnificent occasion with many VIP's attending. Particularly memorable was the 400-strong contingent of young people from all over the Diocese who gathered on Napier's Marine Parade to walk with their offerings to the Cathedral.

In his unfinished memoir Lesser writes:

> "When I came to the Diocese there was about £900 only in the Cathedral re-building fund, but with the approval of Synod, not always easy to accomplish, and with the vision and persistent endeavour of Dean O.S.O. Gibson, we had been able to achieve our objective. We had said 'the stones cry out' and the cry was heard and answered mightily. Thus, it was that the Cathedral was packed with some 1800 people for the Consecration, which was a colourful exciting hour-long service televised and sent out on radio. The guests included the Prime Minister, Mr Holyoake and Mrs Holyoake, the Leader of the

A Likely Lad

Opposition, Mr Kirk and Mrs Kirk, Sir Walter Nash M.P., civic dignitaries and prominent citizens from all walks of life, and many of those whose small but highly valued gifts had made the day possible. Other dioceses were represented by their bishops and other churches were represented, including the Roman Catholic Church. Prior to the service some 400 young Anglicans had marched along the Marine Parade to the Cathedral to bring their gift and exhibit their commitment to the Gospel. My words in the sermon were that it would simply be a mere travesty to consecrate a building and have it filled with people who were not prepared themselves to be consecrated anew and to translate a vision into a reality."

Dean Childs, Archbishop Lesser, Dean Emeritus O.S.O. Gibson in the new Cathedral 1967

Cathedral Re-building

The televising of the service, a first for Hawke's Bay,[353] must have been a stressful experience and certainly entailed a pile of extremely detailed correspondence between Charles Harrison, director of the Provincial Broadcasting and TV Committee, and Archbishop Lesser. The service was also fully described in a newspaper report explaining all the symbolism attached to the Archbishop's actions.

> "During the act of consecration Dr Lesser laid his hand on the northern wall and traced the Cross of Consecration which has been carved in a block of gold and red sandstone from Liverpool Cathedral. As he made the mark of consecration he said 'This dwelling is God's habitation. It is a possession above all price which must not be spoken against.'"[354]

Sadly, Bishop Panapa was too ill to attend. He had read the lessons at both earlier Services of Dedication, and his presence on this significant occasion was greatly missed.

To complete and consecrate a Cathedral a mere twelve years after the laying of its Foundation Stone was an amazing achievement for the Diocese, and a tribute to Bishop Lesser's determination, inspirational leadership and energy. Rarely does a Bishop have the privilege of laying the foundation stone of his Cathedral and consecrating it. As he hoped, the Cathedral rises from the place of former tragedy to be a sign of resurrection and hope. It is a "building with a sense of awe… which of itself commands a sense of worship," testifying to the presence and power of God in both city and Diocese.

Chapter 7: Church Union

It is difficult today to comprehend how much time, energy and intellectual rigour was expended in the Church Union movement of the 1950s and 1960s as the negotiating churches struggled to develop a basis on which they could unite, in the process giving rise to what has been described as "the most comprehensive statement on New Zealand ecclesiology ever produced."[355]

Bishop Lesser was closely involved in those discussions from the mid-1950s, although a Scrapbook item from 1953[356] referring to a decision by the Congregationalists to "engage in future talks with Presbyterian and Methodist churches and to support proposals to invite other communions to enter into discussions on faith and order," suggests an earlier interest, unusual in this country's Anglican leaders at the time.[357]

Two questions arise from these years of involvement: what did he really hope for in terms of a united church? And after all this commitment, why did he later withdraw support for the Plan for Union, the product of so many years of painstaking discussion and negotiation?

In Nairobi he had worked happily with the Presbyterian minister, especially in providing support for the troops, and he had also been involved with the Nairobi Council of Churches. In New Zealand he found a similar organization, the "official expression" according to the preacher at his Consecration, of the "growing desire for increasing understanding and co-operation between our own churches and the other non-episcopal churches."[358]

Napier itself with an active branch of the National Council of Churches and particularly warm relationships between the churches, offered encouragement to anyone interested in ecumenism. This supportive environment, along with his positive Nairobi experience and his natural inclination for Christian fellowship, all contributed to his willingness to be part of the movement for "increased understanding and co-operation" in his new country.

By the time Lesser entered the process as an official representative of the Anglican church, the movement was well under way among four of the non-episcopal churches in New Zealand. The Methodists, Churches of

Christ, Congregationalists and Presbyterians had begun talking to one another in the 1940s and had established a Joint Standing Committee (JSC) by 1951, but the Anglican church had been rather slow off the block to join in, one of the reasons being that its governing body, General Synod, met only every three years. However, in 1955 the first tentative steps were taken when it appointed Lesser to chair a Commission to investigate what was happening in Church Union talks in New Zealand and within the Anglican Communion, a motion he himself had proposed. The terms of reference are significant: whatever the initial enthusiasm for Church Union, at this stage Lesser and the Church of the Province intended to keep in mind the rest of the Anglican world.

Before his official involvement, however, the question of Anglican involvement in Church Union arose at his 1953 Diocesan Synod. Christchurch Synod, knowing that the Anglican church was about to be invited to join in the negotiations and also that General Synod was not due to meet for another two years, had passed a motion urging "a prompt and positive response to that invitation from the Primate, or other authority such as the Standing Committee of General Synod," and asked other dioceses to support it. At the Waiapu Synod the pre-emptive motion was replaced by a bland request that the Primate "communicate with the Archbishop of Canterbury so that any action that the Church of the Province may contemplate, may be of assistance to the considerable preliminary work which the Archbishop of Canterbury has himself initiated."[359]

The expected invitation did arrive in 1953 but as the Christchurch Synod had feared, it was not dealt with until the 1955 General Synod meeting, putting the Anglican church even further behind the other churches in the journey towards possible union. However, that Synod agreed that a "carefully selected Commission" be set up to examine what the JSC had achieved and to investigate what was happening in the Anglican Communion worldwide.[360] It also accepted an invitation from the National Council of Churches to send 36 representatives, selected by the Bishops, to a second "Faith and Order" Conference, an important forum where negotiating churches wrestled with questions of denominational theology and practice.[361]

As Chair of the Commission Lesser reported to the 1958 General Synod very succinctly, but in speaking to his report, he also moved successfully that the Archbishop be requested to "appoint representatives of the

A Likely Lad

church for the purpose of entering into exploratory conversation with the Joint Standing Committee on Church Union." At this stage, he seemed to be a prime mover within the Anglican church towards Union, though the speech accompanying the report was careful in tone, setting out the pitfalls ahead for Anglicans. Synod warmly commended the speech and ordered it to be printed for wider circulation.[362]

"Our first task," he said, "within the Ecumenical Movement is to study the differences in character and personality in the different churches and to understand them better and to learn to love one another as we are..." "The reunion towards which we must move contemplates and prepares for reunion of the Church as a whole, catholic and protestant. No other kind of unity is conceivable." He defended the Anglican, Catholic and apostolic tradition as "the only tradition that has any historical claim to use the word 'ecumenical' since it was ecumenical for the first 15 centuries of Christianity" and stressed the need to face the differences in belief instead of pretending they did not exist, particularly the question of the three-fold ministry and bishops, warning:

> "Theological implications will be of paramount importance. We dare not substitute enthusiasm for theology. To move ecumenically is to move theologically otherwise we are in danger of becoming mere fraternizing federalizing, pan-Protestants."[363]

The reference to three-fold ministry and bishops was a reminder to Synod members that the Anglican church claimed a ministry going back to the apostles of the early church through their bishops – the "Apostolic Succession." The Protestant churches, having done away with bishops, could not make the same claim. Therefore the ordination of their ministers, and the sacraments they performed, lacked authority in the eyes of some Anglicans.

Though the validity of ordination might not seem a central point of Christian doctrine in New Zealand today, it was a difficult question to circumvent and was one of the most obvious signs of separation.

The Anglican church, whose own ordinations were not acceptable to Roman Catholics, felt itself caught in the middle between two opposing traditions. On the one hand it saw itself as Catholic with historic links to the pre-Reformation church; on the other hand it was also strongly scriptural and held to much that the Reformers had died for, and two letters from *Church and People* representing each of these emphases pasted in side by side in a Scrapbook[364] show that Bishop Lesser was well aware of passionately-held differences of opinion among both clergy and laity.

He was again appointed to chair the Commission with its terms of reference now enlarged to "entering into exploratory conversation with the JSC," and was well aware of how time-consuming this work could be, writing in his pastoral letter 28 January 1959, "As I was appointed again as Chairman of this committee, you can imagine that there will be a very onerous responsibility resting upon us, and our deliberations will occupy considerable time."[365]

And undoubtedly they did. After preliminary conversations during 1959 with the Chair of the Joint Standing Committee, the full Anglican committee met in August to prepare for their first JSC meeting in February 1960. They went as Observers only but were invited to deliver two papers on the episcopacy, the major issue to be faced in any negotiations. Lesser as Chair of the Anglican group resisted the desire of the JSC for immediate action but expressed the hope on behalf of the committee that this "discussion is but the first." There is little doubt that Lesser's open and warm personality would have encouraged a friendly atmosphere at those early meetings, when relationships were being formed.

Reporting on this meeting to the 1961 General Synod, Lesser puts it in context. The other negotiating churches, having already agreed "in principle" to Union, had prepared a draft Basis for Union, naturally without reference to bishops or the three-fold ministry as understood by the Anglican church. Lesser sets out the dilemma for an Anglican church believing itself to be both Catholic and Reformed, reiterates the arguments for the historic three-fold ministry and refers to the fact that,

> "for the first time since the Reformation the Archbishop of Canterbury has called on the Pope, thereby… reminding us that our Church, catholic in its very nature and origin, meets the historic Churches of Christendom in equal terms; Reformed, it understands and appreciates the position of the Protestant Churches."

He again warns of the danger of giving the impression that Christian differences either do not exist or do not matter, but is willing to place some of the responsibility for schism at the door of the Anglican Church

A Likely Lad

and offers his listeners a different and somewhat startling perspective on the much-vaunted "Apostolic Succession:"

> "We are indeed in the Apostolic Succession – Judas betrayed Christ and sold him, Peter denied him, the others ran away in his hour of need – we are in the Apostolic Succession, deeply in it. May God keep us in it more worthily."

His conclusion returns to the initial premise:

> "We feel that our Church has maintained its system of three-fold ministry, and it has preserved, as the spinal column of its life, the principle of sacramental initiation and growth within the Church, which is the differential feature of essential Catholicism as contrasted with essential Protestantism. There we stand, we can do no other."

Again, Synod members were so impressed with Lesser's speech accompanying the report that they asked for it to be printed for wider readership.[366]

This General Synod moved forward to the extent of appointing an enlarged Commission on Church Union, approved the steps already taken by the representatives appointed in 1958 and requested parishes "take continuing note of the activities of the Commission and engage in similar exploration of this vital matter as opportunity is afforded."[367]

Unfortunately, "opportunity did not afford" very often for most parishes, and it seems that the vital educational process stalled here. Unless a vicar was really keen on ecumenism, most parishes simply went on as before.

This was as true of the Waiapu Diocese as elsewhere. For one thing, the Diocese during these years, was very focused on re-building its Cathedral. Moreover, there do not seem to have been senior clergy who were enthusiastic enough to take a lead, so the "vital matter" was often relegated to the side-lines of parish life. While the 1963 Waiapu Synod asked the Bishop to appoint a committee "to arouse in the members of the church in the Diocese a concern for and knowledge of the factors involved in union," the committee, duly appointed in 1964,[368] never seems to have met: at least there are no reports from it for either 1964 or 1965, though it surfaces in 1966 for the purpose of receiving comments and suggestions on the Joint Statement on Faith, *The Faith we Affirm Together*, put out by the Joint Commission on Church Union.[369]

Church Union

Lesser himself, however, continued to take a leading part in negotiations as Chair of the Commission, attending the third series of talks in 1962, even though by then he was Archbishop. He also became Vice-President of the National Council of Churches in 1961 and attended a Conference of Churches and Missions in the Pacific held in Samoa in April of that year. Later in the year he was a delegate to the World Council of Churches Assembly in New Delhi, and in 1962 attended the East Asia Christian Conference Consultation in Christchurch when the distinguished theologian D.T. Niles was the main guest.[370] So his ecumenical experience and sympathies were being significantly extended.

In 1964, General Synod made the important decision to join the formal negotiations and Lesser continued to chair the Commission. But as time went on, it is clear that Lesser, now Archbishop, was concerned at the pace of the movement towards Union and tried to slow it down. Anglicans had entered into the talks after the other churches and there was some catching-up to do. He knew very well that the average Anglican in the pew had much to learn, not just about the issues involved with Union but also about their own church; he wanted them to be informed, to know what they were gaining and what they might be losing in a united church, and he was desperately keen to avoid division. Some clergy too, both in Waiapu and throughout the country, were equally hesitant, if not actually opposed.

A point of crisis for the Waiapu Diocese seems to have occurred at a Clerical Conference at Taupo in 1966, following a paper billed as *The Theological Barriers to Re-Union* presented by Archdeacon Waymouth, the Provincial Secretary and Lesser's right-hand man. Lesser wrote later to clergy:

> "At subsequent group discussions and in plenary session it was patent that a deal of obscurity persisted, and it was equally obvious that this uncertainty would be aggravated in the minds of the 'ordinary' Church members… **All** our church members should have as full a knowledge as possible as to what is transpiring."

He urged that,

> "every opportunity be taken to impart the fullest information to all congregations and that Clerical Archdeaconry meetings, parochial annual meetings, vestry meetings and congregational meetings should engage in full discussion, not excluding joint

meetings with negotiating churches. When the time comes for our Church to make decisions, they must be **informed** decisions and not just relics of prejudice or overeager desire for novelty. Will the Clergy therefore give a strong lead in this matter so that approval or criticism may come from prayerful and considered judgment."

A p.s., presumably from Lesser also, recommends, very surprisingly, two pamphlets: one is *The End of the Anglican Church* by Harold Miller, a regular columnist in *Church and People* well-known for his opposition to Church Union; the other *Forward with Caution* by Gary F. Waller.

Whether the full discussions that he envisaged took place is unclear, but at least archdeaconry meetings were held to discuss *The Faith We Affirm Together*, a publication from the negotiating churches. The ignorance of many lay people about their own beliefs, and the general lack of enthusiasm for Union in the reports from the archdeaconries confirmed what he himself was feeling. Lesser's red pencil has highlighted many negative phrases such as "fragmentation might result from too hasty a union;" "heavy theological language for laymen to cope with," and "The group had not all agreed on the phrase 'Act of Commitment' and preferred 'A declaration of Intent' to avoid suggestion of finality."[371]

He was able to refer to these comments in his address to the 1966 General Synod, where he again stresses

> "the vital importance of our people addressing themselves to the deep questions involved… A truly informed opinion in the rank and file of our Church members is essential to a true assessment of what lies ahead of us… We should refuse to be stampeded into precipitate action."
>
> "It would be a calamity if a type of spurious union was achieved which left unmoved a great body of regular and nominal churchgoers…"
>
> "I desire that we should move together as a family and some members of a family take longer to ponder a question than others; but that does not presuppose their answer is either inadequate or wrong."

He again reminded his hearers of the Anglican church's relations with the Orthodox and Roman Catholic churches, referring to recent meetings between the Pope and the Archbishop of Canterbury, and further retreated from the current process by introducing a new and somewhat irrelevant dimension to the whole ecumenical discussion:

> "There is a temptation to suppose that if we can somehow contrive the various Christian bodies to unite, we shall have achieved Christian Unity, but I am convinced that spiritual revival is more important than Christian unity and such unity will never be achieved apart from such revival. The question of church unity is not whether money will be saved, but whether men will be." [372]

While the growing warmth between Rome and Canterbury was welcomed in New Zealand, it probably added further complications at the time to the Church Union negotiations for some Anglicans, who felt themselves caught in a strange ecclesiastical 'ménage à trois' with Rome and the non-Episcopal churches. In Waiapu itself, the parish priest in All Saints Taradale and a priest at the nearby Catholic Seminary were establishing avenues for dialogue, with the Archbishop's blessing.[373] While union with Rome was never under discussion, these new developments were a constant reminder of the ideal "united" church Lesser and others dreamed of.

In addressing his own Diocese in October 1966, he again discourages the organic union which was being envisaged, saying,

> "Mere organizational togetherness is not unity as Christ knows it. The branches may not touch each other, but they can still be one in the Vine."

He did not want "a quick union of churches which has been achieved through half-digested overtures."

> "The deep theological questions of unity must be faced squarely – or the resultant church would be inadequate for its task and sooner or later disintegrate and the last state would be worse than the first."

He went on to raise what he claimed were "lesser difficulties" such as,

> "What will we do with the thousands and thousands of pounds worth of hymn books which belong to the several congregations? What robes will the clergy wear? What will happen to all the Cathedrals?"

To many practical minds in his audience, such questions would have been far more crucial than the "deep theological questions of unity."[374]

A Likely Lad

He could have also raised the question of women in the priestly ministry, a matter which had not yet been discussed by Anglicans, and the heresy trials of the Presbyterian minister Lloyd Geering, which also contributed to the sense of trepidation some Anglicans felt about Church Union.

However, in May 1967 the five churches did enter into an *Act of Commitment* in Wellington Cathedral.[375] Lesser remained concerned at the speed of movement and to the Waiapu Synod in 1967 said,

> "The rank and file of all the constituent churches need to fully appreciate both what they are contributing and what they are forfeiting in the cause of unity."[376]

Continuing to urge a more cautious approach, he addressed General Synod in May 1968,

> "We should be more concerned with the direction than the speed of the movement to Unity."

> "We must gather all our spiritual resources and heritage and see that nothing of eternal value is withheld from union nor sacrificed to achieve it…"

> "The average member of our own Church has not given the serious attention to what is involved with union which it merits."

The throwaway line about hating to see a "supermarket Church with a big business and no soul" was the sort of one-liner the media loved, making the headlines and doing nothing for Church Union.

He was also anxious that the 'new' church should be in communion with other Anglican provinces, meaning that certain elements of Anglicanism must be retained, and he was very opposed to setting a timetable for action:

> "It appears to me to be insulting to the Holy Spirit. We ask for His guidance and to be led into the truth, and then we tell Him how much time we will allow Him to complete His work."

After pointing out that the other four negotiating churches have had 20 years of working together, he produces another quotable line:

> "It is one thing to rock the boat; it is another to torpedo it."[377]

He might have felt slightly more reassured about Church Union after the 1968 Lambeth Conference which issued some positive statements on Church Union, such as "The conference felt Christians could not properly fulfil their ministry in a disunited church," and recommended that Intercommunion be allowed in certain circumstances.[378] On the other hand, the whole Lambeth experience would have deepened his appreciation of the Anglican tradition and reminded him of the value of belonging to a historic worldwide communion, all of which risked being lost in a united New Zealand church.

A year after the Lambeth Conference he, along with 24 other Archbishops, was asked by the Archbishops of Canterbury and York to comment on the proposals in England for an Anglican-Methodist Union. His guarded response indicates the same lack of enthusiasm for organic union in that country as he was showing in New Zealand:

> "As an outsider and as an observer it would appear to me that there is still a not inconsiderable residium of opinion which is yet unconvinced, and it would be presumptuous for me to express an opinion as to how best to deal with the situation."[379]

Nevertheless, the Waiapu 1969 Synod rather belatedly exhorted "all church members to give the most serious study to the Plan for Union during 1970"[380] and at least one archdeaconry did organise a day for study of the Plan.[381]

Meanwhile, apart from the Plan for Union, other significant ecumenical ventures were developing such as the Joint Board of Theological Studies, established in 1968, and the *Christian Life Curriculum*, an ecumenical resource for Christian Education, and although he was by now backing off the idea of organic union, Lesser was supportive of these, particularly commending the latter to General Synod 1968, describing it as "so full of promise" and expressing the hope "that clergy, synodsmen, and vestries within the Diocese would give the new Curriculum every opportunity of proving its worth."[382]

Yet he was wary of working formally with other churches in practical matters unless Anglicans were involved from the beginning. A plan for a joint building programme with the Methodist and Presbyterian churches in the new suburb of Greerton in Tauranga was discouraged:

> "Obviously a good deal of spade work has been done by the other two churches and I do not think we should commit ourselves until we are well versed in all the implications." [383]

On the other hand, he suggests to the vicar of Te Puke that the churches might "unite in the creation of a small building for common use" in the new area of Papamoa as none of them were big enough at the time to build separately[384] and he encouraged the joint use of buildings in Turangi.[385]

However, it is clear that as the decade passed, Lesser continued to retreat from the imminent prospect of Union as proposed in the Plan for Union. The matter of the episcopacy in the Plan was of special concern, he told his 1970 Synod. Presbyterians, he claimed, were not at all keen on the idea, and he felt the rôle of the Bishop had been weakened to the point that it was hardly recognisable to Anglicans.

> "Some have said the name of a Bishop is in the Plan but only in the form of a pale ghost."[386]

And he again diverts attention from the theological discussions by suggesting a "spiritual unity" through deeper devotion should be the aim.

"Spiritual unity" had indeed been growing over the decade among the congregations of the different churches, some of whom had been meeting for joint prayer and study over months or even years, but Lesser was cautious about endorsing combined services as regular events in parish life, and was certainly opposed to sharing Communion at this stage.

Gisborne had had a combined mission leading to a greater spirit of co-operation between the churches, and in March 1965 the vicar wrote seeking permission for an exchange of pulpits, a Ministers' Communion Service "at which all are free to come to the holy table who wish," and a High School service which he wanted to share with other clergy. Lesser replied opposing the Ministers' Communion Service as "I think that this is anticipating events and ought not at present to take place." The exchange of pulpits, and the service for the High School with other clergy preaching or reading a lesson, were both acceptable, but "I imagine that these services would be infrequent."[387]

Inevitably the division at the Lord's Table was being felt quite painfully especially at events like the Ecumenical Youth Conference in 1965 and the call to share Holy Communion was becoming more insistent. Such was the pressure from the young that Lesser felt obliged to write[388] in the national Anglican newspaper *Church and People* on behalf of the Bishops to say, "The New Zealand Bishops are not unmindful of the growing concern of young people over church unity." He sets out the different views on Intercommunion but concludes, "Present Anglican discipline does not allow intercommunion except in certain circumstances but the whole position is being considered by a commission set up by General Synod."[389]

But this was not good enough for some Anglicans who felt that the exclusive nature of the Eucharist was at best, unfriendly, and at worst "downright unchristian,"[390] and judgemental. One clergyman felt strongly enough to bring a motion to the 1967 Waiapu Synod asking that the Anglican Church welcome at its altars members of the negotiating churches who were communicants in their own church.[391]

The "spirited debate"[392] that followed highlighted the two opposing views on sharing the Communion: one that it should be the result of Union, not a tool towards it; the other that by sharing at the Lord's Table, people could experience a sense of meaningful unity which would put into perspective the less important points of division. After some senior clergy had spoken against the motion, Lesser made a statement saying he wanted to await the report of General Synod which had a commission on the topic.

> "There are those who desire only this inter-communion and who have no interest in the search for union, and I believe that we ought to be clear what our final object is. My own object is complete unity of all Christian Churches without exception."

He suggested that supporting the motion might have a delaying effect on "the ultimate cause of unity;" on the other hand, if the motion were defeated "it would give a wrong impression of the spiritual intent of Synod."

> "There are still many people who are keenly desirous of union who maintain that intercommunion is the seal of union and not the means of its accomplishment and I number myself with them."

The motion lapsed as a result of an amendment "that this Synod recognises its deep longing for the day when members of the churches at present negotiating for union will be able to receive Holy Communion together, but affirms its belief that no steps should be taken at this stage to hinder the movement towards union," which was subsequently carried.[393]

It is typical of Lesser that he wrote a conciliatory note two days after that Synod (13 October) to the vicar concerned.[394] "May I take this opportunity of writing to you a simple personal letter to express my keen appreciation of what I regarded as magnificent action on your part in

A Likely Lad

the manner in which you dealt with the situation which arose during the Motion you proposed to Synod." He was glad Synod had expressed its appreciation of the vicar's magnanimity and he admired the vicar's reaction to the situation. The vicar responded, "I can't tell you how much I appreciated your letter about my Motion to Synod," adding that he had had no intention of splitting Synod, and bowing to the Archbishop's presumed superior knowledge in the matter.

Not everyone was convinced by Lesser's arguments, however, and he was besieged with many requests for combined services, including shared Communions. Aware that his position gave his utterances particular authority, he was very careful to follow the protocols established by General Synod and consistently refused permission for shared Communion services on the grounds that he did not want to pre-empt the forthcoming General Synod decision. Only once did he allow it, as a climax to a series of inter-church studies and prayer on Church Union, preferring that option to a combined service on World Communion Sunday – which would have set more of a precedent as it would recur each year.

However, by 6 May 1969 he allows for more freedom of the individual's conscience, writing to a vicar who wanted a combined Communion service for Red Cross in his parish:

> "It is not possible for me to say that you may invite members of other churches to partake of the Holy Communion (at a Red Cross service) and all I can say is that it must be left to their own consciences as to what they do. The whole question is before General Synod and I do not want to anticipate their judgment."[395]

Dannevirke parish was particularly persistent in wanting a shared Communion service with the local Methodists, with whom they were working closely. They had already combined Youth and Young Adult work and wanted to do more together, especially hoping to share a regular monthly evening Holy Communion service. A contributing factor to the desire to work together was the unequal weight of pastoral care carried by the two clergy: the Anglican was over-loaded and the Methodists were a small congregation, so the possibility of the Methodist minister taking some Anglican funerals was suggested to the Archbishop as a way of easing the situation.

Church Union

Early in 1970 Lesser spent time with the vicar discussing co-operation between the two churches and a formal letter followed dated 19 March declining permission for the Methodist Minister to perform "Anglican funerals in the Anglican Church with the Anglican form of service," and asking him to take no action until after General Synod "when I will write to you again." The sharing of the Holy Communion is not directly addressed at this point.

The parish pursued the matter after the 1970 General Synod with the Parish Secretary writing on 25 May 1970: "In view of the General Synod approval of the principle of admission to Communion in special circumstances, it is hoped that a combined Communion Service once a month could be possible" and ending, "The Methodist church is a small body and as our vicar is without assistance the kind of co-operation the Vestry envisages would be of mutual benefit to both clergy and their congregations."

After seeking urgent advice on these requests (27 May 1970) from Bishop Allen Johnston, Chair of the Commission on Church Union at this time, the Archbishop wrote (12 June) that after "most serious and prayerful consideration" of the two requests, he had turned them both down.

Regarding the shared Communion services, he did not think "General Synod envisaged a regular service of the nature proposed." As for the sharing of funeral services, he wrote from his own experience of how "happy working relationships" could change when personnel changed and "endless trouble could ensue" for the parish if it was committed to the arrangement.

Undeterred the vicar wrote (29 June) saying the Vestry had asked the Church wardens to pursue the matter with Lesser. The letter ends, "You may think the matter is closed. Vestry is disappointed, (as I obviously am) and would be grateful if you would give further consideration to what we believe would help the total work of the Church here."

A month later, having heard nothing back, the parish addressed a 'Memorial' to the Archbishop (27 July 1970) asking him "respectfully to reconsider your decision on the question of intercommunion with the Methodist Church in Dannevirke." It is a beautifully set-out three-page document on high quality paper, with fourteen bullet points, but unfortunately Archbishop Lesser was ill for a month, and the parish had to be content with a letter from the Vicar-general dated 29 July acknowledging the Memorial and saying, "As you are no doubt aware the Archbishop has been ill and has been ordered a period of complete rest."

Over a month later on 7 September 1970 Lesser answers the June letter from the vicar, Brian Davis,[396] explaining that he has been ill for some weeks, and has only been back at work one day. He writes,

> "After prayerful reflection I am willing for the monthly services, at which the Methodists join you in your church, to be a service of Holy Communion during which the Methodist congregation would be free to make their communion if they so wish and are eligible to do so."[397]

This carefully-worded ruling allowed Lesser to satisfy to some extent the parish's persistent aspirations in a diplomatic compromise which by-passed who was to judge the Methodists' eligibility to receive Communion, avoided comment on the Methodist minister's ordination, and ignored the possibility that Anglicans might want to reverse the situation and receive Communion in the Methodist church.

Of course not all the clergy were as enthusiastic about Intercommunion or Church Union as Dannevirke's vicar. Some were feeling decidedly uneasy. One wrote in November 1969 to Lesser referring to a colleague,

> "who seemed worried and unsettled with regard to possible developments of a United Church, a feeling that to a great extent I myself, and no doubt other clergy, must be feeling at the present time."[398]

Archbishop Lesser therefore had reason to feel concern not just for laity who might feel perplexed and opposed to change, but also for clergy who might worry that should Church Union become a reality with its joint use of buildings and changed boundaries, their jobs might be on the line. He himself notes with wry amusement in a letter to Stephen Waymouth, his Provincial Secretary and confidante, that "on the basis of the Plan for Union I have already overstayed my welcome as Bishop by two years!"[399]

At his last General Synod in May 1970, he again stressed the need for wide participation in discussions on the Plan for Union, asking for the coming year to be set aside for "deep consideration of all the issues involved and their repercussions." He believed the Anglican church had much to offer union, but introduces a digression becoming familiar to his hearers:

"Until we are fit for unity with our blessed Lord, we cannot be fit for unity with anybody else. The whole essence of union is renewal."

He quotes an anonymous source as saying, "I am prepared to let Anglicanism go when I see something better: at the moment I only see something different" and in a typically pithy quote advises them as they give "serious thought during this year to the Plan for Union" they should, "beware of George Bernard Shaw's dictum that 'people do not change their minds, they merely rearrange their prejudices.'"[400]

In spite of the Archbishop's warnings, the 1970 General Synod gave permission for a referendum to be held on the Plan for Union, and Intercommunion became acceptable if the president of the Eucharist was an "ordained minister." This of course begged the question of what constituted an ordained minister, and some, including senior clergy in Waiapu, continued to hold firmly to the view that ordination by a bishop was the only valid one.

At his own Diocesan Synod, which was to be his last, he continued to recede from the formal relationship envisaged in the Plan for Union, suggesting instead that "a form of federalism might best suit the current mood," and as people were now able to share Holy Communion, "in God's good time, the present urge towards fuller participation with other Christians would result in the congregations themselves demanding organic union."[401]

But the mood of the majority was to pursue the path which they had, belatedly perhaps, begun to follow, and Synod gave "general approval" to the Plan for Union, ignoring the Archbishop's warnings.

In the end, he retired before the vital vote on the Plan for Union was taken, although it is worth noting that Waiapu Diocese as a whole voted in favour.

Lesser's early involvement with the Ecumenical Movement and the Joint Standing Committee shows initial enthusiasm for Church Union in New Zealand, and a warmth towards Christians of other denominations, balanced with a deeply-held conviction of the value of his own church with its dual Catholic and Protestant heritage. However, for various reasons, that initial enthusiasm cooled as the prospect of organic union came closer. By nature cautious, he preferred to move slowly, anxious to keep in step with the wider Anglican Communion rather than to

A Likely Lad

be isolated in the vanguard of such a radical change. It is clear that he considered the process towards Union too hasty and was deeply concerned that many members of "the family" would either be left behind or completely alienated; and he was quite opposed to certain aspects of the Plan, particularly the rôle of the Bishop. But in the end it is possible that the non-theological factors involved – Anglican tradition, buildings, jobs – were as decisive for him as they were for many others.

As we know, organic union was not achieved but the current warm relations between the churches owe much to the years of study, prayer and personal encounter arising from the negotiations for Church Union when congregations discovered how meaningless denominational boundaries could be. Perhaps the Archbishop was right in thinking that in "God's good time... congregations themselves will demand organic union."

Chapter 8: Change in Church and Society

Lesser's term as Archbishop coincided with radical changes in Church and society in a decade associated in the popular mind with the Beatles, protest movements, 'free love' and drugs. For the Church it was a decade that initiated an on-going process of modernization, at least in appearance. While this process was deeply upsetting for some people, there were no doubt others who would have liked more fundamental changes in the Church to help them deal with new challenges to their theological concepts.

The modernization began with the Bible, continued with the Lord's Prayer and for Anglicans culminated ultimately in the revision of the 300-year-old *Book of Common Prayer*, beloved by many. The radical questioning about the nature of God continues to this day, but in the early 1960s the so-called 'new' theology represented by books such as J.A.T. Robinson's *Honest to God*, opened exciting doors for laypeople, encouraging them to share in conversations usually confined to theological colleges.

How did Bishop Lesser relate to change in general? The consensus is that he didn't seem to be "too keen" on some of the changes in the 1960s and may have been relieved to retire before the Church Union vote.[402] The young vicar of Norris Green, described as "always happy to try out new ideas" and "unconventional to a degree" may have become more cautious with age and experience; more accurately perhaps, the "new ideas" he reputedly accepted so happily were merely superficial wrappings of the same message, carrying no threat to fundamentals.

While realizing that change was inevitable for both the world and the church, he preferred to consider all the possible ramifications before accepting it, aware, as he wrote years later in his retirement, that "to change is easy: to improve is difficult." [403] And he reminded his 1966 General Synod that while "'the other disciple may have outrun Peter' …we require to know of a certainty that he has landed at the feet of His Lord."[404]

A further insight can be found in his reply to a vicar who wrote that though the 1968 Synod had been very happy, he had reservations about some of its decisions: "It seems to me we are coming to terms with

A Likely Lad

the world rather than proclaiming Christ and Him crucified." Lesser answered, "Like yourself, I thought we had a happy Synod, but I could not give my complete approval to all that this changing world demands."[405]

His address to the 1968 General Synod is also revealing:

> "A temper of mind which seems to find increasing support in our churches is that we should make Christianity relevant to modern man. I cannot see why we should not use all our energies to endeavour to make modern man relevant to the claims of Jesus Christ, for that was His own way… Of course, we know that times change… but I deprecate the inclination to the watering down of our faith so that we do not offend anyone."

At the end of his address to General Synod in 1970 – which was to be his last such meeting – he said,

> "These are days calling for action, days of unending change. To resist change or fail to condition ourselves to a changed environment means death: but to accept change uncritically and merely for the sake of change can be no less fatal."

He then went on to make a critical comment on workplace chaplaincies, one of the new forms of ministry the church was experimenting with in the hope of reaching outsiders. "We are aware of an increasing desire to exercise a specialist ministry, both within and without the Church. They recognize they will know more and more about less and less, but they do not always appreciate that they will know less and less about more and more."[406]

At his last Diocesan Synod he warned of "cataclysmic changes which appear to some people to leave them just isolated on a very small island in a sea of complexity," making it even more necessary to "remind ourselves of One who is constant, yet is the great Contemporary of every age."[407]

However, change was indeed inevitable, with the first significant one of the decade being the use of the 'new' Bible, the Revised Standard Version, in church services. The RSV was familiar to many from frequent use in non-statutory services and study groups, but it is not surprising that Lesser, who probably knew much of the old 'authorized' version by heart, was lukewarm about this change. However, his only comment to General Synod 1964, which authorized its use, was restrained:

> "I sincerely trust that I shall still be able to read the Holy
> Gospel for Christmas Day in its familiar form."[408]

As to the "bewildering multiplication of versions of Holy Scripture…" which developed over the following years, he avoided recommending any one version by suggesting

> "The best translation is YOU. It is for us to be living
> advertisements for Jesus Christ, for what we are speaks so
> much more loudly than what we say."[409]

The new Bible was the first of many changes. Two that followed were more contentious and difficult: the revision of the old *Book of Common Prayer* and the Lord's Prayer, both of which had been in exclusive use for hundreds of years. The 1964 General Synod Commission appointed to work on the revision of the whole *Prayer Book* started with the Communion service, and various experimental forms were being 'tried out' in selected parishes in the following years.

These experimental liturgies and other 'modern' services to replace traditional Evensong, were welcomed and used by the organizers of the large annual Youth Services from 1967 onwards, and Lesser seemed to have no problem with that. Nor did he object to the inclusion of some of the popular religious songs of the day, though he worried whether the congregation would know them well, writing to one of the organizers, "I am only too willing to conform to the pattern which you set and assume the young people will know the songs."[410] By 1970 he was even "quite willing for them to use the New Zealand Liturgy set to the American Folk Mass" and to allow the Communion table to be brought forward from the High Altar to the nave, "though doubtless you will be in touch with the Dean concerning this."[411]

However, permanently replacing the *Prayer Book* with a new service was another matter. He urged General Synod in 1966 to think carefully: "Anything that has been in the 'family' for upward of 300 years is not lightly discarded whilst at the same time a veneration beyond merit is sometimes afforded." He was more direct to his 1966 Diocesan Synod saying,

> "There are very many who devoutly believe that the proposed
> Liturgy enriched by experimental use will lead to a fuller
> offering of meaningful worship. There would be many also who
> did not wish for change in the Liturgy."

A Likely Lad

For himself, he said, he would be happy with one small change to the 1928 service: replacing "Or This" after the first Post-Communion prayer with "And This"[412] an alteration having no effect on the overall service apart from lengthening it. He warned them that,

> "The new form of Communion service if approved would be the most radical change in the service for 300 years,"

adding,

> "The Revised Liturgy would not save the world unless together with the revised Liturgy there was also a revised dedication of ourselves."[413]

At General Synod in 1970 he remained unenthusiastic about the "new" Liturgy, finding it "questionable" whether its use had greatly increased the attendance of young people at Holy Communion, as some had claimed it would. "Adherents and opponents do not appear to fall into any easily classified grouping."[414] And his reservations were made clear at his Diocesan Synod in the same year:

> "Liturgical revision is of primary importance since our worship must reveal the perfection which is of God. It is unnecessary to add that at present we have not achieved it. Contrary to Scripture, I think that in some cases the old bottle is too good for the new wine."[415]

As far as the Lord's Prayer was concerned, he, like many others, was not impressed with some of the versions appearing over the decade. In his address to the 1970 Diocesan Synod he confessed "For my part, I could not readily use the Lord's Prayer as printed." He would have liked an agreed form:

> "It is most stultifying to attend different churches and not know how to say your Saviour's words,"

but he did not like "Do not put us to the test and deliver us from evil."

> "Our blessed Lord was put to the test with a vengeance and we have no right to ask to be exempted. What I would like to see is 'Strengthen us in temptation.' The 'test' has overtones in New Zealand and South Africa."[416]

The modernization of the Bible, the *Prayer Book* and the Lord's Prayer were all necessary and visible efforts by the church to keep in touch with the world.

Change in Church and Society

But the really significant change occurring in this decade was invisible and neither the Synods nor the Archbishop seemed able or willing to deal with it. Many people were no longer satisfied with the traditional ideas of God they had been taught and were looking for something that fitted better with the reality of the modern world. Yet Lesser, like others in the Church hierarchy, seemed uninterested in what the 'New' Theology was saying, and it rated only a passing mention in his address to General Synod 1968:

> "with some theologians suggesting God is dead, whereas it is not God but our faith that is dead."[417]

And when his Presbyterian friend Rev Bob Foster asked him what he thought about "all this modern theology" Lesser replied, "I believe the Bible still means what it says."

However, it wasn't only the Bible, liturgy and theology that were receiving a makeover in the 1960s but also Church discipline and practice, a comparatively easy area of reform.

The Church's attitude to divorce was becoming a major pastoral problem for clergy. Divorce was more common and more sociably acceptable, yet divorced people were not supposed to receive the bread and wine in the Communion service, and every parish priest had faithful parishioners who were hurt by this exclusion from what had become the most meaningful act of worship the Church offered.

In 1964 the Bishops discussed this matter at their annual meeting against a background of information from Australia, the 1958 Lambeth Conference and articles in the *Church Times*.[418] They set up a careful process whereby a divorced person wishing to receive Holy Communion would speak to his or her vicar, who would then apply to the Bishop on behalf of that person for permission to receive Communion.

Lesser received three or four such requests each year but would not deal with individuals who tried to bypass their vicars and approach him directly, seeing the process set down as an opportunity for the vicar to make contact and exercise some pastoral care. He answered one such direct request in a typically friendly and tactful way:

> "From what you say, it would appear that you will now be regarding St ---- as your parish. Have a word with your vicar and ask him to send me a supporting letter. You can tell him

> you have advised me of the position and that I just require his letter of support to place the matter formally in order."

Later on came the question of re-marrying divorced people in church, a proposal which faced more serious opposition from some clergy. To his 1968 General Synod, Lesser said, "The question should not be viewed emotionally or purely theoretically." It was about real people and "God cares for people." However, he went on to say, "The fundamental question is not our compassion but God's will."

It was a question facing many parts of the Anglican Communion and Lesser made extensive enquiries as to what was happening elsewhere, in turn fielding requests from around the world for information on the New Zealand practice.[419] While he was aware that both the USA and Canada had already made changes in their practice, the Church of England was still "exercising its mind" and he would have liked to delay any decision in the New Zealand church until "all existing information relating to marriage discipline" was brought to a future General Synod through a specially set-up Commission.[420] However, General Synod showed a willingness to act more promptly and the proposal was sent for discussion and comment within the dioceses, with a final decision expected at the next meeting of General Synod.

Re-marriage of divorced people was a step too far for some clergy, who were ready to resign if the Church went down that track. In his own diocese, Lesser reminded a vicar who felt that way that the proposed legislation would allow for priests with a conscientious objection NOT to have to marry such people.[421] He sets out a detailed process for clergy to follow in a pastoral letter, suggesting questions to ask the couple intending marriage, and reassuring clergy that the Bishop will be the one who refuses permission, not the clergyman. He ends:

> "We shall all, no doubt, find difficulties as we deal with this completely new situation, and I hope you will feel free to discuss any problems at all in this connection as they arise."[422]

Interestingly for someone who enjoyed constructing new liturgies, he saw no need for a special service to mark the end of a marriage – a "loosening of Marriage Ties" – as one priest suggested to him.

Meanwhile the church was also reviewing the place of Baptism and Confirmation as a means of entry to church membership. The traditional practice of the Anglican Church was to baptise infants and later prepare

Change in Church and Society

young people for the rite of Confirmation which gave admission to Holy Communion. This had worked well enough in an age of faithful church attendance but as the 1960s rolled on, some vicars began to worry that baptism had become a meaningless social ritual, often carried out at a small private ceremony rather than within a normal congregational service. As early as 1951 there was an expressed concern to "restore to its rightful dignity the sacrament of Holy Baptism," and while some efforts were made to do that, not much changed over the ensuing years, although the concern remained. Eventually in 1969 Waiapu Synod passed a motion asking General Synod to "explore the theology of Baptism and Confirmation in relation to the need to commission laity for their task in the world."[423] General Synod 1970 passed the question back to the dioceses encouraging experimentation.

Those actions were of little immediate help to the vicar of Otumoetai, a fast-growing suburb of Tauranga, who wrote in frustration to his Bishop in December 1968:

> "I have baptised 40 babies in the last year and a few months. Of the 80 parents 14 were regular churchgoers, 10 are occasional, several have left the district and the remaining 50 I have never seen before, have never seen since and do not expect to see until the next baby to be 'done' comes along."

He was very unhappy about the situation and was planning to put a stop to it by insisting that at least one parent come to four classes to discuss the Christian faith before baptism could take place. He also wanted to ensure that the rite was "conducted within the framework of a service of corporate worship." He sought the Archbishop's support for these plans but also asked,

> "How far do I go? If a parent refuses to accept instruction, do I baptise the child willy-nilly?"[424]

Lesser replied with his usual promptness a few days later (18 December 1968) saying he would "find it impossible publicly to support the suggestion fully whilst recognizing the difficulties... Without being in any sense unwilling to grasp a nettle, for my own part, I am sure that the results which you regard as your goal can be achieved in other ways." He gives an example from his own experience of a neighbouring vicar who refused to baptise, marry or bury anyone where the family were not regular communicants. This had led to endless difficulty and embarrassment in Lesser's parish, as it might do for "a neighbouring vicar who may view things differently from you." He suggests ways to prevent the situation arising, such as prior notice of baptism being required, preferably on a printed form. He also points out that "we are not capable of assessing what God himself does for the child…" and ends,

> "Admittedly this question is capable of a number of different approaches. Knowing you to be such an honest man I recognise that your view is utterly and sincerely held, and all I would do, with the greatest humility, is to suggest that there may be shades of light grey as well as white and black."

And signs off as usual, "As ever affectionately…"

While some churches offered a non-sacramental service to mark the momentous event of the arrival of a child, the Anglican church had no suggestions to make at this stage. One vicar had a family wanting an alternative to infant baptism, so he wrote asking about the possibility of a service of Dedication, but Lesser replied, "There is no service for the dedication of a child in the Church of the Province but only baptism." "… but as you know, the whole question of Christian Initiation is under very active consideration."[425]

Similarly, Confirmation, although very meaningful for some, had become a somewhat automatic procedure for any young teenager claiming attachment to the Anglican Church. A complete re-think of both services was much needed in the interests of preserving the integrity of the Church's practice. By 1970, General Synod agreed to the experimental use of a revised order of Baptism and Confirmation, and children who had received some teaching about the meaning of Communion could receive the elements before being confirmed, which it was assumed would become a more adult commitment.

It is not clear what Lesser thought of this change. Confirmation was an episcopal rôle and having carried out thousands of confirmations over the 23 years he might well have had misgivings about the effects of this change to the status and function of the rite.

The Ordination of Women was another issue arising in this decade. Lesser paid respectful attention to women, often acknowledging, as he did at his first Synod, the "incalculable debt" owed to clergy wives who "…with a good heart… do impossible tasks" and he would thank them publicly for their hospitality, admitting that "Although I try not to be too much of a nuisance I do realize that one more in the home means extra work."[426]

Change in Church and Society

He also frequently paid tribute to the support of his wife Beatrice, and as the father of a daughter would have resented any perceived slight to her or to other young women. In fact, he assured the girls of Napier Girls' High School at their prizegiving that "Women have a vital place in the world today and are increasingly taking the reins of power throughout the world."[427]

But it never occurred to him or many others in authority to involve women in high level church administration or any formal "up-front" ministry. The highest office given to a woman in Waiapu seemed to be the appointment of Phyllis Oxford as a Diocesan representative in 1959 to a committee looking at establishing a Youth Training College.[428] In 1960 in a first step to equality, he suggested a committee set up to look at vicarages should have two women on it with Mrs Lesser and Mrs Waymouth being the suggested names.[429]

But the issue of women in the ministry wasn't going to go away. Although there were some deaconesses in New Zealand, and Waiapu had been extremely glad of their services,[430] they had become much fewer over the years and it was Deaconess Lewis, originally from England, who revived interest in the Order in New Zealand, describing herself as a "rare bird" and hoping the Order would not become extinct. She was permitted to speak to Synods around the country and her gracious presence did much to encourage a mood of acceptance and even of welcome to the rôle of the deaconess. By 1964, General Synod had devised a service for "the Form and Manner of Making of Deaconesses,"[431] a slightly adapted version of one used in England.

Although this step was supposedly not a 'backdoor' way of introducing women priests, it certainly encouraged everyone to question the existing order. The media continued to be interested in the matter of women priests, and quizzed Lesser on it after the Toronto Congress in 1963. He told reporters that although the question of women priests had not been raised at the Congress, it had stressed the need for women to take a greater part in the affairs of the Church. However, ordaining women as priests would be "such a major change that he did not think any Province would act unilaterally without a full discussion with the Bishops," implying that the New Zealand church would wait till there was wide agreement in the Anglican Communion.[432]

A Likely Lad

Again asked the question after arriving home from the 1968 Lambeth Conference, he said the Conference had not been conclusive on the subject, although it recommended that deaconesses be accepted as of the same order as deacons "and in effect this suggested there was no obstacle to women being eligible for the order of priest." He did not believe, however, that women priests were "necessarily an answer to the shortage of priests in Waiapu and elsewhere." There was "quite a feeling" for the ordination of women priests but at the same time there still remained "quite strong feelings against the proposal, particularly among women themselves."[433]

However, in 1970 General Synod authorised "duly qualified" women to preach, share in the conduct of liturgical worship, baptise, read the Epistle and Gospel and help in the distribution of the elements – in fact every task carried out by the priest except consecrating the elements of bread and wine. Moreover it agreed that Diocesan Synods should consider the question of the ordination of women to the priesthood, and prepare their findings for a Commission yet to be set up. Waiapu Synod in October of that year agreed "in principle" to the ordination of women to the priesthood,[434] and in 1977 two women were ordained by Bishop Paul Reeves in a first for New Zealand.

Although he was lukewarm about women priests, Lesser gave unequivocal support to the new women's organisation formed after the New Zealand Mothers' Union took unilateral action and broke away from the world-wide organization. A team of MU leaders, including Beatrice Lesser, had gone to England in 1968 to argue for a change in the rules of membership, but had been forced to return disappointed, so the more inclusive Association of Anglican Women was set up. Some clergy saw this disaffiliation as a serious break with the Mother Church of England and were upset by it, but Archbishop Lesser spoke strongly in favour of the new movement at the 1970 Diocesan Synod:

> "There were those who considered that this significant world-wide movement had a great responsibility towards other women than those who were happily married. Accordingly, the Association of Anglican Women has been formed and includes within its ranks Mothers' Union, Family Fellowships, Young Wives and such Guilds as desire to be affiliated. It is my wish to commend the Association to my fellow workers and to wish it every success since now there is provision made for all women."[435]

Change in Church and Society

Contentious issues however were not limited to liturgy, marriage discipline or church practice. One of the early controversies Lesser had to deal with arose in the 1950s from a renewed interest in the Church's Ministry of Healing after centuries of neglect. While no fundamental change was implied with this re-awakening, some tactful handling was needed when it first appeared on synod agendas.

The Diocesan 1952 Synod was no exception with a Māori priest expressing fear of a return to "tohunga-ism."[436] Others associated it with superstition or phony "faith healing" so Synod cautiously agreed to set up a committee to "study" the matter.

The committee's report in 1954 stated that they "accepted the fact that certain people had been given the gifts of healing," which may well have been the focus of the long discussion held, but in the end Synod received the report and "recommended it to the attention of church people in general and clergy in particular."[437] The committee also recommended certain authors to read, among whom was a Dr Christopher Woodard who had established some reputation as a medical doctor and Christian faith healer.

The committee made a similar report to the 1958 Synod[438] but fell silent for some years, probably because of some disquiet with "faith healing" as personified in the same Dr Christopher Woodard, who visited New Zealand in 1958 but was later declared persona non grata by the Archbishop of Canterbury himself.[439] A Letter to clergy headed "NOT TO BE COMMUNICATED TO THE PRESS" dated 7 January 1959 from the New Zealand Primate contains strictures from Canterbury against inviting Dr Woodard to take part in services in New Zealand. Clergy are "not to invite Dr Woodard to preach in their churches or to hold services or meetings in their churches or church halls." In addition, Lesser issued a clear press statement that Dr Woodard had not been invited to take any services in any church in the Diocese.[440]

After this episode, the Diocesan committee went into recess, but in 1966 the Bishop was asked to re-constitute it. Much of its work from then on focused on developing chaplaincies in hospitals,[441] but there was still some interest in the non-medical side of healing and the 1970 Synod agreed that the Archbishop should ask a "recognized specialist… to conduct seminars or services relating to the Ministry of Healing in each archdeaconry during 1971."[442]

A Likely Lad

Those were some of the more contentious issues within the church which Lesser as Bishop or Archbishop had to manage, but there were some minor changes which he was happy to support. A simple one was to change the official name of the church from "The Church of the Province of New Zealand commonly called the Church of England," to the "Church of the Province of New Zealand commonly called the Anglican Church." In his Synod address the Archbishop said,

> "A title which has come down the years is not lightly to be despised. But an old suit of clothes although frequently esteemed by the wearer, is not always the object of approbation by the beholders… It is for Synod to determine the change and if it be in the suggested form, I would give my unqualified support."[443]

Weddings in Lent, traditionally frowned on, was another minor issue awaiting change. Lesser considered this example of church discipline worthy of respect but capable of being adapted to pastoral needs. Almost the first clear direction Lesser gave as Bishop in 1947 was on weddings in Lent in a pastoral letter to clergy.[444] While he believed then that "it would be indefensible to refuse to marry someone in Lent," he says people should be educated so that they understand not to ask for it.

As the years went on, the situation became more confused for clergy as the neighbouring diocese of Auckland had relaxed its rule and Waiapu people who subscribed to Auckland newspapers would read of weddings in Lent and ask why they were refused one. The issue smouldered away for a few years until in a letter dated 10 December 1969, he tells clergy that "in future weddings could be solemnized in Lent." Interestingly he notes that "our Roman Catholic brethren have no ban on weddings in Lent and may even have Nuptial Mass."[445] He seems to have come to this decision through a quick process of correspondence with the Archdeacons before the final letter giving permission was sent out, a mere 15 days after the initial approach – an example both of his work ethic and also of the excellent postal services of the time!

Weddings in general, though hardly problems, could be tricky to handle. A young woman in a small town wanted to get married in her godfather's beautiful garden, and her godfather was a person of some local significance. To the vicar's well-reasoned request that it might happen, Lesser replied,

> "With regard to the request of Mr G… we normally solemnize
> all weddings in church. Exceptions are occasionally made
> where people may be 50 miles or more from a church."

He refused to sanction the wedding in the garden and helpfully suggested:

> "After the church wedding the bridal party and friends can
> then go to Mr G's lovely house and enjoy the glorious grounds
> for the reception and photographs."[446]

Another wedding, this time between an Anglican and a Roman Catholic, caused a delightfully complicated situation illustrating the kind of relations which sadly existed all too often at that time between the Roman Catholic and Anglican churches. The bewildered vicar sought Lesser's advice. Clergy were not supposed to marry un-baptised people and the groom, though from a Catholic family, had not been baptised. His mother however was now insisting that he be baptised by a Roman Catholic priest – but the priest was unwilling to do this simply in order for the man to get married – in the Anglican church! The vicar's proposal was to marry them but to place an obligation on the groom to get baptised as soon as possible AFTER the wedding. Lesser replies,

> "Although I dislike marriage of un-baptised people because it
> seems to remove any possibility of regarding the marriage as
> sacramental in any way, yet it would seem in this case to be the
> only honest course and therefore I would not disapprove of it."

He also, shrewdly, warned against placing an obligation on the groom concerning Baptism after marriage as if the mother still insisted on a Roman Catholic priest doing it "that could involve at some time or other pressure from some other priest to have the wife join her husband."[447]

However, while there were enough difficult decisions and a superfluity of change within the church, issues outside the church were even thornier to deal with! Although Lesser said he believed the "Church had every right to speak out soberly, courageously and courteously on the issues of the day" because "religion affects every fibre of life,"[448] he was well aware of the difficulty of making public statements on behalf of the Church, having been the Chair of the Church's Provincial Public and Social Affairs Committee for a short time.[449] He was not known for making pronouncements on social issues, a position defended by the editorial in the *Daily Telegraph* at the time of his resignation.

A Likely Lad

> "Perhaps if he has not been so outspoken on worldly matters as have some of the Bishops… when he has spoken, the impact has been the greater."[450]

It was difficult for clergy to get it right, as he had implied when speaking to a Church of England Men's Conference in 1948:

> "When I was in Nairobi, if I pointed out things that were necessary to improve living conditions, it was said I was dabbling in politics. If I did not do so, others said that I had not the guts."[451]

On the one recorded occasion when a parish AGM did write to him expressing concern over public statements made by prominent Anglican speakers, (which they obviously disagreed with) his reply, headed "Personal" is succinct:

> "I have received mention of some of the statements made by visiting speakers, and I have noted what the motion passed by your Annual Meeting has recorded. Whenever opportunity is afforded me, I make representations which I think are not altogether unhelpful."[452]

And that was it.

He was unequivocal, however, on one of the big issues being debated in the first year of his primacy: the abolition of Capital Punishment. In 1961 the Waiapu Diocese voted for abolition "after a long and stormy debate,"[453] which the President tried to close down twice without success. The Committee on Public and Social Affairs had issued a statement with a minority of 3 dissenting, supporting abolition of the death penalty in all cases. Archbishop Lesser agreed with them: "While recognizing the fact that there are members who sincerely support conflicting opinions in this matter, I myself subscribe to the majority view of the committee." He gave his reasons:

> "For about 8 years I served as chaplain to a prison which held about 1000 prisoners and almost unanimously the opinion was held by staff members that capital punishment should not persist."

> "My own personal opinion for what it is worth is that our country should dispense with capital punishment… a deterrent at best but by its very nature not remedial and the whole emphasis of penal policy is now rightly based on remedial measures."[454]

Change in Church and Society

Other issues of the time which concerned Christians were the Cold War with its associated nuclear arms race, apartheid in South Africa, especially in relation to playing rugby with that country, and the Vietnam War.

On the Cold War, the Iron Curtain and the Nuclear Arms race – issues preoccupying the minds of many at the time – he had little to say. However, the common term 'Iron Curtain' did supply apt metaphors, and he also found it useful to compare the commitment of Communists to their ideals with that of many Christians to theirs.

> "Communists will work – and I mean WORK – for a mere pittance and readily inflict hardship on themselves, their wives and families, even to risking everything that you and I hold dear, in order to further their cause,"

he wrote in a letter accompanying an appeal for the Bishop's Fighting Fund in 1953.[455]

The spectre of nuclear destruction, a real concern for many, seems not to have worried him. In a 1954 Easter sermon he said,

> "The common people of the world are gravely disturbed by the world trends with the coming of the H-bomb. If it were called by another name beginning with the same letter, it would be a more accurate description. When the hell bomb is a relic in an underground museum in a race of troglodytes, the Christ will still shatter the tombs and rise in the hearts of men,"

and went on to declare that compared with the recent "worst electrical storm in living memory in Hawke's Bay" it was just a "damp squib." And at the Laying of the Foundation Stone of the Cathedral in 1955, he compared atomic power, which "could only be handled behind walls of lead" to the power of the Christian faith: "If we are humble enough and sincere enough, we shall build here a real power-house."

Six years later, asked for comment on the threat of nuclear war still facing the world, he replied "What is there to say? The position is so difficult and so much is going on in the background of which we know nothing. What then can be said, other than that we hope not?"[456]

The allied issue of testing of nuclear weapons in the Pacific was similarly ignored in his public discourse, apart from a comment to the Church of England Men's Society that there was "no more inappropriate place for nuclear bomb tests than Christmas Island," and a comparison between the 1962 test and the birth of Christ, "an explosion with greater power, but his was a creative one."[457] A few years later, after consultation with the other Bishops, he went as far as signing an open letter to French President de Gaulle supporting moves to halt nuclear testing in the Pacific.[458] As the letter had been framed by the Campaign for Nuclear Disarmament, it was a strongly-worded document and no mere formality.

Sporting contact with South Africa was another thorny issue, first appearing on Synod agendas in the 1950s. Although united in their opposition to the apartheid system in South Africa, synods – like the whole country – were often divided as to the most effective tactic to bring about any change. Those who believed themselves better informed were confident that eliminating sporting contact, especially in rugby, would be a step in the right direction; others claimed either that it was better to maintain the contact to show, "our good example of race relations" or that cutting sporting ties would make no difference.[459] The 1958 Synod passed a motion to the effect that if Māori were not considered for inclusion in the 1960 tour, then the team should not be called the All Blacks nor wear the traditional All Black uniform.[460] It was a cautious motion, described by its mover, Watson Roseveare as "gentlemanly," but there was some dissension even so.

Lesser took some lead as Senior Bishop in 1960, offering a prayer for use for all the people of South Africa. It asks that "God will inspire all who bear the grave responsibility of government with wise judgment that they may help to build a brotherhood of man in the Fatherhood of God. And may we all be set free from the temper which refuses to forgive and has no wish to forget, and for the lack of faith in Thy power to change men's hearts."[461]

Later in the year he wrote an article for *Church and People* headed "Fundamental Problem in South Africa."[462] In it he addresses the contentious issue of sporting tours, without giving a clear answer. However, he says "Apart-hate" is against Christian conviction – "God is colour-blind" – and describes apartheid as "a fundamental problem which is no nearer to solution…" Showing awareness of racism in New Zealand, he continues,

> "We should not judge another country if we are not in
> good shape ourselves. On the other hand, while no country
> appreciates criticism from outside, there are times when silence
> is not golden, it is just yellow."

Change in Church and Society

Rugby tours of South Africa were again on the agenda towards the end of this decade provoking equally robust discussion. Lesser consistently supported Synod motions against sporting contacts with South Africa, but it was not an easy situation as some prominent Māori in the 1960s publicly supported the tour.[463] In 1970 General Synod attempted to pass a motion criticizing the forthcoming rugby tour of South Africa but it was defeated by one vote in the House of Laity.

The Vietnam War provoked the most personal controversy for Lesser. The first question regarding it was whether New Zealand should be involved at all. The Primate issued a full statement which in essence deplored war but realized that in "this big issue there would be diversity of opinion sincerely held by both sides."

> "If the House should determine to send NZ troops to Vietnam to engage in the Vietnam struggle while at the same time constantly making every effort to resolve the situation by negotiation through every conceivable means at its disposal, then, realising that the government has information which is not available to the average New Zealander, I would personally, with sadness, concur in the decision. I would earnestly hope and pray that negotiation which can offer the only permanent settlement, will be pursued vigorously, unremittingly and patiently until the conflict is replaced by a negotiated settlement with honour."[464]

The Christian community and others continued to urge for an early settlement of the conflict. In 1965 all the churches combined to make a statement:

> "The lead given by Mr Holyoake and the action proposed by the conference of Prime Ministers now meeting in London with a view to making peace negotiations possible for Vietnam will have the support of people of goodwill throughout the world."

It went on to ask for prayers in churches and in homes "in support of those who go and those to whom they go in their endeavours to find a peaceful solution to the conflict in Vietnam."[465]

Lesser received some personal criticism for what some regarded as a weak stance against this war. To one he answered, "You have been kinder than many people in that you have signed your letter," and admits to "being forced into actions which one recognizes as being lower than the

A Likely Lad

highest but better than the alternatives." He thanks another writer for his letter and says:

> "I fully appreciate the stand you make according to your conscience and am sure you will recognize a like liberty for those who differ from you."[466]

In March 1966 he was invited to sign an open letter in the *Listener* on behalf of the Anglican church but declined, saying, "As I have already indicated my sorrowful acquiescence to military action in Vietnam I cannot accede to your invitation but thank you for the courtesy of extending it." Similar sentiments were expressed in an undated statement headed simply "Vietnam" in which he speaks of resisting the desire to rush into print and simply repeat "parrot-like phrases which merely deplore war." He does not subscribe to the Pacifist position:

> "I could not think it practicable in the present state of human development to leave a country defenceless."

He points out that there are other conflicts in the world – naming Israel and Egypt – which are also to be deplored; and reminds readers that there are so many shades of grey in world relationships and no black and white.

The National Council of Churches was particularly active against the war, writing to the Prime Minister at the time, and receiving a five page letter in return. As the war continued, with its graphic media coverage, the controversy grew very bitter. The NCC met again with Holyoake, and in 1967 Australian church leaders also joined in criticism of the war. This made it harder for Lesser to stand apart, but he reiterated "that he had no wish to be drawn into a debate on the issue." He did not sign a statement issued by the NCC and when questioned on that decision by the editor of *The Young Anglican* he replied that "it was fruitless to apportion blame" and "no problem is black and white."[467]

However, he was unequivocal in his stand on some issues, one of them being euthanasia which arose briefly in the late 1950s following the publication of an English doctor's memoir. Unsurprisingly Lesser was clearly opposed to this when asked for his opinion as a church leader:

> "While recognising the sincerity of those who publicly approve of 'voluntary euthanasia' I personally would not subscribe to its tenets. Once legalized euthanasia is common, it could easily become the handmaid of the unscrupulous."

Change in Church and Society

His fundamental objection was that he did not believe that human beings had the right to take a life, and,

> "even if we had, we would frequently be bad judges of timing. During a discussion I had on this question with one of the most eminent physicians in another country, he reiterated what had been said by another distinguished member of the medical profession. On a number of occasions, he had been earnestly requested to give a lethal drug and had consistently refused to do so. In almost every case he had received, subsequently, sincere thanks for having disregarded the request."

Lesser went on to quote the physician's experience of someone near death with an "incurable" disease, when the only expectation of the attending doctor was that he would alleviate excruciating suffering.

> "Just as death appeared imminent, the disease exhibited signs of recession and a steady recovery was maintained. Subsequently specialists of the highest repute were unable to detect any signs of the 'incurable' malady and the patient recovered full health. Had euthanasia been resorted to, a life would have been destroyed that later was of considerable value to the community."[468]

He was equally clear in his opposition to the development of the big lotteries such as the *Golden Kiwi* which was a feature of this decade.

Under the headline "Primate sees danger in £60,000 prize," Lesser writes that he is "convinced that a move to increase the prize – a 'mammoth Golden Kiwi' is undesirable." He backs this up from the "sad results in his parochial experience" where "'success' was a synonym for 'disaster.'" He opposed state sponsorship of the lottery as it "cast an aura of respectability over gambling," ending:

> "If we as a community have this money to spare then let us… apply our common wealth to relieving the sore plight of those who will never know the advantages which we so richly and bountifully enjoy."[469]

The ethical dilemma of applying for funding from the proceeds of these lotteries was a natural consequence. Whakatane parish was considering applying for a grant for resurfacing tennis courts and asked the Archbishop's advice. In reply he quoted a similar request from the Provincial Youth Council to the Bishops, who advised that an application for lottery funding should not be made on the grounds that "most of the Diocesan synods had expressed opposition to gambling." "They have asked the Public and Social Affairs committee to discuss the whole question."[470]

There were some issues, however, he felt he could publicly support without offence to anyone. One was world hunger, and he wrote regular recommendations for the annual door-to-door appeals of CORSO, at that stage an apolitical organization. A column headed "At your door… a dying child" appeared in the Napier *Daily Telegraph* on 27 May 1965 urging people to imagine a hungry child at their door with "wide eyes filled with sadness and hopelessness" instead of "a bright healthy New Zealander."[471] He also for some years filled a twenty-minute slot on the Napier 2YZ radio station in support of the "Freedom from Hunger" campaign.

Similar support was given to the National Council of Churches' Christmas Bowl Appeal, and in 1969 he allowed a petition to increase New Zealand's Overseas Aid to be circulated, writing:

> "So far as I am concerned I see no objection to your circulating copies of the material you have sent me to the clergy of the Diocese. Please forgive my apparent laxity in reply as I unfortunately had a few days in bed."[472]

It was perhaps typical of the way he worked that many of his strongest comments on this world problem were made almost as asides in his many Christmas messages to Rotarians, when he would remind his listeners of the millions who would eat no Christmas dinner nor receive any Christmas presents.

For a person naturally disposed to caution, the period over which he presided as Primate must have been especially difficult. The pace of change was alarming, yet he was unable to halt the stampede. He could of course influence what happened in Synod, and did so, but in the end the mind of Synod was decisive. In his Diocesan Synod, he had the power of veto, but if Synod seemed to be favouring a particular choice, it was probably not in his nature to use that power. At General Synod, where the really important changes happened, his voice was only one among the Bishops, so there was less opportunity to control the processes, even if he had felt it right to do so.

In the end, his strong sense of the Church family, his understanding of the rôle of the Bishop as a focus of unity, and his desire to work collegially led him to a passive but reluctant acceptance of changes that were in his view both too radical and too hasty.

A Likely Lad

Chapter 9: The Province and Beyond

Knowing that he was to be appointed Senior Bishop from 1 March 1960,[473] Lesser warned his clergy in a January pastoral letter,

> "Without in any way attempting to stress the added work which will be involved, I would mention that the committee appointed by the General Synod to engage in exploratory conversations with the Joint Standing Committee (representing four other communions) begins its discussions in a two-day meeting at Feilding in February. The Board of Missions did me the great honour of appointing me as Chairman of the Executive of the Board. With the very full programme of work which is normal to the Diocesan commitment and the extra duties involved in a Provincial capacity, it will readily be appreciated that this year will make heavy inroads on time and energy."[474]

While he had acted as Senior Bishop for some months during the absence of other bishops at the Lambeth Conference[475] in 1958, 1960 was a more realistic experience of the "heavy inroads on time and energy" which were to come. During that year he "revealed his gift for leadership" according to Bishop Kempthorne, and it was no surprise when he was elected Archbishop during the 1961 General Synod meeting in Nelson.

The coincidence of the former Archbishop dying two days before the Synod gave a certain drama to the meeting, intensified no doubt by chartered plane flights across Cook Strait for the funeral in Wellington. Lesser as Senior Bishop delivered his presidential address to General Synod at 11 a.m. on Monday morning, flew to Wellington to give the eulogy at Owen's funeral at 3 p.m., and on Tuesday morning was elected Archbishop by his brother bishops.[476]

Lesser was the first Bishop of Waiapu to become Primate, and the first to be elected from outside of "what the four main centres like to call the four main centres" as he would often teasingly remark. It was an exciting moment for Waiapu, and the Diocesan Synod in welcoming him as Archbishop rejoiced in the honour it brought to Waiapu – though Bishop Panapa could not resist reminding him that he was "still the lesser

The Province and Beyond

half!" According to a newspaper report, Panapa's words of welcome were supported in traditional style:

> "Before the Archbishop could reply the Māori ministers rose and sang a song of welcome followed by a vigorous haka." [477]

His election was widely welcomed elsewhere in both church and state. Dean Chandler in his weekly column wrote,

> "The new Archbishop has a gift for friendliness and an approachability that will never be lost no matter how deeply involved he may become with the Church's business…"

He adds "A sense of humour is a divine gift," and tells the story of an Electoral Synod in Hamilton at which Bishop Lesser was presiding.

> "Suddenly the Synod Hall was plunged in darkness and a voice came out of the darkness exclaiming, 'I am but a 'lesser light!' At that instant all the lights came on amid loud laughter and Synod proceeded."[478]

The *New Zealand Herald* editorialised with enthusiasm:

> "Christian folk extending far beyond the congregations of his own communion will wish Archbishop Lesser well in the high office to which the church has called him… He possesses an intellect and wit to match his fine qualities as a churchman; and he has proved himself to be no denominational reactionary."

Although "he is not a high officer of state as is the Archbishop of Canterbury" the position is one of "exceptional influence,"

> "as sufficient of the English tradition remains to make the leader of the Anglican Communion in New Zealand an accepted witness of the Christian faith whose words on spiritual and moral issues are listened to with respect… Archbishop Lesser has already revealed his gifts of tolerance, understanding, humility and humanity. The Christian virtues stamp his life. His leadership has always been exercised not so much by exhortation as by example. His church will owe him loyalty and love; and the other churches have occasion already to regard him as a friend."[479]

Nearer to home, Napier's *Daily Telegraph*, after extolling the achievements of the Bishop's career to date, ended with a typical push for completing the Cathedral:

> "Perhaps his home diocese can best recognise the honour accorded Bishop Lesser by fresh efforts to complete rebuilding of the Cathedral. In a land noted for its uncompleted cathedrals, the completion of the task would acknowledge an objective close to Bishop Lesser's heart and provide a church worthy of the spiritual home of the Primate of New Zealand."[480]

In an interview with the monthly *Church and People* the new Primate expressed optimism about the Province, basing this on a "deeper spiritual perception throughout the Province and greater cohesion and unity of action between its seven dioceses… There is more complete personal dedication, which is the secret of advance," and stewardship campaigns now emphasised that "the first gift should be oneself." In answer to the question of what the greatest need of the Province at this time was, he replied,

> "To become one family. Provincially we can achieve more than we can by working as seven separate dioceses."

And creating that sense of the Provincial family was something he continually strived for as Primate.[481]

By 1961 Lesser had been a bishop for 13 years and had accumulated considerable experience in the work of the church beyond his diocesan boundaries. He had served as the Chair of the 1946 ongoing Provincial Advisory Council on Māori Educational Problems,[482] was a member of the Provincial Committee on Public and Social Affairs from 1955, and Chair of it in 1961 when its rôle was clarified,[483] and was Convenor of the important Commission on Church Union at the time of his election. His year as Senior Bishop had given him some experience in balancing the demands of the Primacy with the rôle of Diocesan Bishop: he told his Diocesan Synod in October 1960 that he had tried during that time to fulfil all the "normal Diocesan engagements as usual" with "only three of these being undertaken by my Brother Bishop of Aotearoa." So he was more than ready to take up this new challenge.

Some assistance for him was available in the form of the Provincial Secretary of the time, Laurie Wilson, but that position was very much a part-time one. When Wilson resigned, Lesser asked Archdeacon Stephen Waymouth with whom he worked closely in Waiapu, to apply for the job, although "the stipend was ludicrous" and the work "heavy" especially at certain times. The transfer took place in 1962, when Waymouth received a wooden crate and six cartons of Provincial records

The Province and Beyond

in preparation for the 1964 General Synod when he was to take over officially.[484] Waymouth served as Provincial Secretary and Treasurer, still on a part-time basis, until his sudden death in 1969, and his advice and support were invaluable to Lesser over those years.

The Province in his care, known officially in 1961 as *The Church of the Province of New Zealand commonly called the Church of England*, consisted of seven New Zealand dioceses and two associated Missionary Dioceses: Polynesia (mainly Fiji and Tonga) and Melanesia, mainly the Solomon Islands and Vanuatu, today an independent province. It was an area both geographically huge and culturally diverse, with enormous challenges of communication and transport.

The two Missionary Dioceses enjoyed a somewhat ambiguous relationship with New Zealand at this time, with representation at General Synod but no right to vote except on matters directly relating to their affairs. It was easy for them to feel neglected by "big brother" over the seas, and if the Province as a whole was "outlying" as Lesser once described it, these two dioceses were even more on the edge. In his charge to General Synod 1961, Lesser, referring to the martyrdom of Bishop Patteson in Melanesia, quoted the closing words of a sermon from the legendary Charles Fox: "Only once in these 100 years has a Bishop of the Province of New Zealand with which we are associated, come to visit us. We are too far away." Lesser asked, "Whose heart could not be moved by these words?"

Far away they were, but Lesser was aware of the need for inclusion and made several visits over the decade. Travel around the whole of this "outlying" province was always going to be time-consuming, tiring and expensive, causing the 1964 Standing Committee to express concern about travel costs, "which had increased greatly with the growth of provincial work."[485]

However, travel both within the country and overseas was largely unavoidable. In his first year as Archbishop, Lesser represented the New Zealand church at a Pacific Council of Churches conference in Samoa, and later at a World Council of Churches Assembly in New Delhi.

While he may have chosen to attend these gatherings, other occasions soon followed where his presence was obligatory. As Primate he had to officiate at Consecrations of bishops, with two of these occurring in 1962: McKenzie as Assistant Bishop in Wellington in February 1962

A Likely Lad

and Vockler in Polynesia in March 1962, for his first official visit to that Diocese as Primate. A year later he travelled to Honiara in the Solomon Islands, where he consecrated two Melanesians, Leonard Alufurai and Dudley Tuti, as Bishops in a world first, at a service attended by about 2,000 people. During this visit he spent time with Dr Charles Fox, and visited both the theological college at Siota, and the Melanesian Brothers in their headquarters at Tabalia-Kohimarama.[486]

More Consecrations and Enthronements followed during the next seven years when there was quite a procession of Bishops in and out of their Chairs: Peter Sutton in Nelson, Alan Pyatt in Christchurch, Monteith as Assistant Bishop in Auckland; Manu Bennett as Bishop of Aotearoa in 1968, and Walter Robinson in Dunedin after Allen Johnston moved to the Waikato. He was again in Polynesia when Fine Halapua was made Assistant Bishop in Tonga in 1967 and spent a further week in that diocese when Bishop John Holland was enthroned in Suva in 1969.

As Primate he was also expected to visit every diocese in the Province over time, in order to be officially or "liturgically" welcomed. In 1962 he visited the Waikato, Christchurch, Wellington, Nelson, Auckland and Dunedin dioceses, and represented New Zealand at a special General Synod of the Australian Anglican Church.

Wellington welcomed him with a fanfare from a military band: "a glorious surprise" said the Archbishop, cleverly picking up on the military theme with the challenge that "the trumpet call be sounded by men and women, boys and girls on this side of life, not the other." Preaching with "vigour and simplicity" he threw down another challenge, in which he included himself: "If we had to get a warrant of fitness in our lives as we do for our cars, I would be going around sometimes without it. Would you?"[487]

The Auckland visit included the dedication of the married men's flats at St John's College, and a trip to Whangarei. The visit to Melanesia at the end of 1963 completed the "round" and he was able to tell his 1964 General Synod that it had been his "joy to visit every one of the nine dioceses in our province during the past three years."[488]

Apart from these official visits much other travelling was required, as the engagement list for 1966 reveals.[489] The year started with a Te Aute Trust Board meeting on 2 February, followed by a week in Auckland for a three-day "recruitment" conference at St John's College and a meeting of the Joint Committee on Church Union (JCCU). Then it was

The Province and Beyond

back to Porangahau for two days before heading to Wellington for CMS meetings. The list goes on to include the major feast days of the Church, (he would preach at 7 a.m., 8 a.m., 11 a.m. and 7 p.m. for example on Easter Day,) over 30 Confirmation services; meetings of General Synod, the Bishops, Board of Missions, Standing Committee, St John's College Trust, the JCCU (again), the CMS (again); monthly meetings of Te Aute Trust Board; a three-day Hui Topu at Tiki Tiki; three Youth services at Gisborne, Tauranga and Napier, school prizegivings at St Mary's Stratford, and Wairoa College; visits to the Māori Mission at Frankton, Dedications and Jubilees inside and outside the Diocese; hosting Bishop Chandu Ray, Mother Zoe of the Community of the Sacred Name, and the Bishop of Melanesia; a MU festival, a broadcast, three Debutante balls and, finally, preaching at the Provincial Youth Conference at Massey on 28 December.

A sentence at the end of this list points out that only "the major contracted engagements have been listed and these may be subject to alteration if Provincial commitments unexpectedly intervene. Many engagements cannot yet be listed." Among the latter would have been the consecration of Allan Pyatt as Bishop of Christchurch, and certainly many other engagements had to be included as the year continued. Little wonder that the Synod that year wanted "urgent steps (taken) to provide assistance in his work as Bishop of Waiapu (should it be deemed necessary)."

While the list above gives some idea of the range of his activities in a particular year it does not fully indicate the extent of his preaching and speaking engagements over the decade. These were often associated with festive occasions such as the dedication of Wellington and Nelson Cathedrals, a Patronal Festival in Stratford, or 100 years of Christian witness in places as far afield as All Saints' Dunedin or St Peter's Cathedral in Hamilton. He was in demand for any big event such as the International Rotary Conference in Napier in 1963 and the National Ecumenical Youth Conferences, or for a smaller one such as a stewardship campaign in Te Awamutu where they found him "warm-hearted, practical and down-to-earth."[490]

Apart from these tasks which could be considered inherent to the position, there were a myriad other demands on him as Archbishop. He was invited, for example, to lead many organisations such as the National Council of Churches, becoming Vice-president and later president, continuing an association which had begun at his first General Synod in

A Likely Lad

1949,[491] and was frequently asked to be Patron of others, accepting both the Boys' Brigade and the Bible Society.[492]

As head of the Anglican Church, and as predicted by the *New Zealand Herald* editorial, Lesser also acquired a national profile, becoming the voice and face of "the Church" on many community and state occasions, such as the 129th celebration of the signing of the Treaty of Waitangi – not yet a national holiday – and the Captain Cook bi-centenary celebrations in Gisborne, both in 1969. It seemed automatic that he had a rôle in the nation's sacred and secular rituals such as the funeral of Prime Minister Sid Holland in August 1961[493] and the Opening of Parliament; he was invited to lunch with US President Lyndon Johnson, where he said the Grace;[494] Government House hosted him more than once,[495] and he joined official parties on significant state occasions such as the Queen's visit in 1963.[496] In fact he almost seems to have followed her around the country on that visit, starting in Napier with the presentation of military colours, and lunch on board the *Britannia* before going to Wellington for a Civic welcome, the opening of Parliament and a church service; then to Christchurch for a Royal Concert and a Cathedral service at which he preached, and finally a State Dinner.

Much the same itinerary was followed again in 1970, with the state dinner being in Auckland on Maundy Thursday. It seems only Archbishops could say Grace on these occasions and the one Lesser wrote for this dinner reads:

> "As on this night our Lord partook of a meal, the Last Supper, so may we in our plenty remember before Him all those who suffer in mind and body and offer Him our thanksgiving for these good gifts with which we are so richly endowed."[497]

But as the "face of the Church" he was careful to avoid making pronouncements on potentially divisive issues in the name of the Church, though very happy to accept other tasks such as delivering a Christmas message to the whole country, or encouraging a Christian response on a national level to such matters as feeding the hungry overseas.[498]

Within the Church there were enough potentially divisive issues. As Archbishop, one of his chief tasks was to preside over General Synod, its Standing Committee meetings, the annual Bishops' meetings, and at least the more significant Provincial committees and Trust Boards associated with the management of a large and many-faceted institution.

The Province and Beyond

He was also a member of other Commissions and committees, such as the 1958 Commission considering Māori representation at General Synod. While the Archbishop did not necessarily chair every committee or Board, he probably felt the need to keep up with the work of the more significant bodies as he apparently did with the Provincial Board of Christian Education.[499]

Presiding over General Synod had its challenges. The church was entering a period of turmoil as it tried to keep up with what was happening in society, and General Synod was the only forum where any significant change for the whole church could be implemented. It was an unhurried process: General Synod met only triennially until 1964, giving time if necessary, for diocesan consultation on matters under consideration before coming back to General Synod for further discussion, amendment, approval or rejection. Even after 1964 when meetings became biennial, movement was still slow, and some issues required much negotiation and diplomacy. At that time the dioceses tended to operate in isolation with each guarding its independence and ethos closely, so it was always difficult to build the same sense of family within the Province that had largely been achieved in Waiapu. "I have worked and prayed incessantly to the end that we should become a family of worshippers and believers," he told his 1966 General Synod.[500]

But even within a family of "worshippers and believers" there can be disagreements, and it was a continual struggle for Lesser to get a consensus on the many important matters facing the Church in this decade. Apart from the Church Union proposals, other issues on the agenda included re-marriage of divorced people; revision of the old familiar prayers and liturgies; an Enquiry into Trends in Māori Work; dissatisfaction with the practices of Baptism and Confirmation; the rôle of women in ministry, and the development of specialist ministries such as chaplaincies to hospitals and workplaces. Long and occasionally stormy debates attended some General Synod gatherings. The 1970 General Synod, for example, went on for five long days, ending at 12.10 a.m. on the last day – or night – and included debates on Church Union, the new liturgies, the ordination of women, Intercommunion, the work among Māori, the theology of Baptism and Confirmation, and the Rugby tour of South Africa!

At such times it must have taken all Lesser's diplomacy to keep "the family" together. Speaking at the 1972 General Synod following his retirement, the new Archbishop, Allen Johnston, paid tribute to his "endless patience and good humour" and his striving to "keep the unity of the Spirit in the bond of peace."[501]

Lesser's personal view on any of these matters is sometimes quite clear, and at other times may be guessed at, but he was generally careful not to state openly his opinions in his addresses to Synods, instead using these as opportunities to challenge, exhort and encourage.

There was always a good quote, a story or some memorable line to take away. In 1961 he reminded members,

> "This session will be profitless unless it is evident to all whom we meet that we have not only been to Synod, but that we have been with Jesus. St John writes: 'Then came Jesus forth wearing a purple robe and a crown of thorns.' Brethren I frequently come forth wearing a purple robe. I wonder if I would do so if it were necessary to wear the crown of thorns as well."[502]

On the topic of training for the ministry, he quoted approvingly an older ordinand he had known in Africa,

> "who feared theological training produced conformists, devoid of vigour and freshness, with all the corners and sharp edges nicely smoothed off… and a horrible 'professional' relationship with God, in place of a direct knowledge of faith…"

Like this man, Lesser did not want "a supply of well-tailored deacons guaranteed safe politically, economically innocuous, socially amenable and devoid of all dynamite."[503] Dynamite was somewhat lacking in most parts of the Church of the Province in his view.

To his 1964 Synod he said,

> "There are those who vehemently assert that the primary and possibly the sole concern of Synod is business. I heartily concur – but only if we remember that it is the 'King's business.' A new birth in an outlying part of an outlying Province two thousand years ago brought hope to the world on Christmas Day. Pray God that a new birth in this, an outlying province of our Communion, may, some two thousand years afterwards, bring fresh hope to a world hiding itself behind iron curtains of fear and death. Men draw curtains to mark death, let us raise them to mark a new life."[504]

The Province and Beyond

In 1966 he compared the apathy of the contemporary church with the commitment of the early church:

> "We are in a minority. This means we must have the spirit of the early church of whom it was said, 'These are the men who are turning the world upside down'. But instead of providing a meal for a hungry lion, we are ignored."[505]

While arriving at a consensus from General Synod was understandably hard, even getting agreement on an issue from the seven Bishops was not always easy. Alcohol use was one example. Some pressure was brought to bear on Lesser to sign a public statement on behalf of the Church deploring the way alcohol had become the 'drink of choice' at all social occasions. Correspondence continuing for months shows a lack of agreement amongst the bench of Bishops on the wording. Writing to the Bishop who was the most supportive of signing the document Lesser said,

> "I am firmly convinced that we ought not to make constant public statements and that when we do make a statement wherever it is humanly possible it should be clear, unequivocal and positive."[506]

The only public statement he seems to have made about addiction makes no mention of alcohol but simply deplores all drug-taking, ending "All God's gifts are for use, not abuse."[507]

The annual Bishops' meetings, held in Napier during his presidency, were no doubt busy for the men, but must have been exhausting for Mrs Lesser who provided all the meals and hosted three of the visitors, according to the following letter:

> "We regret that we can accommodate only the Bishops of Wellington, Waikato and Dunedin in our home, but all meals will be taken with us and suitable accommodation provided for other bishops."[508]

However, the friendly hospitality no doubt contributed to the collegial nature of the meetings.

Agenda items were sought before the meetings and all Bishops shared fully in decision making. The agenda might include arrangements for a visit from an overseas bishop, the marriage discipline of the Church; whether it was permissible to celebrate Holy Communion in Polynesia with roti instead of bread; a request from the Christian Pacifist Society

A Likely Lad

to support a statement on the Vietnam War; chaplaincies, possibly interdenominational, were desired in hospitals, the military, prisons and ideally the universities; there were plans for an "all-Aotearoa" Hui Topu at Kohupatiki in 1967 and a possible Billy Graham Crusade; Baptism and Communion services were being revised in Polynesia, and there was interest in forming a religious order for men.

Besides all the Anglican issues a remarkable amount of interchurch correspondence and activity, generated in part by the National Council of Churches and Church Union negotiations, had to be dealt with.

Beyond the Province, there were reports to read, questions to answer, information to absorb and pass on as appropriate (for example the Archbishop of Canterbury was setting up an Anglican Centre in Rome) and advice to give.

Always inclined to work collegially, it became even more necessary for Lesser to share the load of authority as old certainties gave way to new complexities. Was it permissible in this age of inter-church relationships, for example, for the Auckland prison chaplain to give non-Anglican prisoners Holy Communion? A trivial worry in our eyes today perhaps, but no doubt a real question for the person concerned at the time. Bishop Gowing sought guidance from the Archbishop on this; Lesser wrote to the Chaplain at Christchurch prison asking him what his practice was and passed this information on to Bishop Gowing without comment.[509]

Sometimes an apparently straightforward matter could produce "voluminous" correspondence over a period of years. An example is the question of re-printing the *Māori Prayer & Hymns* book (1953). The Society for the Promotion of Christian Knowledge wrote in 1966 that their stock of *Māori Prayer & Hymns* was running low and did the Province want a reprint? For a variety of reasons, there was no clear and simple answer to the question: some Māori were critical of the existing books and wanted a revision and more hymns included, which would drastically alter the costs; the context of Church Union negotiations and the revision of the *Prayer Book* added a complicating factor; arrangements for local sales and distribution were confused, and to cap it all SPCK had staff troubles and lost sight of the order for about a year. While in England for the 1968 Lambeth Conference Lesser took the trouble to visit the SPCK; by then of course the price had gone up![510] In the end it was decided to order a reprint of 1,000 copies and to set up a committee "to consider desirability of revisions, additions, deletions and general format."[511]

After one such meeting he writes to thank his brother bishops "for their valued willing assistance" and adds,

> "I am constantly aware of the encouragement and support of my brother bishops and without a ready realisation of their unremitting prayer to God for me and the work which I attempt, I would find the task beyond my strength as it is so frequently beyond my capability."[512]

Meanwhile among all these church and state commitments, he had a diocese at home to manage – and a Cathedral he was anxious to complete!

Beyond the Province

As Primate he was responsible for maintaining international links with other Provinces, other world-wide churches, and most especially, with the office of the Archbishop of Canterbury. He was naturally the first contact for any enquiry about the Anglican Church in New Zealand, including the surprising number of clergy who wrote asking for work in this country! It was his responsibility to organise visits from overseas bishops or people such as Reverend Edward Marsden, who came with his family in an exchange visit with Canon Sam Rangiihu as part of the Samuel Marsden commemorations in 1964.

This was a big event, attended by many leaders of Church and State and there are pages of memorabilia in Scrapbook 10, including a booklet of Māori hymns and a charming photo of the Archbishop and Bishop Gowing wading ashore at Oihi Bay, holding their shoes and briefcases in each hand. Lesser as Archbishop was very much part of the happy four day event, taking early morning Communion Services, preaching at the Sunday service and writing a message in the souvenir programme.

Other visitors during this decade requiring care and attention were the Archbishop of Canterbury in 1965, the Bishop of Coventry, and the Archbishop of York in 1967. As well, the Bishops of Karachi, Iran, Hong Kong, Bendigo and Victoria-Nyanza all came at various times for short visits.

Not only did he receive such guests on behalf of the Anglican Church in New Zealand, but he was also expected to represent his church to the rest of the world. This might mean writing an article for the English

Church Times about the New Zealand Church,[513] in which he explains the differences between the latter and the established Church of England, describes the place of Māori in church and society, and sets out the hopes and problems of the "small province in a distant land."

It might mean a trip across the Tasman to attend a significant meeting of the Australian General Synod[514] when, coincidentally, he was given an Honorary Doctor of Theology from the Australian College of Theology.[515] Or it could mean a journey halfway across the world to an international pan-Anglican gathering in Toronto.

But as well as the Anglican connections it was an age of ecumenical conferences and his first trip overseas as Primate was to Samoa for the Conference of Churches and Missions in the Pacific in April 1961, the first of its kind, which he said had "opened up enormous possibilities to the churches in the South Pacific,"[516] hardly surprising perhaps with the eminent scholar Hans Rudi-Weber leading the Bible studies and Bishop Lesslie Newbigin, President of the World Council of Churches, playing an important part.

In the same year he attended the World Council of Churches Assembly in Delhi in November, preceded by a four-day Missionary Conference where preparation was made to integrate the work of the International Missionary Council with the World Council of Churches, a "highly significant" step in his view. While at the Assembly he was hosted by the NZ High Commissioner Sir Guy Powles,[517] and enjoyed hospitality from various dignitaries including an Indian MP.[518]

His 153-page report on the Assembly typically starts with a light-hearted reference to being addressed in his WCC mail as the "Most Reverent" commenting that he assumed this was to be his expected attitude throughout the Assembly. The folder includes significant papers given at the WCC Assembly, some much underlined, like the interview with the delegate from the Russian Orthodox Church on the relationship between the Church and Communism, and a paper on the laity. Personal encounters with some of the impressive delegates, and a meeting with an African friend who had listened to his broadcasts from Nairobi Cathedral are also recalled.

He was especially impressed by Pastor Martin Niemoller and quotes him:

> "I cannot believe that God died for Martin Niemoller if I did not believe that God died for Stalin too."

A message which he brought home and later applied to the New Zealand context was "Our brethren in Christ are given to us, not chosen by us."

And instead of visiting the Taj Mahal on his one free day he chose to accept the offer of his hosts and used their chauffeur and car to visit a number of villages where he was able "to ask many questions through my interpreter" and "see much of the life of the people which intrigued me greatly."[519]

To the press at home he said the delegates "had had their sympathies immensely widened." The Russian delegation, attending for the first time, had seemed very friendly and Archbishop Nicodeme of Moscow had made it clear that the church was free: "Preachers were able to say what they liked in the church." And the idea of the West ruling the East was "as dead as the dodo." The Eastern churches, he said, were playing an increasingly significant part in World Council policies. He was particularly impressed with the Indian Deaconess who said,

> "There is no church too young to have nothing to give, and no church too old to have nothing to learn."[520]

To *Church and People* he said, the most significant aspect of the Conference was that the leaders of such diverse churches from so many countries were able to meet and talk...

> "I believe this was more significant than even the important papers and reports that were presented. We were able to get to know people, and particularly people whom you knew held certain views you wanted to discuss."

An hour's talk on the Assembly to a church group in Hastings was enthusiastically received.

"The Archbishop brought the city, the conference and the personnel immediately before our eyes. And, as is so characteristic of the speaker, whenever anyone began to wonder why church hall seats have to be so unyielding, a well-timed spark of humour would relieve the tension. Then back to the real purpose and message of the Conference."[521]

His first pan-Anglican gathering was the Toronto Congress in 1963, the second such Congress to be held. Every diocese was invited to send a bishop, a member of the clergy and a layperson, and Lesser headed the New Zealand delegation of 23. The Lessers attached some well-deserved holiday time to the trip, and left in June 1963, stopping overnight in New Delhi to renew acquaintance with the High Commissioner there.

A Likely Lad

The holiday time included a formal occasion when the Archbishop of Canterbury conferred the degree of Doctor of Divinity on him,[522] but more importantly provided a chance to renew links with family and friends for the first time since 1947. Naturally they paid visits to the family church of St Simon and St Jude and Lesser had the special delight of preaching in his beloved Liverpool Cathedral.[523]

They left England for Canada in time to attend a conference on 5-8 August of the Advisory Council on Missionary Strategy, in Huron, London, Ontario, and as Huron College was celebrating its Centennial there was a special Convocation Dinner and other quite grand festivities.[524] Archbishop Lesser was also part of the Anglican Consultative Council meeting before the Congress to prepare documents for the approval, or otherwise, of the Congress.

While in North America they were able to pay a quick visit to their daughter in New York where the Archbishop preached at the Cathedral. As usual there was a good quote, with the headline,

> "Archbishop finds the church lukewarm,"

and the supporting sentence,

> "the Archbishop… feels that the trumpet has gone out of the Christian orchestra."[525]

This two month trip was both stimulating and relaxing for the Lessers, who for once, had the chance to be tourists for a little while, visiting the Niagara Falls and coming home via a pleasant spot in California. Memorabilia from the Toronto and Huron conferences fills several pages of a Scrapbook, suggesting the importance of the experience to them.

Interviewed on his return home, he focused on the major document produced by the Congress with its cumbersome title *Mutual Responsibility and Interdependence in the Body of Christ*.

> "The essence of the manifesto was that Anglicans in New Zealand and throughout the world should not consider only what was good for their province or parish but what was good for the Anglican Communion as a whole,"

he said.

> "The idea of all sections of the church pooling their resources to take the faith to people could be revolutionary…"[526]

The Province and Beyond

"The greatest impression he had brought back with him was a sense of belonging," he told one reporter. Asked about the ordination of women, he said that was "such a major change" that he did not think "any province would act unilaterally without a full discussion by the bishops."[527]

He believed that "the Anglican Church was in a healthy state and has a much wider vision than many people would imagine," while the opening service with a congregation of 17,000 and a choir of 1,000 voices was "a great moment."[528]

Church Union was also of interest to the press. Lesser quoted the Archbishop of Canterbury's statement at the Congress to the effect that the divided Christian Church would someday be reunited, and pointed to the progress being made in New Zealand between Methodist, Presbyterian, Congregational and the Churches of Christ who "were already considering a motion of union" with "the Anglican Church engaged in 'exploratory talks' with them." [529] He did not go into details with the press, but he met Archbishop Philip Carrington at the Congress, with whom he had corresponded for some time on this subject and whom he quoted approvingly to his General Synod in 1964.

> "We must first get to know one another and love one another as we are, before we start to organize schemes of co-operation or re-union, and we should think in terms of the whole church, not just a half of it or a tenth of it."

The 'calling' of the laity in their everyday working life, and the essential partnership between clergy and laity in the Church's task of evangelism received new impetus from the Toronto Congress.

> "We clergy would do well to remember that in the field of penetrating the 'whole of life' it is we clergy who are the laymen,"

remarked Lesser in his address to General Synod in 1964[530] and it was a subject he enlarged on later in the year when speaking to a Church of England Men's Society on the Congress.

But what most people remember about the Toronto Congress is the Document it produced setting out the theme of *Mutual Responsibility and Interdependence in the Body of Christ*, an impossibly ponderous title which was soon shortened to MRI – initials which Lesser in typical fashion was able to translate as "My Regard Increases" and "Money Really Indispensable."

A Likely Lad

The principle of MRI could, as the 1963 Diocesan Synod heard,

> "completely alter the life of our church. It is no mere call for some slight additional effort on our part but a complete re-evaluation of our discipleship at the foot of the Cross."[531]

Reporting on the Congress to General Synod in 1964, Lesser highlighted the need for more generous giving from the wealthier parts of the church to others less well resourced, remarking,

> "Many of those who promise to give till it hurts seem somewhat sensitive to pain." [532]

In a full report of the Toronto Congress for the October issue of *Church and People* Lesser expands on the significance of MRI.[533] While its title was unattractive, the document clearly set out the new emphasis on sharing, and receiving, resources of all kinds in a worldwide church, rather than the traditional giving to missions overseas. "The old idea of 'giving' and 'receiving' churches was outmoded and irrelevant," wrote the Archbishop.

> "Mission is not the kindness of the lucky to the unlucky; it is mutual united obedience to the one God Whose mission it is… We all stand together to fall, or to rise to fresh heights, therefore we must seek to receive and to share."

The 1964 General Synod set up a Provincial Enquiry into the Needs and Resources of the whole New Zealand church in order to see what part New Zealand might play in Mutual Responsibility within the Anglican Communion, a decision which Lesser described to his Synod as,

> "a kiss such as the Prince gave the Sleeping Beauty to revivify her, or it could be a kiss of death. So it is with this challenge to our spiritual life… There is a Spanish proverb which says, 'A rising tide lifts all the boats.' This expresses to my mind the heart of mutuality. We rise together and we fall together; we live together, or we die by ourselves… The resolution will be just words if that is all it means to US. If it is words seen in the light of Him who is the Word it could lead to resurrection, and the Church could earn the opprobrium of the early Church, that once again it was turning the world upside down. To do that we must ourselves be converted, and that is what so many of us dislike… The mind and the spirit and the knees and the pocketbook are all connected. The **whole** boat is lifted by the rising tide… There is nothing new in Mutual Responsibility.

It is just that we have grown accustomed to our religion and it no longer has a 'cutting edge' for us. It is like a man starting on his married life with high hopes and deep understanding and permitting it to become commonplace and taking his wife for granted, until the day he stands on the edge of a six-foot hole in the ground... Mutual responsibility challenges us to rethink what Jesus Christ means for us personally and corporately, and what we are doing about it."[534]

In bald terms MRI did mean increased giving from countries like New Zealand, considered a member of the richer group, and the Province pledged to give an extra £100,000 over the next five years, inviting the dioceses to accept their share. While some parishes in Waiapu struggled with the new challenge,

"towards the end of the decade impressive amounts were being raised for mission projects beyond New Zealand's shores."[535]

Over time the more holistic approach to church giving as a stewardship of talents, time as well as money became well accepted, and certainly was in line with Lesser's thinking about Christian commitment.

The Archbishop might well have welcomed some MRI within his own Province where some dioceses were much better endowed than others, hinting this much to General Synod in 1966 when he told them that he prayed "for the day when the Province will look at our common needs and meet them from our common resources."[536] But that prayer remained unanswered in his time.

Lambeth Conference 1968

Lambeth Conferences held every ten years are important gatherings for all Diocesan Bishops, and Lesser could have gone to the 1948 Conference, but feeling that he had only just arrived, he gave the privilege to Bishop Bennett. He planned to attend the next Lambeth Conference in 1958 but was advised against it on medical grounds as he "was undergoing a course of treatment to rectify the after-effects of an accident sustained some time ago." The accident referred to occurred near Rotorua in 1954, and although he made light of it at the time, and was in hospital only briefly, it was quite a serious accident and did have long-lasting effects.[537] So in 1958, it was again the Bishop of Aotearoa who represented the Waiapu Diocese at the Lambeth Conference and the only Lambeth Conference Lesser attended was in 1968. At that point in time the Bishopric of

A Likely Lad

Aotearoa was vacant as Bishop Panapa had retired in February, and Manu Bennett was not yet consecrated.

Before leaving for Lambeth he attended a Hui Topu in the Bay of Plenty, fitting it in between General Synod and his departure, saying with typical diplomacy that he viewed all three gatherings as equally significant.[538]

On his return, he passed on to his Diocesan 1968 Synod[539] the main messages from Lambeth: "God is; God reigns; God loves," a deliberate contrast with the 'new' theology and the "God is Dead" school of thought. The concept of the Church as a "Suffering Servant" and the idea that the prime duty of clergy was to strengthen the laity for their work in the world were two key insights from the Conference. On the "controversial question of the ordination of women to the priesthood," Lambeth had decided that the theological arguments for and against were "inconclusive" but advice should be sought from the Anglican Consultative Council before taking any action.

In typical style the Archbishop lightened his report with a touch of humour: describing the Holy Communion service attended by 15,000 in the White City Stadium, (used commonly for hound-racing), he said,

> "I stood near the 120 chalices and patens prepared for the communion, and it was a moving sight despite the fact that the counter indicated that winners might be paid out 20 shillings."[540]

And he was still of the opinion that "the most useful parts of a Conference are when it is not meeting."[541]

During the Conference, Lesser, like all the visiting bishops was invited to preach at different churches. Lesser asked for an East End church in London and was given, appropriately, St Simon and St Jude; he was also invited to preach at St Paul's London[542] and at Lichfield, important to the New Zealand Church as the home and last resting-place of Bishop Selwyn.

After the Conference, he was again pleased to preach at Liverpool Cathedral, at two of his former parishes, Holy Trinity in Formby,[543] and St John the Evangelist, in Barrow-in-Furness, and also at churches in Southport, Beatrice's hometown.

There was time, too, for some socializing, with a Diocesan function to "welcome him home" at Meols Hall, the home of Col. Roger Fleetwood

Hesketh and Lady Mary Hesketh, a historic manor house (now a wedding venue but still owned by the Hesketh family according to its website), where "the Archbishop greeted everybody there himself, which was a nice gesture," said the Archdeacon responsible for the function.[544] And once more there was a chance to renew some old friendships. A cheerful photo of three couples shows Lesser with two former fellow undergraduates at Cambridge, one of whom entertained the other two "at his home at Wisbech castle,"[545] an ancient castle in East Anglia dating back to Norman times.

The Conference would have strengthened the ties that already bound Lesser to the Anglican Communion and particularly to Canterbury as its head. In his own Cathedral, symbols of those ties were all around him, reminding him of a heritage which would find little place in the united New Zealand church envisaged by the Church Union negotiations.

His last overseas trip as Primate took him to Australia in 1970 to attend on behalf of Māori Anglicans the presentation of a beautifully carved font to the parish of Parramatta as thanksgiving from the Māori people for the first missionary to New Zealand, Samuel Marsden.[546] This appears to have been an idea first put forward by Bishop Hulme-Moir in 1964, the year of the 150th Marsden Celebrations, but the idea was a long time in fulfilment and the file on this project is an inch thick. While Waiapu Māori were keen, others were not quite so enthusiastic; what form the gift should take was problematic, and when it was decided on a carved font, some thought the fee for the carver was "exorbitant." It was in the end, an important and successful bi-cultural occasion: Bishop Manu Bennett came supported by a party of fourteen, and preached the sermon, the service included three hymns in te reo, and other leading figures in the Māori church from both New Zealand and Sydney attended.[547]

Archbishop Lesser's visit was extended to include a preaching engagement in Sydney's Cathedral and an Anzac Day celebration in two churches in Canberra, where he preached.

By 1970, his age, some ill health, and the unexpected loss of his right-hand man Stephen Waymouth in mid-1969, were beginning to make the physical, mental and spiritual demands of the task almost overwhelming, and it was not surprising that the 1970 General Synod proved to be his last.

A Likely Lad

Lesser's gifts of "tolerance, understanding, humility and humanity" referred to in the *New Zealand Herald* editorial marked his primacy. He successfully balanced, or juggled – at some cost to himself and with considerable support from others – the demands of the position with the functions of a Diocesan Bishop, including the mammoth task of building a Cathedral, "maintaining contact with parishes and pastorates while also keeping the Diocese aware that it was part of the wider Anglican Communion in New Zealand and around the world."[548]

As someone who could be relied on to speak in appropriate and lively fashion on any occasion, he was invaluable to the Church's public image. His approachable, affable, 'down-to-earth' style presented a human face of the institution to the country, contrasting with the popular image of an aloof body largely uninterested in matters of everyday life.

Chapter 10: Bishop and Man of Many Parts

The Bishop

A prime task of a Bishop is to care for the clergy – in the words of a traditional title, to be 'Pastor pastores.' It was a rôle at which Lesser excelled, with much evidence of his care for individuals and the group. One of his first acts as Bishop was to write to his clergy, assuring them of his understanding and support,[549] and he continued to keep in touch with them through pastoral letters, written every few months in the early years. These typically gave news of the Diocesan family, or brought messages of encouragement or challenge, in which he would always include himself.

As the years passed and his workload increased, especially after his election as Archbishop, these letters became rare, but he continued to deal as promptly as possible with individual questions or problems, always signing himself "As ever affectionately…"

He normally stayed at the vicarage during his annual Confirmation tours throughout the Diocese so was able to get to know his clergy and their families well, and letters to individual clergy would often contain a personal touch: a query about someone's health, or congratulations on an achievement. Having the Bishop to stay could be a little daunting for the younger clergy and it must also have been hard at times for the Bishop, but it all helped to build a sense of the "Waiapu family" that he was so keen to establish. One clergy family, new at the time to Waiapu, has fond memories of his arrival for a Confirmation, bearing a box of chocolates for them, saying casually "A man in the street gave them to me!" The vicar's wife later chastised herself for not realising the unlikelihood of this but was taken unawares.[550]

Staying at the vicarage also enabled him to keep an eye on the standard of his clergy's homes, a practical task he shared with the Archdeacons, and when a new vicarage was being planned in a certain parish he was insistent that it fulfilled the Diocesan requirements, as opposed to the cheaper mass-produced house the vestry were hoping to build. Although it was shown that changes could be made to bring this house up to the required standard, Lesser was still concerned about the durability of the building and according to notes taken at the meeting, asked if any Vestryman lived in one! Answer "No."[551]

While new vicarages were expected to meet certain standards, older ones were often rather run-down, and as the standard of living throughout the country rose steadily, clergy housing came under more scrutiny. In 1966 Standing Committee recommended certain "furnishings" which parishes should supply within five years, in a list which is a sobering reminder of the standard of living for some families at that time. It included "an electric stove, refrigerator and washing machine, adequate wardrobes and bookshelves, power points in every room, and floor coverings limited to, say, the study and semi-public room… linoleum in the bathroom and kitchen."[552]

Other practical support for clergy came from his awareness of their often straitened financial circumstances: he recognised that working in God's service was

> "the job to which we are called, so poorly paid, perhaps, but so richly rewarded, most certainly."[553]

One of his early pastoral letters includes a reminder[554] to the Parish Wardens of the English tradition of giving the Easter offering to their vicar, pointing out that it is "impossible" for the vicar to ask for it. Though this was not a well-established practice in New Zealand, there were no doubt clergy who welcomed the reminder! And the vexed question of clergy stipends was frequently on the Synod agenda, especially in years of rapid inflation.[555] Lesser was loyal to his clergy on this, as in other matters. When the 1951 Synod was to debate an increase in stipends, he assured members that "not one single clergyman had mentioned it" to him, and he was taking "sole responsibility of referring to the matter." "No clergyman asks to live in luxury," he said, "but he cannot do his best work if he is worried about giving his wife and children what they need."

He also tried to ensure that they took their annual holiday, asking clergy to let him know if they were unable to get away for a break.[556] One couple who wrote to say they had taken a month's "enforced holiday" as they had both been "over-doing it" received "a small cheque… to help put you both on your feet again" with a request "to try not to overdo it" when back at work. "I know that this is hard for people with consciences like yours, but I would ask you to try to be a little more indulgent with yourselves."[557]

Bishop and Man of Many Parts

Older clergy, especially those facing retirement in difficult financial circumstances, were another concern, and he spent time ensuring they were aware of any entitlements due to them from Church or State.[558] Over the years his efforts, strongly supported by later Bishops, the work of Standing Committees and competent laymen, resulted in much improved pension arrangements for clergy and widows of clergy.[559]

At the other end of the clergy demographic he took a strong interest in ordination candidates in whom he saw potential. One such was John Bluck from Nuhaka, later the 14th Bishop of Waiapu, who remembers with gratitude Lesser's faith in him as a prospective ordination candidate when others in authority questioned his suitability. From the first formal interview with John as a sixth-former in 1960, through years of study at home and abroad, until his ordination in 1970, Lesser continued this friendly support, offering encouragement, practical help and gentle suggestions for future plans, even though he struggled to understand John's interest in pursuing new and innovative models of ministry beyond the parish one. A parish, he assured John "is a microcosm of life." Clearly, he wanted John back in Waiapu! When John's ordination service was approaching, his home parish of Gisborne naturally wanted to claim the occasion, but Lesser insisted that it be at the Cathedral, explaining that arrangements had already been made and "moreover this will be my last ordination and as I have had a peculiar interest in John's career I want him to stay in our home at the time of his ordination."[560]

The tremendous hospitality shown by him and Beatrice was a powerful symbol of his care and his sense of the Diocese as "family."[561] The Synod Garden Parties, to which all members of Synod and their spouses were invited, were legendary; in addition, every Synod member was invited at least once to lunch or dinner at Bishop's Court during Synod.[562] But Bishop's Court hosted many other gatherings, such as the pre-Christmas party for clergy families, when even the smallest member was made welcome. One guest remembers the children being given chocolates, and his nearly 2 year-old "expressed her appreciation by crawling around the room untying the shoelaces of all the clergy." Her parents tried to stop her "being a nuisance" but the Lessers were insistent that she be allowed to go on with the activity.[563] Older children from those times remember

> "a friendly cheerful jolly man with a distinct and strong voice and an interest in building dolls' houses. We used to go there

for annual Christmas afternoon teas (delicious!) and the dolls' house was always there to admire in its absolute perfection!"[564]

Young people from the Cathedral were also hosted for fun games and "great suppers"[565] and many others have "happy memories of the friendliness and graciousness shown to them by both the Bishop and Mrs Lesser."[566]

Ordinands almost always stayed at Bishop's Court during their three-day ordination retreat,[567] conveniently close as it was to Ormond Chapel where they would go for services and addresses. The Rev Bruce White, like all who shared this experience, remembers the expanse of food, and a Communion service during the retreat when the Bishop simply came forward from the nave to be the server when needed.

"He was worshipping there like one of us, giving dignity to a humble and useful rôle."

He does not remember any conversation about ministry or possible future plans, but there were a lot of jokes![568]

Creating a sense of family was a challenge, given the geography of the Diocese with its widely separated centres of population and Lesser must have felt people were tiring of his repeated use of the words as he said, perhaps defensively, to his 1954 Synod:

"If you feel that I use that phrase too much (i.e. the "Diocesan family") then all I can add is I will cease when I feel it to be a reality."[569]

That he had some success was, and is, gratefully acknowledged by both clergy and laity. [570]

That sense of family, allied with his own cheerful warm disposition and approachability, probably prevented too many interpersonal problems from arising; certainly, Lesser disliked any signs of conflict and strove to avoid unpleasant situations. However, priests who did have some troubles in their parishes could expect a sympathetic hearing and sensible advice from their Bishop. If he felt there was hurt or division within the "family" at whatever level, Lesser's style was to reconcile opposing parties if possible, write a soothing letter, give people time to cool off, and/or offer alternative ways ahead. The kindly letter[571] written to Harold Titterton after the 1967 Synod debate on Intercommunion is an example (see Chapter on Church Union), as are letters to those concerned about

Bishop and Man of Many Parts

marrying divorced people,[572] or to the vicar dissatisfied with baptising babies he rarely saw again.[573]

There were of course still minor rows from time to time. Difficulties arose in one parish when a well-loved priest left for the mission field but maintained contact with former parishioners through a circular letter describing his work, which inevitably led to donations from his correspondents. The new vicar, unhappy that this was causing confusion in the parish which was already committed elsewhere under a Diocesan programme, complained to the Bishop, who asked the offending priest to stop sending the letters, pointing out that they were the equivalent of a pastoral visit, not considered appropriate. His letter ends,

> "It is my hope that this does not sound niggardly for that is not its intention. *All I desire is happy relationships* (italics mine) which I believe could be maintained were you to send the letters to *Church and People* where they can receive wide coverage and to friends in parishes other than your last one."

This was done, but it wasn't quite the end of the story as a former recipient of the letters complained bitterly to Lesser in a six-page letter full of sorrow and indignation, which was answered courteously, much to her relief![574]

Dissension can also arise from public statements made on behalf of the Church, and one unhappy parish complained to the Bishop about "reported statements on moral issues made at student functions by Anglican speakers particularly the Rev Paul Ostreicher and Dr Leslie Paul." As the offending Dr Paul had already taken part in the Clergy Conference in April and been invited to preach at the Cathedral by the Archbishop, the complaint was not well-timed,[575] and Lesser's reply was brief, simply noting the contents of the letter, ending "Whenever opportunity is afforded me I make representations which I think are not altogether unhelpful." [576] And that was it.

However, there were times when Lesser could not assist the clergy with their problems. One vicar, quite anxious to move for the sake of his children's education, requested this four times over a two-year period, but Lesser could not help him as there were no parishes vacant at the time.[577] More seriously when a priest was suffering from a lengthy illness, whether mental or physical, there seemed to be very little that the Bishop or the Diocese could do. One parish shared the suffering of its vicar as he

A Likely Lad

struggled for over a year with a mental health problem,[578] and some felt that the Bishop and church authorities could have done more to help the parish over this painful time.

A similar health problem seemed to be looming in 1969 when Lesser heard that another vicar had been ordered by his doctor to take some time off.[579] Bishop Lesser wrote a sympathetic letter to the priest concerned, hoping that the "enforced rest" would refresh him, and telling him not to bother answering the letter, which was just to "assure him of the prayerful good wishes of Beatrice and myself." The vicar was back for lighter duties within a few months, was "very appreciative" of Lesser's "thoughtfulness towards us during the past few weeks,"[580] and not surprisingly paid him an exceptionally warm tribute on his retirement.

In later years the provisions of the Pension Board fortunately enabled the Church to give greater assistance to other clergy and parishes in difficulties.

A more public breakdown in relationships, however, came when the former vicar of Otane, Arthur Westley, brought a case of damages against the Archbishop and four others. Westley came from England to take up the position in February 1958, and appears to have been well treated by both the Diocese and the parish, with the Diocese paying the total fares for both him and his wife and the parish supporting him in the purchase of a second-hand car – a huge concern in those days of import restrictions.[581]

However, all did not go well, and although claiming that 95% of parishioners supported him[582] he resigned in 1960 amid sufficient controversy for the tabloid *New Zealand Truth* to run the headline "Parish Disgusted at Way Vicar Was Treated." Because he had trouble getting another position, Westley alleged in 1962 that four men on the Vestry had conspired to cause disruption in the parish and to defame him, and that one of them had conspired with the Archbishop to prevent him, Westley, from obtaining further employment after his resignation.

The original claim of £44,000, later considerably reduced to £15,000, made good headlines, and the case dragged on for months as Westley's Counsel kept producing more affidavits. Even the Judge seems to have found it a confusing set of circumstances, one being that the letter of resignation had not been signed by Westley but by his wife, leading the Judge to wonder if that raised a question as to whether the Plaintiff had actually resigned! In explanation, Westley said that for some time his nerves had been very bad, and he generally typed his letters, with his wife quite often signing them for him, which he "did not think was a criminal offence."

The case was eventually withdrawn by Westley's Counsel, and in a masterly understatement, the Counsel for the Defence said, "It is clear that there has been during Mr Westley's term of office at least some dissension."[583] Although Westley had left the Diocese by the time of the legal conflict it can't have been pleasant to see the headlines in national newspapers, and the parish was left in an unhappy state.

While clergy families and Synod members formed the core of Diocesan family life, Lesser's concept of the Diocesan 'whānau' had much wider parameters. He took an especially close and prayerful interest in Te Aute and Hukarere schools, but the five Mission Homes, run by dedicated and poorly-paid women, and the two Hawke's Bay Children's Homes, all received attention, with the handmade Christmas cards from the children being appreciatively preserved in the Scrapbooks. In fact, anyone, however 'ordinary' with links to the 'Diocesan family' was of interest to him. There are Scrapbook items, for example, about the Golden Wedding of a Gisborne couple where the husband was verger of Holy Trinity for 25 years,[584] and another about the bus driver, retiring after driving the Napier-Taupo road for 25 years, who remembers Lesser as a regular passenger who

> "always cracked a joke and made everyone comfortable so that it was a pleasure to have him on board."[585]

A personal note to Napier historian A.M. Anderson wishing her a happy 80th birthday and thanking her for all she had "done to set forth Church work and so ably and acceptably" is another example of his attentive care of individuals,[586] a care not confined to Anglicans. His Presbyterian friend, the Rev Bob Foster, having expressed some anxiety to the Bishop at leaving family behind when he went to study for the ministry at Knox College Dunedin, was "touched and cheered" to receive a letter from Norman Lesser on his first morning there.[587]

Clearly no single person can meet every individual's expectations of pastoral care, but Lesser as 'Pastor pastores' achieved a standard difficult to match, and the many tributes on his retirement further testify to the extraordinary support he and Beatrice provided.

A Likely Lad

A bishop must be more than a pastor, however. He or she is seen as a leader and a figure of some authority within the church, and another traditional title 'My Lord' clearly suggests this. This title, never strictly appropriate in New Zealand as it stems from the historic seats held by some English Bishops in the House of Lords, seems antiquated today, but in Lesser's time was in regular use. While there were other titles he did not wish to claim, one being 'Father in God,' he accepted without demur the formal 'My Lord' and later, on becoming Archbishop, 'Your Grace.'

The authority conveyed by the title 'My Lord' is most obvious when the Bishop is presiding over the Diocesan Synod. According to all accounts, Lesser was an excellent manager of Synods: "We got through the business," said Archbishop Brown Turei. Even his first Synod was highly praised: the vicar of Opotiki, writing in his parish newsletter, said,

> "The Bishop was in great form and conducted Synod very well indeed. He was always at ease and master of the situation. In fact, we might say he was on top of it and flashed back with his ready wit on several occasions."[588]

Other comments support his efficiency as President. "He had a light touch but was always formal, enjoying a joke or a quip."[589] In fact, Archbishop Brown Turei remembers Synods, unusually, as "a lot of fun" under Norman Lesser, while a parish magazine described them as "always extremely happy affairs" under his presidency,[590] and the 1966 Synod gave him "a spontaneous and lengthy ovation for his patient, tactful and efficient chairmanship." Lesser's addresses, a term he preferred to the traditional "charge," were undoubtedly instrumental in achieving that happy atmosphere, setting the tone with a mix of humour and memorable quotes, exhortation and challenge.

His reputation as a chain smoker also lent some piquancy to Synod procedures. Many have noted that Synod would move into committee as often and as soon as possible, leaving non-smokers to watch with interest as to who would light up first.[591]

> "He was a stickler for the rules but if some debates were going on too long he would call for an adjournment and was first out the door to light up his cigarette… and as things got longer in Synod, his patience became shorter."[592]

The one day of the year that he didn't smoke was Good Friday, which a well-intentioned vicar discovered to his slight chagrin. Bishop Lesser was preaching in this parish on Good Friday morning as had become his custom, and after lunch at the vicarage, he was offered a cigarette, which was refused in what seemed an "agonising" act of self-sacrifice.[593]

While he accepted the respectful title 'My Lord' without question, Bishop Lesser understood that

> "the mana and authority of a bishop is not bestowed merely through consecration but must be earned among the people."[594]

Norman Lesser earned respect for many reasons, but among them was surely his formidable work ethic, perhaps more accurately described as a sense of his whole life as vocation. Work for him extended well beyond office hours and he would type very rapidly with two fingers on his little Underwood[595] at home at any hour, with scarcely a correction needed. Thorough preparation was a hall-mark of his working style as the much-annotated Synod papers and Orders of Service testify.

As well, he could skim-read yet pick up every detail or error, noting points even the Diocesan Secretary has missed, and corrections, annotations and other markings are found on the most trivial items in the scrapbooks as well as on more significant papers.[596] Other people's mistakes, such as the wrong date on an Order of Service, would be politely noted in a p.s. as a "slip."[597] In addition he was prompt and business-like in dealing with correspondence, and unfailingly courteous in his style, apologising for any delay in replying to a letter, or for not signing a letter personally "due to absence from the office" or even for dealing with three matters in one letter.[598] His ingrained habit of courtesy led him to thank people great or small for any contribution they made, from the Governor-general coming to the end of his term, to the maker of the jam tarts he enjoyed.[599]

There is no doubt whether as 'Pastor pastores' or as 'My Lord' Lesser set himself high standards and the task could have been overwhelming without support from other clergy and Diocesan staff. Lesser's team of Archdeacons, Canons and the Dean certainly shared the load, with senior clergy such as Canon Gardiner taking responsibility for the Children's Homes and the students at St John's Theological College in Auckland.[600] Archdeacon Stephen Waymouth was especially helpful with his long experience in General Synod affairs and legal training, and in a letter to him covering a number of points, Lesser thanks him for

> "being willing to have his brains picked so frequently and to such good purpose."[601]

A Likely Lad

Although quite different from Lesser, the two worked closely together particularly when he became Lesser's Provincial Secretary, and his sudden death in mid-1969 was devastating. In a tribute to him at the 1969 Synod, Lesser described him as,

> "a dear friend, whose judgment I trusted and whose affection I valued immensely. Frequently I still find myself going to the phone to consult him, and moving back saddened..."

Another immensely valuable member of the team was the Diocesan Secretary, who often went the extra mile, with Les Nash's work in handling all the accounts for the re-building of the Cathedral being particularly significant.[602] Such support was essential in a diocese with small, distant and isolated parishes.

Yet despite his own high expectations of himself, there is no hint of any criticism of clergy whose own standards might not be as exacting. Only in retirement was there an occasion when he did show disapproval. While preparing for an 8 a.m. service one cold winter morning both he and the vicar he was assisting became concerned that the young curate had not turned up for duty. The vicar remembers:

> "As the Archbishop began the preparatory prayer the outside vestry door burst open and the curate stumbled in, looking somewhat dishevelled and began ratting through the wardrobe and struggling into his alb. 'Sunday, bloody Sunday!' he muttered loudly, not realising that the Archbishop was in the room. Norman paused in his prayer and looked at me disapprovingly – the nearest I ever saw him express an opinion. He, by contrast, was always an immaculately groomed and dressed man, and always punctual."[603]

In that respect he fitted the image of the 'Lord Bishop' and some saw him as a traditionalist, interested mainly in preserving the status quo. Like other bishops of the time, he wore the English bishop's garb – the, apron, cutaway coat and gaiters – for formal social events such as the frequent debutante balls, or even at a school prizegiving, though he was capable of making a joke that he and Beatrice could share the same fear of a ladder in their stockings![604]

Yet in other ways he was unlike a "Lord Bishop" or other senior clergy of the day, who are remembered by the Rev Bruce White as "coming from a very cultured ethos, mostly from the UK, and smoking pipes," delivering sermons which were "not spell-binding." In contrast, he says, "we warmed to Lesser's humour, the way he often joked at his own expense." He was small – they needed to place a box in the pulpit of St Matthew's so he could be seen!

> "As young people we were engaged by his story-telling. The stories often had a sting in the tail and carried a clear message like a parable."

He recalls a sermon on vocation to the ordained ministry, and a pleasant incident when the Bishop stood talking to a group of boys beside his car, "a green Holden sedan, much like our own family cars. He showed us the mitre, a cast emblem screwed to the bonnet of the vehicle. A small thing, but he had a twinkle in the eye as he chatted to young people."

Confirmation for this teenager was a stirring occasion,

> "with parents and extended family proud and affirming, loud organs, big crowds, the Bishop preaching boldly, meaningfully – and always some laughs."

He was also unlike other Bishops of the day, remembered by Archbishop Brown Turei as "almost like gods." Although he might be addressed as "My Lord" Lesser had an ease of manner, remarked on from the moment of his arrival and illustrated in the encounter with the boys, which enabled him to relate comfortably to a wide range of people in spite of that title. Kingwell Malcolm, the architect of the Cathedral, said,

> "He could talk at my level and never mentioned religion when talking to me."[605]

In fact he could talk to anyone.

> "You saw him around Napier to say 'hello' to, which helped to build up the family feeling of Waiapu. To me he was the face of the church. He was very much loved and respected."[606]

"He was a man for his time, certainly a character who took centre stage wherever he went."[607] Others agree: "He had a big presence. He seemed able to project out in a way few people can, especially of his size,"[608] and Rev Bob Foster, recalling the farewell to Ron Hay, minister of St Paul's Presbyterian church in Napier for 24 years, says,

> "I think it was Lesser's last public outing. The Asher Hall was packed. Ron Hay was much loved but Lesser was the star turn."[609]

Yet although affable and not at all a formidable figure, few people could say that they knew him well. Bill Bennett found him a "hard man to

A Likely Lad

decipher;" he was always formal and courteous, but "I could never tell where he stood personally on any issue." Barrie Allom thought he was "a shy man who had developed a surface expertise in social intercourse" and as a Bishop he was "a friendly but elusive figure."[610] "He was quite a private person for all his outward bonhomie."[611]

What did he do for relaxation and refreshment? While there appear to have been few holidays away from home in his working life, he would occasionally feel the need to be among a larger population and he and Beatrice would drive to Wellington for a short break, go to a movie, have dinner, see another movie, perhaps stay the night and drive home the next day.[612] He clearly found relaxation in his demanding hobby of model-making, while Beatrice provided wonderful care and support, and he would be the first to claim that the habit of prayer and bible reading gave him spiritual sustenance.

Whatever his means of renewing himself, the fact that he gave the Diocese of Waiapu nearly 24 years of dedicated service is remarkable. His energy, drive, passion for the Gospel, ability to inspire others and his willingness to stick to the task are some of his gifts the Waiapu Diocese remembers with gratitude.

The Preacher, Orator, Wordsmith and Wit

Lesser was more than "My Lord Bishop" and a superb pastor, however, and his portrait is incomplete without some insight into other important aspects of his life: his gifts of preaching and oratory, his love of language, liturgy and story; his enjoyment of wit and humour, and his skill as a craftsman.

Lesser was tremendously popular as a preacher and speaker. People came in droves to hear him preach, knowing they would get a laugh, find some memorable phrase to hang on to, and receive inspiration for their Christian journey. One woman was heard to say,

> "I would go and hear him preach even in a dog-kennel!"

For at least one boarder at Napier Boys' High School, attending the almost mandatory Cathedral services every Sunday,

> "If Norman was preaching, that was the highlight of the week. He preached with passion and humour, a rare blend at the time."[613]

Sermons were for him an opportunity to evangelise, rather than to teach: "He knew his Saviour and proclaimed him constantly"[614] and he had a "great gift with words."[615] So the traditional exposition of a Biblical text was not for him, and Barrie Allom, having absorbed "instruction on sermon preparation" as a theological student was startled but impressed when he first heard Lesser.

> "He broke just about every rule in the correct way of constructing a sermon, including starting his address with five jokes in a row! Yet he captivated his audience… he was a great storyteller and moral pointer…"[616]

"Whenever he conducted confirmations you could guarantee that the church would be full to overflowing."[617] This was true also of the Youth Services, begun in 1951 in Napier and held around the feast of St Barnabas, 11 June, to commemorate Lesser's consecration. Huge numbers of young people from all around Hawke's Bay came to these highly successful annual fixtures, with extra seats having to be found to accommodate them all, and it was the same story in Gisborne and Tauranga.

Men too, in their hundreds – 500 was common – regularly came to hear him preach at the special Services for Men, organised by the Church of England Men's Society,[618] which again became annual events until his retirement.

What were his secrets as a preacher? One was his instinct for choosing references that would resonate with his congregation, particularly noticeable in his addresses at the Youth Services. In 1953 he used the recent coronation of the young Queen and the successful ascent of Everest as touchstones for reverence and aspiration; in 1958, he quoted a popular song of the day, the refrain of which was "To know him is to love him, and I do," saying,

> "Let us turn from the ridiculous to the sublime and apply that to ourselves and the Young Prince of Glory."[619]

The Dedication of the first part of the Cathedral in 1960, and the continuing growth of the building in the years following, were opportunities to remind the young people sitting among the on-going construction work to "dedicate themselves" or "to build up a temple in their own hearts and lives."

A Likely Lad

He was sensitive not just to the demographics of his congregation but also to the place they called "home." At Whakatane to lay the foundation stone for a new church, he noted the rock and waka at the town's entrance and seized on them to make a comparison with Christian symbols:

> "Something of great importance to the people of Whakatane stands at the entrance to this town; it is the rock and the canoe. But today we are establishing a far greater Rock – the Rock of ages. And with it goes a far more important canoe – the Ark of the Kingdom of God."[620]

His lively mind and wide-ranging interests encouraged him to pick up on a new trend or phenomenon and use it effectively, as he did when instant coffee first appeared:

> "People have become accustomed to instant tea, coffee, rice and the like. Now they want instant religion – something to pull out of the bag when the unexpected occurs."[621]

When the corner grocery store became a supermarket he used the word to describe the possible future united church, saying he didn't like the idea of a "supermarket" church, "big business and no soul."

Current events and world affairs could also be used to make an effective point in a speech or sermon. The Iron Curtain, an ever-present feature of life at the time, served him well as a metaphor for the way people lived even in non-Communist countries.

> "We live behind our own Iron Curtains, smug and complacent. God is longing for us to allow Him to tear them down."

And the Royal Visit in 1963 was an excellent 'hook' for his Christmas message to Napier Rotary: "But Christmas was the supreme Royal Visit. We say we couldn't care less: Christmas says God couldn't care more."

He did not preach at length, observing the advice he himself gave to others:

> "If you don't strike oil in 15 minutes, stop 'boring'"[622]

and knew when to break up a speech or sermon with a joke or a story to keep everyone's interest. But the punchline of the joke would often be followed by an evangelistic message:

> "A representative of a 'particular' type of Christian met a humble follower of our Lord and asked him, 'Have you found the Lord brother?' and was doubtless somewhat dumbfounded

> to receive the reply, 'I did not know he had been lost.' He is never lost but we cannot always say the same of ourselves."[623]

But above all Bishop Lesser understood the power of the story and was a master raconteur, with a sense of the dramatic and a rich stentorian voice, used to great effect. As Archbishop Brown Turei commented there was rarely the traditional exegesis of a Biblical text, nor do people remember him preaching on any of the issues facing the church or society at the time – apart from the need to evangelise.[624] But everyone remembers the story-telling, the moral tale, pithy aphorism or personal experience which were all part of his repertoire.

> "He had the ability to communicate a simple and devout faith through the stories he could tell with such force."[625]

It wasn't just the content of his sermons, but also the delivery which made him such an effective preacher. "He had a fund of wonderful stories, always illuminating. He acknowledged he had a book of them but it was the way he told them that was so effective."[626] Many of these anecdotes, told in the dialect and style of the Liverpudlian working man which he imitated very well,[627] referenced his experiences in England such as a visit to a "slum home" and some people found that while they "made you laugh at the time, afterwards you could remember very little about them."[628]

The theology behind his sermons was simple: the love of God for all people, the need for us to love and serve him in return – something we should feel so passionate about that we would exhort others to do the same. His style remained the same throughout his episcopate, and as the years progressed even his most ardent admirer would agree that the sermons became a series of stories or "pointed anecdotes" as one journalist described them, but they were still memorable.

Well-known and well-used as he was as a preacher, he was also the "go-to" man for many secular occasions when a witty and wise word was required, ranging from a social evening at a local school in his first year as Bishop to large occasions like an International Rotary Conference. He frequently addressed school prizegivings, was a favourite for any Civic celebration, and a regular for annual Christmas messages to both Napier and Hastings Rotarians. While these Christmas messages to Rotarians were not sermons, he seized the opportunity to remind them of the real meaning of the festival: "Christmas – a creed to live by or a cult to indulge?"

Or,

> "Many who will buy Christmas spirit will forget the spirit of Christmas."

And he was often able to insert a telling point on some world issue, such as world hunger and race relations:

> "The average New Zealand family would spend more this Christmas than the average Asian family would spend in 1963,"

he told them that year.[629] In 1965 he referred to race relations in the USA, where Negro children in Alabama were walking to school with tanks and armed forces standing near: "I suppose the Statue of Liberty dropped its eyes."

Prizegiving speeches were almost as frequent as Christmas messages and were enjoyed by pupils and parents alike. He usually focussed on the broad purpose of education – "to teach you how to live, not how to make a living" – or the need to have high ideals. Occasionally religion would be included as a necessary part of a good life as he did once at Wairoa College, using the image of the three-legged stool as an example of stability and balance, the three legs being the school, the home and the church. "The home," he warned, "could become degenerate and become a house – a filling place by day and a parking place by night."[630] Again, there would be a memorable phrase for the pupils to take home, such as telling Napier Boys' High School pupils that they should aim to "put more into life than they take out of it."[631]

As he did with his preaching, the message on secular occasions would be astutely adapted to the audience and situation. Civic services to celebrate the centenary of the Hawke's Bay Province, or to mark Napier becoming a city in 1950, included suitable references to past heritage, along with exhortations to keep striving for future greatness. A few favourite quotes would reappear on these occasions:

> "Hats off to the past; Coats off to the future;"

or,

> "We do not just inherit traditions, (or history) but we also make them (or it.)"

Underlying his effectiveness as a speaker and preacher, in addition to his strong faith, wonderful voice, and well-developed sense of drama, was his fascination with language. He was a master of rhetoric, defined by

Aristotle as "the ability to identify the appropriate means of persuasion in a given situation" in both writing and speaking. He could, for example, issue an order without appearing to do so, as in this communication to the organisers of a Youth Service: "No doubt you will be in contact with the Dean about…;" or to the clergy: "I know I do not have to ask you to pray for…;" or "It is certain that you will remember our Synod in your daily prayers."[632] He knew how to use different linguistic devices and understood their effect. When he told new members to the 1961 Synod, "It is our hope that you will find the experience interesting, the effort worthwhile, and the results rewarding," he was well aware that the sentence structure in itself gave the words added weight and dignity.

Antithesis and balance were other favourite techniques, as in

> "The Christian must have a heart that can be broken, and a courage that can't;"[633]

or as in one of his favourite prayers:

> "That we would be worthy of our privileges and equal to our opportunities;"[634]

or

> "Although we may be a small country, we can still be a great power;"[635]

or

> "Some think religion is a safe way of dying but it is really an adventurous way of living."

For the founders of St Hilda's College in Dunedin "stumbling blocks became stepping stones,"[636] a phrase he used later to refer to the pioneers of Hawke's Bay who were "vintage people." "For them difficulties were but opportunities and stumbling blocks but stepping stones."

Another effective device was to take a stock phrase and give it a surprising new twist. If New Zealand was "God's own country" then it was time "we started doing something for the Owner!" "Silence is not always golden; sometimes it is just yellow."[637]

> "Christmas is either lip service or life service."[638]

To the young people at the service of Consecration of the Cathedral he said, "You do not go out to preach the Gospel; you go out to BE the Gospel!"

A Likely Lad

His interest in language led him to comment with some asperity at times on contemporary usage: "Nothing is simple today. Everything is super. We never talk of informing someone; it's communicate..."[639] He once roundly criticised "gobbledegook" and jargon, saying he had recently received lengthy information which might well have been reduced to one sentence. "Ordinary language seemed to be at a discount," he said, and suggested that modern jargon might turn Shakespeare's famous "The quality of mercy is not strained; it droppeth as the gentle rain from heaven upon the place beneath" into,

> "The basic confrontation of essential reconciliation is not ruptured, But loses altitude simulating condensed moisture of the atmosphere falling visibly in separate drops emanating from celestial otherness."[640]

Above all, he enjoyed raising a laugh through a pun or witticism. While one of his clergy thought "humour characterised him but also concealed him,"[641] John Bluck as a young man found him a

> "figure of life and energy and laughter in an otherwise rather solemn and dour church."[642]

Humorous self-deprecation and frequent plays on his name were hallmarks of his style, such as the introductions of himself and Beatrice: "She is Mrs Lesser, I am far – the – Lesser!" and the clever definition of the Synod Garden Party as "the evil of two Lessers."

In fact, he seems to have been born with a quick quip coming out of his mouth. "His repartee was sometimes quite brilliant especially when he was with his fellow countrymen when they would spark off each other."[643]

Bob Foster, his Presbyterian friend, remembers asking him if Beatrice, a most conscientious hospital visitor, managed to speak to all the Anglican patients in hospital. "Oh, she even talks to the Presbyterians!" responded Lesser. "He never lost a chance," says Bob.[644] And when Synod received a message from a somewhat "fiery" clergyman now living abroad wishing them a "peaceful Synod," Lesser suggested he should have replied, "It was. You weren't here!"[645]

The ready wit could be a little scathing at times. A letter appealing for the General Diocesan Fund assures readers that,

> "We will be glad of the widow's mite, but not from a millionaire's widow!"[646]

Bishop and Man of Many Parts

And about "giving till it hurts," he said, "Some people seem to have not much tolerance of pain."[647]

Or,

> "Many people who say 'Our Father' on Sundays live as orphans for the rest of the week."[648]

Occasionally the sharp comments are attributed to "someone" as in:

> "Someone has said, 'I notice that many of those who affirm that they are willing to shed their last drop of blood for a cause, are mighty shy of shedding the first!'" [649]

To Napier Rotarians he commented "sarcastically" on Cecil B de Mille's forthcoming film, *The Ten Commandments,* saying, "I wonder who he will choose as his stars to illustrate the seventh Commandment. Perhaps the cinema authorities will sell copies of the book of the film in the foyer!"[650] The humorous riddle ending this same speech had a characteristic evangelistic postscript after the punchline:

> "What is the difference between a Bishop and a bookmaker? Answer: None. They both want the outsider to come in. But God prays that all will come in."

His wit could be turned against the perceived shortcomings of the Church as in his alternate version of *Onward Christian Soldiers,*[651] or the short prayer,

> "May God use us in this Synod to become His Body not His corpse!"[652]

or the comment to his 1960 Diocesan Synod,

> "Our lay terminology is more suited to a nursing home than to an army. The church militant sounds like the church convalescent."[653]

And like many clergy he was capable of making irreverent fun of the more esoteric religious rituals. The Presbyterians had bought the old Pro-cathedral and the minister asked Lesser, coincidentally sitting next to him at the barber's, what sort of procedure might be appropriate to mark the transfer, as the building had already been consecrated. Lesser replied,

> "Oh, just sprinkle some Dettol on it and it should be all right!"[654]

A Likely Lad

Even serious addresses and dignified occasions were lightened by a witty comment or 'one-liner' as he did at his last Synod, when with Mrs Lesser by his side, his response to the farewell speeches included,

"I took Orders in 1925 – and I've been taking them ever since!"

And any address to the august General Synod could be broken up with some humour. Speaking about the need to change with the times, he quoted James Thurber: "Let us not look back in anger, but around us with awareness," adding, "A sensitivity to our total surroundings is a work of real discipleship, even if we are not able to say with a Bishop who knew his diocese well that he knew every crook and nanny!"[655]

This mingling of the serious with quicksilver humour was at times a challenge for reporters. Although they loved the one-liners, they were sometimes forced to resort to general statements such as,

"The Archbishop's remarks were, as always, punctuated by scintillating wit amongst many worthy words. He spoke on the World Council of Churches Assembly in New Delhi last November and even on this serious subject found place for appropriate splashes of humour."[656]

The report in the Opotiki newspaper describing his speech at the Centennial of the Church of St Stephen as,

"sometimes solemn, occasionally humorous, always thought-provoking"[657]

neatly summarised what many others had found to be true.

Apart from finding humour in words themselves, Bishop Lesser delighted in unfortunate juxtaposition of lines and mis-spellings, examples of which are found throughout the Scrapbooks. His quick eye and quirky sense of the ridiculous noted "Gird up your *amour* bright" for a Men's Service with an exclamation mark and the word "sic" beside it;[658] and in another service sheet he wickedly linked the direction "Here follows the Sermon" to the first line of the hymn immediately following it: "Awake! Awake!" Newspapers too could be a fertile source of amusement with wildly inappropriate juxtapositions of headlines with photographs, such as "Left a Trail of Bad Cheques" alongside a photo of Lesser and the visiting Bishop of Iran; or the headline under a photo of two smiling Lessers: "Two Accused for trial on Bank Robbery Charge."

Whether humour "characterised or concealed him" or whether he simply believed "joy to be part of the Christian faith" as he wrote of Bishop Panapa, Bishop Lesser's ability to raise a laugh and lighten a solemn occasion remains one of his enduring legacies and one for which he is remembered most fondly.

The Liturgist
Lesser had always been aware of the power of words to awaken and strengthen a sense of the Divine and had enjoyed putting together services of worship. While at Norris Green he had compiled service books for both the Sunday School and the Girl Guides and his year at Liverpool Cathedral, under Dean Dwelly, famous for creating fresh and innovative liturgies, would have further encouraged him in this activity.

During his time there he preserved a collection of services, most relating to Liverpool Cathedral, but some of personal interest only, such as his Institution as vicar of St John's, Barrow-in-Furness and his own marriage service. These Orders of Service, bound rather amateurishly into three volumes, travelled around the world with him, enabling him to refer back to the reading and blessing used in a 1929 Service for Scouting when planning for Baden-Powell's funeral in Kenya over a decade later; another has his hand-written notes on it indicating it has been adapted for use in the Church of the Good Shepherd in the Waipawa parish. Clearly the many examples of Installations, Inductions, Dedications, Laying of Foundation Stones, and Memorial Services have served as models for him, while the other special occasion services which Liverpool Cathedral hosted, like the annual one for Seafarers, the Jubilee for a University, or the celebration of a centenary of the Railway, would remind him of the diverse opportunities for worship a Cathedral could offer the community.[659]

His interest in creating liturgies continued in Waiapu. Although busy enough as a new Bishop, he undertook additional initiatives in his first months, producing a Cycle of Prayer for Waiapu clergy, which listed every church in the Diocese, including the two churches named for the Brazen Serpent. He also compiled a service to mark the Silver Wedding of the King and Queen on 26 April 1948[660] and offered this to clergy for their use, with a request for feedback on "how the congregations have reacted to such a service," and a copy even went to the Palace.[661]

A Likely Lad

However, he was planning a much bigger project, as he tells his clergy in a pastoral letter of 4 March 1948: "In my spare (!) time" (sic) he was "developing ideas for a whole list of occasional services" for which he has received "encouraging co-operation and permission from the Dean of Liverpool ("a leading liturgiologist (sic) at Home"), the Bishop of Lichfield, and the Student Christian Movement Press Ltd." The Table of Contents[662] lists 49 topics for special services, 8 collects and 35 "Prayers for Several Occasions." And clergy are asked to contribute any "services which might be of help to fellow priests in their ministry."

Although this ambitious project does not seem to have been completed, he later composed a Litany for Clergy[663] titled *Many Things to Say* based on over fifty sayings of Jesus followed by a petition particularly apt for clergy, such as the one responding to Jesus' invitation to deny yourself and take up the Cross: "That we may never equate petty annoyances with carrying our cross." One of Lesser's favourite prayers is also included: "That we may be worthy of the privileges we have and equal to the opportunities with which we are presented."

While he did not manage to complete the book of occasional services he had optimistically started in 1948, he continued to find time to write or at least adapt forms of service for every kind of occasion, large or small, whether for the centenary of the constitution of the Diocese in September 1958;[664] or an important moment in the life of the community, such as Rotorua becoming a city; or an occasion of more limited interest such as installing a new headmaster at Te Aute,[665] or the Opening of the War Memorial Cricket pavilion at Hereworth School.[666] All of these services with their apt prayers and readings show a keen appreciation both of the uniqueness of each event and its wider context. A particularly nice example is a version of the Beatitudes found under the heading "A Prayer for Children everywhere" in the Dedication service of the new St Hilda's Children's Home in Waipawa, when presumably some children would be present:

> "Happy are they who are kind to dumb creatures, for they are the children of the good Father who made all things,"

and,

> "Happy are they who laugh when they feel like crying, for they shall be called God's heroes."[667]

Bishop and Man of Many Parts

Even when there were already Provincially-approved forms of service available for ceremonies such as the Laying of a Foundation Stone for a church he preferred to design his own or at least put his mark on the standard one in some way. When a vicar wrote saying he would "prepare an order of service as from the booklet *Special Orders of Service* for the dedication of the new vicarage" Lesser responded,

> "I think the enclosed Form of Service is desirable and leave it to you to decide… about the two hymns…"

> "This has been the general form of service for dedication of vicarages for some years now in this Diocese. To save expense there is no reason why the form may not be cyclostyled."[668]

As someone with a love of words and a passion for spreading the Gospel, he probably saw these special occasions in the life of a parish as a God-given opportunity for a fresh, meaningful and relevant way of presenting the Christian message. However, while he enjoyed designing appropriate services for such events, he was not at all interested in modifying the established *Prayer Book* services, which he found entirely satisfying. And he does not appear to have contributed to the more experimental liturgies and services which the organisers of the highly popular Youth Services[669] were beginning to use, apart from one occasion when he offered two hymns he had written.[670]

His enthusiasm for putting together different services was not matched by all his clergy and an amusing exchange of letters between Lesser and the vicar of Wairoa shows the more conservative position of some. Wairoa parish was going to lay the foundation stone for the new Church and Lesser wrote to the vicar regarding the service:

> "In case the enclosed copies of services are any use to you I am sending them along… These service forms are not the Laws of the Medes and Persians but must serve as pointers for your own desires in the matter. Although I do not wish to obtrude myself in any way, I shall be only too delighted to offer any help I can give."

Eight years later the church was to be consecrated and Lesser again wrote to the vicar saying,

> "Are you contemplating a printed form of service since if you are I have copies of similar services which might save you a little preparatory work."

A Likely Lad

In answer the vicar replied "Thank you for the forms of service. I already have the one used at St Peter's Mt Maunganui. I note however, that both of these forms which differ from each other in various ways contain a number of alterations and additions to the form of 'Consecration of a Church' printed on Pages 20-27 of the Provincial 'Special Forms of Service' and I wonder whether your Grace has any particular preference in this matter." Lesser answered,

> "Noting what you say about the form of service for the Consecration, I would be perfectly willing to confine it to the form printed on pages 20 to 27 of the Provincial 'Special Forms of Service'. If you like this, please act accordingly..."[671]

Craftsman and Miniaturist

"Lesser took delight in delicate and beautiful things made with his hands"[672] and found "complete relaxation in a satisfactory hobby."[673] With little spare time in his busy working life, the bigger creations were mainly completed in his annual holiday, but he would sometimes snatch an hour or two to work on a small piece, enjoying the concentrated effort which took his mind off any ecclesiastical problems.

He first took up this hobby in his pre-war parish of Barrow-in-Furness where no money was available to buy teaching aids for the Sunday School, so he had set about making some. Most of his early creations were left behind in this church, and later ones stayed in the Cathedral in Nairobi, so his claim that his early figures were "hardly recognisable" cannot be refuted, although he admits that over time, he gradually developed his skills.

His creations always fascinated visitors to Bishop's Court and intrigued the media. An extensive article in the local newspaper in

A Miniature Aid to Devotion

Bishop and Man of Many Parts

1950, with the headline "Maker of Miniatures" and sub-headings "Bishop with a Hobby" "Exquisite Craftsmanship Revealed in Remarkable Collection" covers the subject well.

> "He indulges a hobby that is at once a source of creative enjoyment and a test of patience and dexterity. He is a maker of miniatures, some of which are of exquisite craftsmanship. Unlike most hobbies it is not continuously practised. He returns to it during his holiday to add another piece to the ever-growing collection."

The report goes on to describe with great enthusiasm this year's project, a dolls' house:

> "an eight-roomed mansion which took three weeks to make. No details are omitted: a doorbell for the front door and every room fully furnished with its own comforts and requirements. Tiny beads, matches, pieces of fabric and all manner of odds and ends have been transformed into chairs, tables, flowers, desks, and beds. In the kitchen the electric range has its facsimile of a thermometer. Telephones, bedside lamps, clock and even an umbrella stand with an umbrella are strictly to scale. A feature is the study with over 100 books, each separately and painstakingly bound, placed neatly on the shelves. There is a midget ladder for reaching the top shelves, a roll-top desk, and a swivel chair – which really swivels."

Other items which fascinated the reporter were the cigar box, no longer containing cigars, but a pool complete with a boy fishing, a butterfly, and a caterpillar. Another surprise was the Noah's Ark containing 500 animals including some New Zealand species – even the notornis. "The caterpillar of the Monarch butterfly was my hardest task here," he said. "I had to carve in between each little black leg." As well as those miniature creations, there are "several cribs and tableaux figures all with a religious significance, most brought from Nairobi. The prize of this collection is a triptych with three painted panels depicting the life of Christ. Above it is a small crown of thorns, carved exquisitely from wood." Does it take a lot of patience he is asked? 'Patience? Yes of course. But it's a lot of fun.'"[674]

In 1955 another newspaper article on his hobby appeared under the headline "Bishop's Tiny Models Fascinate Children in all Parts of the World."

A Likely Lad

"In one room in Bishop's Court there is a large cabinet that contains a series of triptychs – three panelled altar pieces made of delicate fretwork and carved woodwork. Each represents hundreds of hours of painstaking and careful work…"

"Salvador Dali's controversial painting of the Crucifixion forms the basis of a magnificent piece which the Bishop regards as his most successful work." These were all made using only a fretsaw, a wood knife and a brush, and "his use of everyday materials for the wonderful detailed effects is a tribute to his ingenuity and skill." Another eye-catching work is the model of the 17th century galleon *Ark Royal*, a repeat of one left behind in Nairobi, as many of his creations were. "A model of the model stands on the main deck. A model of the model of the model, which as Bishop Lesser says 'is getting rather complicated,' is on the poop deck."

His "satisfactory hobby" clearly gave much pleasure to this reporter as well as to many others who appreciated the craftsmanship and felt the charm of the miniature.[675]

Miniature decorated egg scene of angels and shepherds adoring baby Jesus

Bishop and Man of Many Parts

Two years later he again featured in the local newspaper when he was the biggest contributor to a display of children's toys in a special exhibition in the Hawke's Bay Art Gallery and Museum.[676] His contribution included a dolls' house in a matchbox and a bigger dolls' house "with modern style furniture and a realistic TV set and phone made with excellent craftsmanship."

The arrival of grandchildren gave fresh impetus to his creative urge. His first granddaughter received another wonderful dolls' house, described in a January 1967 article: "The little house is complete in every detail, even to electric lights in each of its eight rooms and running water in its minute kitchen. It took 18 months to complete. Each room is fully furnished with items the Archbishop has made himself including period antique furniture, a fully stocked refrigerator and stove in the kitchen, and a tv set in the drawing room. In the library a large bookcase fills one wall and holds 300 individually bound books. A swivel desk chair is included in the furnishings. One room is a chapel complete with carved altar and reredos – and the carving is accurate in every detail. On the altar is a tiny chalice. Inside the nursery of the dolls' house is a dolls' house and inside that, another…"[677]

Clearly this demanding hobby brought joy to Norman Lesser and to many others.

But at the centre of his working life was the call to be a Bishop. In this rôle he provided dedicated care of priests and people, preached with vigour and persuasion, managed his Diocese with efficiency and amiability, and was happy to share his wit and wisdom with those about him. He was indeed blessed with a range of personal skills rarely seen together in one person.

Chapter 11: Retirement

In August 1969 Lesser wrote to one of his clergy, in hospital with a bad dose of flu, urging him to be

> "fully rested before engaging in the work again. What seems delay is usually beneficial in the long run. As you have not known what I have done over the past 22 years I am taking advantage of this situation and giving you advice which I have not always taken myself." [678]

A year later, in July 1970, he himself experienced a similar illness, was ordered to take a month off[679] and at the Diocesan Synod in October announced his intention to resign. The period of illness, although not responsible for his decision, he claimed, had given him "time for much prayer and thought." The announcement was not totally unexpected[680] and Synod greeted the news quietly at the time, though tributes flowed in at its conclusion. The Synod Newspaper said,

"While at all times maintaining the dignity of his office, he has the glad faculty of easing any difficult situation with his ready wit, and the apt anecdote."

It went on to refer to the "present oneness of the Diocese" with its "difficult geographical conformation" and the "greater spirit of harmony and unity within the whole Church of the Province."[681] Archdeacon Rowe on behalf of the clergy echoed similar sentiments, referring to his "inspiring leadership, his untiring and

Norman Lesser working on a miniature 1980

Retirement

self-sacrificing pastoral care, and the personal understanding and interest shown to all..." and the lay speaker referred to his gift of diplomacy. Bishop Manu Bennett quoted the proverb which had been spoken on his arrival: "He iti kopara – Kai takirikiri ana i runga o te kahika" ("Small though the bellbird be, yet it may eat from the top of the kahika"), and said the Archbishop had shown "great affection and care of all three Bishops of Aotearoa," a statement endorsed by the "Māori members of Synod who then left their seats for a spontaneous action song."[682]

In announcing his decision to retire, the Archbishop spoke of the "almost cataclysmic changes" pressing upon the Church, one being Church Union.

> "It seems to me that this far-reaching decision should be made by those who are to engage in the completely new conditions which will emerge... Prayer has led me to believe that this is the time for a change to be made, not because I fear work or change, but because I believe that a younger man with greater gifts than I possess, can bring an access of life to a Church faced with unbounded opportunity."[683]

According to an *Auckland Star* editorial tribute to him, this sentence revealed his whole character.[684]

Other editors paid tribute, with Napier's *Daily Telegraph* describing him as,

> "a man who can walk humbly though holding the highest office in his Church...; who can quip his way into friendship, ever ready with a smile (or more often than not, a cigarette), has been blessed with the common touch, not least when 'speaking of things eternal.' He has an intense loyalty to his clergy, is self-effacing in church matters to a degree, and has successfully distinguished between that which lies within the authority of his office and that in which he cannot interfere. The spiritual leader of any community is challenged to walk warily, to weigh his opinions and to be seen to be firm and strong."

His unwillingness to make public statements on issues was commended in an implicit criticism of other Bishops of the time:

> "Perhaps if Archbishop Lesser has not been so outspoken on worldly matters as have some of the Bishops of the Church in the Province of New Zealand, when he has spoken the impact has been the greater."

The editorial went on to highlight the achievement of the re-built Cathedral, the "Archbishop's physical memorial," and "the first Cathedral to be completed in New Zealand this century, paid for and consecrated."

It continued:

> "Memorial though the Cathedral is to his pastorate, the bigger memorial yet is in the respect – indeed the affection and gratitude – in which he is held by those he has helped. A man with the rarest of all gifts, the gift of compassion, he has been very much a people's archbishop"[685]

Interviews with the *New Zealand Herald*, the *Hawke's Bay Herald Tribune* and a radio interview on "Feminine Viewpoint" followed his announcement and an autobiographical article – written in what the *Daily Telegraph* calls "the familiar theme of humorous self-denigration" appeared in that paper, with reprints in the *Auckland Star* and *Otago Daily Times*."[686] He concludes the article with these words:

> "As I lay down my tasks I thank God for the opportunity and pray forgiveness for my failures. So much to do, so little done. There is an old story that Our Lord was approached by those who asked Him what would happen now that He had left His followers and He replied: 'I have Peter and James and John and the others.' The questioners persisted, 'But what if they fail you?' He replied, 'I have no other plans.' In the deepest humility may I say that I have consecrated ten Bishops, ordained many deacons and priests, confirmed about 25,000 people, preached and met thousands and thousands of people and spoken of things eternal. And as I lay down my task, I look to them for I have no other plans."

The *New Zealand Herald* interviewer posed some quite searching questions on how the retiring Archbishop saw the future of the church. Lesser was in general optimistic but said too many priests were opting for a specialist ministry instead of the parish ministry which he thought indispensable. But the church had to "get out and meet people where they are." On church membership he declared, "The church of the future will increase in strength even if it decreases numerically." On social issues, he believed the church had "every right to speak out soberly, courageously and courteously" on issues of the day, because "religion affects every fibre of life." On the future of the Māori people, he said they were going through a difficult time as the result of urbanisation, but "we

Retirement

are interdependent." He confessed to some concern on Church Union that "not enough people had given the earnest consideration to the Plan for Union," that he would like to see, and it was possible that there was "overdue haste on Church Union."

Accompanying the article is a photo of the Archbishop holding a plaque he has carved, with a caption that hints at how time might be spent in retirement:

> "For many years Archbishop Lesser has spent much of his spare time painting and carving. One of his most prized possessions is a large dolls' house complete with a water system, lighting, furniture, and even leather-bound books in the bookcases. It took 18 months to complete."[687]

The *Hawke's Bay Herald Tribune* took a lighter approach, focussing more on his personality and hobbies, and wrote this revealing paragraph: "During his years in office Archbishop Lesser has achieved a reputation for wit and originality which he claims is ill-deserved. 'I'm not really a bit original,' he said, 'but I have a retentive memory and a gift for associating ideas. The art of originality is to remember what you hear but forget who said it,'" a sentence which perfectly illustrates his wit and retentive memory, if not his originality. When asked what his main achievements were he side-stepped the question somewhat by focussing on what the church had done in response to social change, citing "significant and promising progress towards Church union;" revision of the Holy Communion service, and the re-marriage of divorced people as examples.[688]

Individual clergy paid their own tribute in parish magazines. One vicar was particularly warm, writing:

> "For 23 years he has been our beloved bishop and has served the diocese with selfless devotion, and throughout his long and singularly happy episcopate he has brought to his high office the rich treasures of his fertile mind, and because he possesses the human touch and knows the ways of men, he has succeeded in making God real. To clergy and laity alike, it has always been a matter beyond our comprehension that he has carried such heavy responsibilities so lightly. Never has he given the impression that he was weighed down by the magnitude of his office."[689]

A Likely Lad

His retirement took effect from 31 January but there was a "busy round of duties"[690] as well as his "normal engagements" to fulfil before Christmas.

The "duties" included John Bluck's ordination, with its associated three-day retreat at Bishop's Court; the dedication of a memorial window to Canon Button in St Matthew's church, and a final Carol service in All Saints' Taradale, when his own Nativity lullaby, set to music by Peter Godfrey, was sung. An address to the Catholic Men's Association early in December won him a five minute standing ovation – possibly one of his most valued tributes – and Father Ward, in thanking him, spoke of the kindness shown to him and the other clergy, adding, "You gave us the impression that you had waited most of your life to come to talk to us."[691]

Christmas Day itself was, of course, a working day for the Archbishop, with services at St John's Cathedral at 7 a.m., St Augustine's at 8 a.m. and St Matthew's at 11 a.m.

About 1,500 people, including 70 clergy and an augmented choir of 200, attended the farewell service at the end of January at which he preached.

"This is not an end, but a beginning of a new and glorious chapter in the history of Waiapu Diocese," he said. "Your new bishop may serve the Diocese infinitely better than I have done, but he will not love it more." The first sermon he had ever preached had been on the love of God; he returned to that theme, and the need to hold firm to faith in Jesus.

> "We are bedevilled by change… it is important not to think that because a thing is new it is necessarily better, nor because it is old, it is necessarily good."
>
> "The trouble with being a leader these days, as one remarked, is that you cannot tell whether people are following you or chasing you. With Jesus, 'they left all and followed Him;' too frequently we follow all and leave Him."

He asked for support and prayer for the new Bishop,

> "in this diocese so divided by mountains there is only one possible way to succeed and that is by the faith that moves mountains."

Then followed some of his favourite sayings:

> "A river becomes crooked by taking the line of least resistance and so do men.
>
> If you do not stand for something, you will fall for anything.

Retirement

> It is no good singing 'Stand up; stand up for Jesus' and then falling down on the job.
>
> Religion is not a safe way of dying, it is an adventurous way of living, and whilst the Church is looking for better organisation, God is looking for better men and that means you and me."[692]

A typically thoughtful note at the end of the Order of Service lists the names of the members of the 1947 Diocesan Synod who were still living, and assures readers that "All who were able to be present are taking part either in this service or in the farewell Function in the Centennial Hall."

In the evening about 2,000 people filled the Centennial Hall for a Diocesan farewell, where tributes flowed from civic leaders, Diocesan and Provincial representatives, and Father Ward representing the other churches, who particularly mentioned the Archbishop's "friendly manner."[693] Lesser's speech of thanks naturally produced some laughs:

> "Tomorrow I will be what the chiropodists call a fallen arch, and so tonight I would thank you all… yet again for enduring the evil of two Lessers for some 24 years and for doing it so uncomplainingly."[694]

And in thanking them for the gift: "As the teetotaller said when presented with cherries in brandy 'I deeply appreciate the gift but even more the spirit in which it is given.'"

And so, with a customary neat quip, the longest episcopate in the history of the Diocese came to an end, but tributes continued to flow for some time.

Napier City Council honoured him with a public farewell[695] a week later where community leaders, the local Member of Parliament and the Minister of Internal Affairs all paid their tributes. The Mayor said, "The city of Napier has been better and its people feel better because you came to live with us;" and the Minister for Internal Affairs described him as "a loved friend of the people of the Diocese and a respected member of society in Napier," adding that he was glad that in retirement Dr and Mrs Lesser would not be "cut off from their life work or from the ordinary people in life – the people they love." And a park in the new suburb of Tamatea was named the "Lesser Park."[696]

In June 1971 he accepted with pleasure the Queen's Honour of Companion of the Most Distinguished Order of St Michael and St George, and was invested in November.[697] Equally acceptable was the offer of Honorary

A Likely Lad

Life membership from the Hawke's Bay Club, of which he had been a long-time member.[698] Still later he was elected Vice-president of the Fitzwilliam Society,[699] the organisation for the "old boys" of his College at Cambridge, an honour he greatly appreciated.

But it was the tributes of 'ordinary' people which meant most to him. The assertion that he was "very much the people's Archbishop" made by the

*Archbishop Norman and Beatrice Lesser
at the Investiture of the Order of St Michael and St George – 1971*

Daily Telegraph was in line with his own self-analysis in the *Hawke's Bay Herald Tribune* interview:

> "I have always tried to keep very much in touch with the ordinary person – I suppose it's because I'm ordinary myself, and I find it easy."

The interviewer continues,

> "This is probably why the ordinary person in Napier – the taxi driver, the shop assistant, the hotel receptionist, the waterside worker – has such a high regard for Norman Alfred Lesser, Anglican Bishop of Waiapu and Primate of New Zealand."[700]

Perhaps one of the most moving and significant tributes came from an unknown journalist who wrote in the *Sunday Times* of 14 February 1971 under the heading "Mitre and a Human Touch:"[701]

"Norman Alfred Lesser has done a pretty good job for the past ten years as supreme head of the Anglican Church in NZ. But, in an unofficial capacity he has filled an important secondary role for his church: that of a first-class public relations officer." The writer compares Lesser with other heads of the church who, "conscious of the dignity of their office" have become "over-pompous" and have "lacked the human touch."

> "Not so Norman Lesser. He has always been imbued with the common touch, the ability to meet and talk with the ordinary man on his own ground. This, coupled with a deep sense of avocation, a first-class grasp of the Queen's English, competent oratory and a lively intelligence has made Norman Lesser an ideal man for the job…"

> "Busy as he was, he always found time to make himself available to reporters and to answer their queries courteously. We were always sure of a good 'quote' from the Archbishop. And he consistently got a good press."

The writer goes on to say that "not all the good that important men do is generally known," and tells the story of how twenty years before, his photographic premises were destroyed by fire, he had no insurance and wondered whether he should give up photography altogether. "Then came a letter from Bishop Lesser and a cheque for five guineas." Although he had photographed the Bishop at various events,

> "to him I was just another reporter who was not even of his church. I never did cash the cheque. The Bishop's words of

encouragement 'Pick yourself up, it could be much worse, you know,' inspired me to get moving again. That day Norman Lesser won himself a friend."

As organisations with which Lesser had been associated resumed duties for 1971 further tributes were paid. The Anglican Board of Missions recorded their thanks for "the many years of wise and skilful leadership of the Board,"[702] and Allen Johnston, presiding at the 1972 General Synod, said of the former Primate:

> "If I compare his style with *Coronation Street*, we have all delighted in his personal touch, in his seemingly endless stock of anecdotes about ordinary people. Endless also was his patience and good humour. It was as difficult to quarrel in his presence as in Mr Walker's in the Rovers' Return. It may be difficult to define his friendly ministry. It is impossible to forget it. Surely the Church of the Province will want to place on record its tribute to its Archbishop, who alike in his personal dealings and his public office strove to keep the unity of the spirit in the bond of peace."[703]

It was understandable that the Lessers should choose to retire in Napier, contrary though it was to the usual protocol of Diocesan Bishops disappearing from the scene. As they did not own a house, the generous legacy of a property in Sealy Road for "diocesan use" was most welcome and the Lessers moved there shortly after retiring.

He promised "not to be too much of a nuisance" to the incoming Bishop and generally was as good as his word. The only comment he was heard to make on his successor, the 37-year-old Paul Reeves, was "I said they should get a younger man, but I didn't mean THAT young!"

Wisely he kept his distance from the new regime, and the two bishops rarely met. But when the new Bishop and the new Dean made significant changes, in the interests of modern liturgical reform, to the Cathedral in 1973, and turned the Memorial Chapel into Diocesan offices, Lesser found himself very much at odds with the proposals. In a strongly-worded letter he gave his opinion to the Dean, who had asked for it, ("I write now only because you have invited me to do so"),[704] and reportedly only once entered the Cathedral thereafter.[705] His distress is hardly surprising: after all, the building into which he had put so much energy, loving thought and time, had only been completed eight years previously!

Instead, he and Beatrice became faithful parishioners of suburban St Augustine's, where he offered to become the curate for the vicar.

They continued their active participation in church and community, doing Meals on Wheels and visiting the Napier hospital regularly. Care for individuals remained high in their priorities and when the nervous new curate spilled Communion wine on a parishioner's 'Sunday best' dress his chagrin was somewhat eased with the Lessers' kindly words, "Don't worry about it. We'll pay to have the dress dry-cleaned."[706] He and Beatrice also kept a note of significant anniversaries in people's lives and Bob Foster, a Presbyterian ordained later in life, was, like many others, remembered with a phone call on the anniversary of his ordination.[707]

In 1972 he celebrated 25 years since his Consecration as the Bishop of Waiapu and preached at St Augustine's for the occasion. Musing over that quarter-century, he recalled, "In my time as Bishop I saw ten new parishes formed, 13 new churches, 21 new vicarages, three old people's homes built, and the cathedral rebuilt and paid for." He had also confirmed close on 25,000 people and driven about 380,000 miles. The first sermon he had preached had been on the love of God, "and if I were to know that what I was preaching was to be my last sermon, I would select the same subject."[708]

Delivering that "last sermon" still lay sometime in the future. He continued to be in demand as a preacher, and having expressed willingness on his retirement "to be of service to anyone who wished to use him,"[709] he gladly accepted preaching engagements within and beyond the Diocese, including St Chad's New Plymouth, several Auckland churches, and St Paul's Cathedral, Dunedin, where his daughter and family were parishioners.[710] The *New Zealand Herald* found him still quotable with pithy sayings such as "The church that does not reach out will pass out," or "God is looking for labourers, he already has enough advisers,"[711] while the publicity for his visit to St Chad's New Plymouth described him as "a deep thinker," adding reassuringly, "but not a deep speaker!" with "the rare ability of being able to adapt winsome and meaningful illustration to his preaching which is invariably centred around his commitment to the Lordship of Christ and to Christ's love for us."[712]

Rotary Clubs still asked him for a Christmas message, and again there were good "one-liners." He believed New Zealanders were a good-hearted people, "though if a visitor from another planet came here and

A Likely Lad

saw our television, he would think we only drank coffee, ate biscuits and spent a lot of our time avoiding smelling." Talking of hunger in the world, he said, "Yes, there are people who eat regularly – every second day." Agnostics were "people who only mention God when they have a flat tyre," and "If you want to avoid a hopeless end, accept the Christmas Gospel and enjoy an endless hope."[713]

But above all, retirement gave him time for his hobbies and creativity – for making "delicate and beautiful things with his hands." As he remarked, he saw no shortage of things to do. For years he had made models and miniatures, some illustrating bible stories, some mini-sermons in themselves, like "Riches" where the "poor" woman has her Bible, while the "rich" woman has many fine possessions but no Bible; and "Kingship" where a richly-decorated royal throne is contrasted with Christ's Crown of Thorns.

The amazingly realistic dolls' houses, his model of the 17th century *Ark Royal* and the miniature Noah's Ark with its 500 animals, always produced gasps of astonishment and admiration from visitors to Bishop's Court for their rich and intricate detail. Now retired, he could undertake big projects without continual interruption. His first major effort, taking five months, was a model of a village shop, "Ye Olde Shoppe est. 1754," with 200 realistic items – not including the 300 shingles on the roof, or the many pickets of the fence – which, he said were "the only things he got 'fed-up' with making as he didn't like repetitive work."[714]

Not all his work with knife and razor was in miniature however, and over the years he had produced several finely-carved altar-pieces and a beautiful fire-screen decorated with different New Zealand butterflies. In fact, art in all its forms attracted him, and his clever enlargements of favourite *Punch* cartoons had amused and delighted visitors to Bishop's Court. In retirement he took up painting in oils and made very effective copies of subjects that appealed to him, among them the interiors of old churches, the well-known *Praying Hands,* and a wonderful old African face.

Later still in retirement he picked up yet another new and demanding craft with relish, saying he "was only interested in making things that were challenging and difficult."[715] This description certainly seems to apply to the new activity, that of creating tiny scenes within a hinged eggshell. One, a scene from the ballet, *Swan Lake,* contains eleven dancers;

Retirement

another, made for his grandson, depicts a football match: a Liverpool team of course! Challenged to include more figures he managed to fit 130 into his version of the Sermon on the Mount.

His illustrated talk on this hobby to the Napier Collectors group was enthusiastically received with one listener reporting "His eggshell sculptures show a delicate touch and are fashioned with meticulous detail." "These are all so beautifully decorated that they resemble a Fabergé reproduction. Most of his work is done with a pocket razor knife which cost him three pence, but he also uses screwdrivers, water colours, small forceps and a drill." As well as the eggshell scenes, he also "creates Nativity and Crucifixion scenes in walnut halves with tiny matchstick figures which are lifelike." The writer goes on to say that "the Archbishop who is now 77 and Mrs Lesser are examples of how to retire and live happily, provided one has a hobby and a joy and zest for living."[716]

Absorbing as his hobbies were, and pleasant as retirement might be, there were a few who sensed in him some disappointment during these years. Perhaps there were unmet expectations, perhaps he missed the regular contact with large numbers of people and the profile associated with being Primate, even of "a small and outlying province" and his refusal to accept the changes to the Cathedral saddened some of his friends.

Within the general population of Napier, however, he continued to be popular and very "visible." He had always appreciated the importance of being out among people, and firmly reassured his Presbyterian friend, Rev Bob Foster, who confessed to feeling a little guilty on being found in town on personal business when Lesser chanced upon him. "Nonsense!" said Lesser, "You're being visible."[717]

He and Beatrice remained visible in retirement with almost daily visits to their favourite café[718] where they would enjoy chatting with old friends or making new ones. In 1980 they celebrated their Golden Wedding. Interviewed by a reporter from the Napier paper, the Archbishop expressed the view that "A strong Christian marriage remains a stabilising factor even in this permissive society," then typically added a witticism:

> "It was said of marriage that two young people are made one and they go on honeymoon to see which one! But with us we decided we would be just one and that has been the secret of our continuing happiness."

The reporter seems to have enjoyed the visit:

A Likely Lad

> "I spent an hilarious hour or so with Dr and Mrs Lesser in their Sealy Road home this week listening to some sharp-witted anecdotes. It started off with a discussion on how he should be addressed. Should it be Dr Lesser, ('your Associate Editor calls me that because he is mean on space!'), Your Grace ('people who want to get to the top in the church used to call me that') or, 'Archbishop?' 'I don't really mind what people call me although I didn't appreciate being called the late Archbishop shortly after I retired,' he said."

It was perhaps typical of Lesser that the light-hearted interview centred on what words were most appropriate in addressing him, not because he was concerned about titles or status, but because he was fascinated by language. Words, and what could be done with them, had always been a source of joy for him and over the years he had occasionally had the time and impulse to write creatively. In 1967 he produced a poem and hymn for the consecration of the Cathedral, two more hymns for Youth Services, and a Nativity lullaby which Peter Godfrey set to music in 1969.[719] The publication in January 1971 of *Hear, Here!* a booklet of 35 poems ranging in length from four lines to 150 suggests that he had quietly found time to pursue poetry-writing in the midst of a busy working life.[720] In his Foreword to these poems he quotes a few lines he had written forty years previously in honour of his mother, adding with typical self-deprecation,

> "Since that time until very recently I have occupied my time in other realms and some who may read the following may wish that I had continued to do so."

Many of the poems originate from anecdotes which had been part of his repertoire over the years, such as the one telling the story of the Barrow-in-Furness woman who was not going to meet her Maker without her teeth, even if Hitler's bombs were descending. The poem ends:

> "The common people heard Him gladly, 'cause
> He understood their ways, and He still does."

Another poem relies on the challenging aphorism, used more than once in sermons and speeches, supposedly uttered by the hero facing a firing squad, who shouted to those about to kill him:

> "I am dying for an ideal!
> What are you living for?"

The poem continues,

> "The question first came from another
> Whose claim challenged all men as brother

and ends,

> "What are you living for? The zeal
> Of love that does not count the cost,
> Off'ring life though all else be lost?"

Other poems are based on simple personal experiences such as *The Third Time*, describing how the young curate has to knock three times – the last one really loudly – before the householder hears him and opens the door. It ends,

> "My knocks, He says, are not just three
> I knock, and hope, eternally."

Whatever their origin, all the poems aim to illuminate some aspect of the love of God seen in the life and ministry of Jesus, and in the natural world.

No further poems are found after this collection, but he continued to use his skills in language as an occasional contributor to the "Thought for the Week" columns in the *Daily Telegraph* between 1972 and 1984, with special Christmas editorials from 1976 to 1980. One of these, cleverly headed "Thought for Every Day," describes Christmas as a "person-to-person" call. "It is very personal. We are not just the 'last bed but one on the right...' We are not even men and women; we are sons and daughters of God. Christmas reveals the depths of His love. Whittier's dying words were 'Give my love to the world.' These were God's first words and Christmas Day proclaimed them in flesh and blood." He ends

> "The world seems at its wits' end, and the greed of individuals
> and gross attempts at personal gain could do with an injection
> of the spirit of Christmas which gives and asks for no reward
> save the joy of being able to give. In that spirit we wish you the
> true joy of Christmas."[721]

Good Friday and Easter articles were further opportunities to communicate the Good News. In 1972 he wrote two in sequence, one for Good Friday, headed "What's My Line?" – the title of a popular radio programme at the time – and a week later another one on the message of the empty tomb at Easter. The Good Friday one quotes a poem from *Hear Here!*, referring to the soldiers casting dice, "to while away the time"

A Likely Lad

and the crowds who say they couldn't care less, "whilst all the time Good Friday says God could not care more. We are told that Peter followed at a safe distance. Are we like the disciples who left all and followed Him, and then followed all and left Him?" [722]

The "Thought for the Week" columns show he retained his wordsmith's skill with attention-grabbing headlines such as "Cherish the Thought" or "Dead Men Do Tell Tales" and arresting openings like this one for the Advent season:

> "A young person in a Youth group was asked by his Youth leader to imagine that he answered a knock at the door and found Jesus Himself standing there. What would he do? The boy answered, 'I'd be very surprised, but I'd ask him in and offer him a glass of sherry while I phoned the vicar to come quickly.'"

The writer continues with a sentence which might well be interpreted as a tilt at the new Liturgy in frequent use at the time of writing:

> "During this Season of Advent in some *churches where services can still be recognised*… (Italics mine.)"[723]

The columns also confirm that he retained his simple theology. He had never indulged in theological discussion for its own sake, and in fact suggested that theological controversy was in part to blame for the shortage of clergy, mentioning the "recent theological issues which had caused grave questioning in young people's minds," possibly a reference to the controversy going on in the Presbyterian church in the late 1960s. In the same interview he said,

> "I certainly think there should be limits set to theological freedom."[724]

His own writing does not pose theological questions or arguments but simply states in powerful language what he himself believes most sincerely – the basic tenets of the Christian faith. "Look at the facts of people's lives," he seems to suggest in one of his Christmas editorials. While he admits,

> "theology may have enjoyed or suffered change like other facets of history… it is a fallacy to identify all change as advance."
>
> "In the final analysis there does not remain doubt about the quality of life personified in the nativity. Atheist, agnostic and Christian alike agree that the sort of life lived by Hitler and

St Francis are poles apart and it is easy to link one of them with Christmas."[725]

For him, the individual's response to the love of God was all-important and he once told a reporter that "the individual Christian was likely to have more impact than the Church."[726]

His last "Thought for the Week" is dated 2 September 1984 and is on the theme of persistence and dedication in living the Christian life, a "corporate adventure."

Soon after this he was diagnosed with lung cancer. With typical thoroughness and care he tied up a few loose ends, as a letter from the then Bishop of Waiapu dated 31 January 1985 acknowledges papers of "historical value" that Lesser has passed on to the Diocese along with a stamp collection worth almost $1,000 at auction.

He was nursed at home for as long as possible before going into the Napier hospital where he died on 13 February 1985.

His funeral service at an overflowing St Augustine's church was led by three clergy: the vicar, Dan Jensen, Alan Pywell, and the former Dean, Henry Childs, with Bishop Peter Atkins giving the address, Archbishop Paul Reeves in attendance, and many other clergy forming a guard of honour outside the church at the conclusion of the service.

Later the Diocese erected a window in the Cathedral in thanksgiving for his life. One of a series based on sayings of Jesus from St John's Gospel, the words on his memorial are, "I am the Light," a particularly fitting choice for the Bishop who did not want his Cathedral to be "a Gothic building with a sombre interior."

The Waiapu Diocesan Synod, meeting to choose a new Bishop in September 1946, had been advised by the Presiding Bishop Stephenson, to choose a man "who knows in his own heart the power of the Lord Jesus Christ to save and to keep; he must be a man of prayer who spends time with God; he must be a witness to others of God's love and of God's power to save; he must be a lover of souls."[727] He repeated that advice at the December synod which elected Norman Lesser. It seems they took it.

Norman Lesser, CMG., MA. D.D, D.Theol was indeed worthy of the privileges and equal to the opportunities he was offered.

*Portrait of Archbishop Norman Alfred Lesser, 1972.
[John Kinder Library Archives ref: ANG-90-2-40]*

References & Abbreviations

1. Unpublished papers

ANG – Lesser's files in the John Kinder Library

DIO – Lesser's papers in Diocesan Archives

DYB – Waiapu Diocesan Year Books

EP – Elisabeth Paterson for further information and photographs

LC – Lesser's Collection of Services from Liverpool Cathedral in 3 Volumes

NAL – Unfinished autobiography and articles

PGS – General Synod Year Books

SB – The 15 Scrapbooks kept by Bishop Lesser

SC – Standing Committee and Finance Committee Minutes Waiapu Diocese

2. Books

AKD – Davidson, A. K., "Christianity in Aotearoa; A History of Church and Society in New Zealand" Wellington, Education for Ministry 1991

BH – "A Brief History of the Church of St John the Evangelist, Barrow Island" compiled by Martin Hughes and Rev Gwyn Murfet, September 2010

MP – Paterson, Michael, "A Brief History of Life in Victorian Britain" London UK Constable and Robinson Ltd 2008

SWG – Grant S.W., "The Resurrection and the Life" a Centennial History of the Cathedrals of St John the Evangelist 1886-1986," Napier, Dean and Vestry of the Cathedral of St John the Evangelist, 1986

TGE – Bluck, John ed. "The Gift Endures – A New History of the Waiapu Diocese" Diocese of Waiapu 2009

WPM – Morrell, W.P., "The Anglican Church in New Zealand: A History," Dunedin, Anglican Church of the Province of New Zealand, 1973

WR – Rosevear, Watson: "Waiapu: The Story of a Diocese," Hamilton and Auckland, Paul's Book Arcade, 1960

Appendix: Writings, Sermons & Addresses

Poems and Hymns

Poem written for the Consecration of the Cathedral
>Three seconds hell, and down it fell;
>The hopes and fears of many years
>But dust and ashes tell.
>Arise and build!
>Strong hearts so willed;
>Resurrection desolation
>Hath so bravely routed.
>On this day our roundelay
>Of joyous praise we proudly raise
>In high adoration.

Printed in the Order of Service.

Hymn for Consecration of Cathedral
>Consecrate, O Lord this building,
>From it let Thy love o'er flow;
>Take us as we are, and make us
>Vibrant beings all aglow.
>All aglow Lord,
>Action's splendour fortify,
>At this scene of desolation,
>Courage and devotion cried
>Lord for restoration so that
>Now the loss is rectified.
>Consecration.
>Men and building sanctified.
>Thus with hearts firm fixed in Heaven
>May our earthly service be
>Strengthened and supported
>By reliant Faith in Thee
>Who dost give us
>Pledges of eternity.

A Likely Lad

Hymn for Youth Service 13 June 1969

1. Young Prince of Glory, victor
   Of all that drags men down,
   Whose humble, vibrant service,
   Could earn, but scorns, a crown.
   As thorns, not jewels, crowned thee
   So may we dedicate
   Our lives suffused with Calv'ry,
   And all to thee relate.

2. Strong Son of God who gladly
   Became the Son of Man
   That sons of men may likewise
   The sons of God become,
   Blind us with visions of thy love
   Then take our hearts and wills
   Work in them unceasingly
   Till time our effort stills.

3. Youth's vigour, dreams and action
   To right earth's many wrongs,
   Direct, inspire and heighten
   And fill our hearts with songs
   Of courage and endurance
   Despising earthly price
   That by love we gain entrance
   To share God's sacrifice.

SB 13 p 134

Lullaby

Baby Jesus take your rest,
Snuggle in to Mary's breast,
May no fear you betide,
In fond arms you may confide.

Smiles and kisses softly giv'n
Foretaste of the joys of heav'n,
Raven tresses bending o'er,
Prayer, God bless you evermore.

Whispered lullaby so sweet,
Kisses then for two small feet,
Clasp with a so-gentle nod
Dimpled fingers of our God.

Writings, Sermons & Addresses

Selection of Poems published in *Hear, Here!* 1971

Do Not Disturb

"Do not disturb," the ticket hangs
On bedroom doors, that no one bangs,
Disturbing those who "rest in peace"
Before they're dead.

Take up your cross and follow Me
If you would My disciple be.
"Do not disturb," I'd rather not,
Include me out.

When the Last Trump shall rend the air,
And inmost secrets are laid bare,
Shall we not worry how you fare,
Just – not disturb?

The Lost Sheep

"There were ninety and nine that safely lay
In the shelter of the fold." In that day
The shepherd risked life and limb, for to seek
The erring, the wayward, the blind, the weak.
New times bring new manners, and now we see
One safe in the fold, the rest on the lea.
The shepherds no longer go out to seek
The wandering sheep forlorn, but each week
They issue a notice that all lost sheep
At the Parish Office may find relief
If they attend there between ten and four,
Wipe their feet and gently knock on the door.
If the sight of the Good Shepherd is sought
They'll be unlucky, for what He has bought
With His life, He'll be out seeking till found.

What Difference?

When Jesus came to His own place,
He could no mighty work embrace,
Because of unbelief.
Were He to come to Timbuctoo,
Napier, Hastings or Timaru,
Would it be any different?

A Likely Lad

The Cock Crowed

    Whilst Peter thrice denied
    We know the cock crowed twice.
    If cocks kept records true
    Of our base denials,
    They would tally thousands,
    And their myriad crows
    Their throats make sore, and so
    Their accusation silence.

Holy Communion

    As watchmen look for the morning
    So look we for thee, O Christ,
    As skies with sun's light adorning
    With soul purged, seek we our tryst.

    From corn on hillocks wide-scattered
    One loaf taketh shape and form
    Let all divisions be shattered,
    One Body shaping reform.

    Days before us, thou beside us
    There is naught we more can ask,
    For thy power and peace most precious
    Gives us strength for any task.

    Thus surveying Body broken
    Reigning from a wooden throne
    Do we offer thee a token
    Venture all for thee alone.

A Fly

    How aggravating is a fly
    Beyond the reach of hand, not eye,
    All this, when hand is free to move
    To strike, or scare, or just to rove,
    How then, when hands and feet secure
    By cruel nails, how then endure?
    The life blood, lava-oozing sweet,
    From wound deep gashed in hands and feet,
    The sweat of armpits and soiled clothes
    Attracted visits from the fly,

Who could not be disturbed, but by
Convulsive shudders of the frame,
By shaking of tired head, the same
Result as twitching of the skin,
But any movement made worlds spin.
What torment suffered He so well!
To conquer death, there's none can tell.

Easter

Two scarred feet
The scarred earth trod,
Where crossed beams of timber
Had served as a throne.
The lilies of the field rejoiced
To see the Lord of Life
Stride gaily o'er the earth
Where He had been death's hostage.
Death cried aloud to keep its victim,
But conceded defeat
As Love strode shining by.

Pastoral letters to Clergy – Excerpts

3 July 1947

...I am under no illusion with regard to my own ability and am fully prepared to admit that I can lay no claim to being a profound scholar, a great organizer or a skilled committee man. On the other hand, I do sincerely trust that it may be my privilege to share with you in every serious effort to make the mind of our people wise, it's (sic) heart loving and it's (sic) will righteous.

The problems and perplexities, the joys and the encouragements of day to day Parochial life are not unknown to me, and I shall always regard it as a privilege to discuss such matters with any of my brethren who care to seek such discussion either by letter, or better still, by personal contact.

I cannot stress too strongly that I hope to be available so that all my brethren who care to use my services, may find them available at all reasonable times.

SB 1 p 47

A Likely Lad

18 October 1948

…It is a stirring challenge to be a Christian! On the Prayer Cycle that I am to produce for next year, I propose to insert two sentences, the first being a quotation from William Temple's thought, and the second, an idea which for long has been stirring in my mind. I am going to risk this, even if some people think it an impertinence to quote myself after so great a thinker as William Temple.

"Jesus ought always to be put to men, not as a problem, but as a solution!"

With Jesus Christ, as we walk along the way, we find the truth and discover the life, for He is all three.

SB 2 p 34

18 June 1950

…In our prayers, when we remember the men who are mentioned in the Diocesan Leaflet for the day, shall we sometimes try to add all those Clergy who day by day and week by week carry on with very little obvious signs of success, those men who go to one service after another with a mere handful of people, and never fail to recall that Jesus gave one of His most challenging sermons to one woman by a well. Shall we think especially of those Clergy who have little opportunity of meeting their fellow Clergy for comfort (in God's sense) and relief? Shall we think of those Clergy who find the "vision" fading, that God will reveal Himself afresh to them? Shall we pray for those who think they are "successful" and pray that God will lead them again to Calvary, upon which foundation alone, success can be builded?

…Just one personal note. Will my brethren do me the kindness of writing to me *before* I leave home to come to their parishes and let me know what they propose as to engagements. I know that some of my friends think I was vaccinated with a gramophone needle and all I have to do is to stand up and talk. Such is not the case, and like you, I am anxious to think and pray before I speak, and I would value the opportunity of knowing beforehand what is expected of me, so that I can have some degree of preparation of mind and spirit.

SB 3 p 10

21 September 1950

…In about ten days' time, we shall be holding our own Synod in this Diocese. Doubtless there will be many matters requiring our earnest

Writings, Sermons & Addresses

and prayerful consideration and action. Shall we prepare ourselves in the best of all possible ways by asking God that we may be responsive to the promptings of His Holy Spirit, humble enough to seek His Will, and brave enough to attempt to do it. Since before I came, brothers, I have heard much of the "glorious spirit of Waiapu." Brothers, you do not talk much about "things that are too deep for tears." The glorious Spirit of Jesus Christ will work miracles in us if only we will let Him, and then we shall not need to talk of the glorious spirit of Waiapu, because it will be evident to all who come within the bounds of its influence.

In this Diocese we have no great cleavage of "schools of thought," we do not represent (or rather misrepresent) any extremes of opinion, and if only we would agree to be sufficiently humble for God to use us, we might give a lead to men and women who seek God in sincerity and simplicity. God can only fill us with His spirit if we empty ourselves of our own self-sufficiency.

SB 3 p 32

2 June 1951

...A clever saying which I read recently was, "We learn from history that we do not learn from history." How true that is! Down the ages man has allowed his greed and his malice to accumulate until it boiled over in war. The only thing that has changed has been the weapon employed. Whereas in the days of Julius Caesar it cost about three shillings and sixpence to kill a man, the cost in the last war was anything over £12,500. Most truly do we learn from history that we do not learn from history! Jesus Christ gave men a pattern of behaviour to follow, so that there would be peace on earth to men of good will. We, in our blindness, dispense with the good will and ask where is the peace.

If you are lost in the bush of Africa, and have sense, you will go back to the point where you took the wrong turning. Man has not that sense in things spiritual. Why can we not get back to Christ and learn the road afresh, for after all, He told us He was the Way. We have tried most of the other "ways" and where have they led us?

Evangelism is really finding and being found of God.

SB 4 p 20

A Likely Lad

4 September 1951

...May I say that I sincerely trust that none of the brethren will write to ask to be excused from attendance at the Synod service at 10.45 a.m. on Sunday October 7th. I do want us all as a family of God's children to gather together round His Table and gain fresh strength from Him who alone can give it. I fully realise that this may mean providing Celebrations on another day so that people may have a Celebration during that week, but I am convinced that the mere fact of us all being together of one heart will make possible the re-enactment of Acts 2 verse 1 following. There is not one of us who does not feel his own personal unworthiness to be an ambassador for Christ, to be a living, vital agent for the proclamation of the eternal Gospel, and kneeling together and hearing the comforting, strengthening words, we can later rise to our feet, consecrated men, ready to do the bidding of the Lord Christ whom we serve, and whose we are. Ye are my witnesses, says Jesus. Think, my brother, if your witness determines what the world will be – will it become the Kingdom of God?

SB 4 p 29

7 November 1951

...We are all eagerly looking forward to the challenge of Christmas to human life and are praying that we may rise to our opportunities. But just try to imagine that THERE IS NO CHRISTMAS! It is all a myth, and Jesus was never born except in the imagination of mis-guided people. There is no guiding star, there is no stable, there is no song of angels, there are no shepherds to find the Lamb of God, there are no Wise Men to discover the source of wisdom, there is no Maid with courage to say, "be it unto me according to Thy will." There is no story of a prodigal son, there is no story of a sinner who found forgiveness, there is no grave that was burst open to the heavens, and December 25 at night is no longer Holy Night, and certainly not Silent Night.

When we look at it like that, isn't there an awful lot for which to be thankful? So, let us thank God that He was never so great as when He became small.

SB 4 p 44

11 February 1952

The death of George VI meant that a projected visit by Princess Elizabeth was postponed.

...Certain engagements which we all would have kept relating to the Royal Visit, will unfortunately be cancelled. We will all remember

Writings, Sermons & Addresses

in our prayers, our Queen facing such heavy responsibilities under such a strain of sorrow yet supported by both human and Everlasting Arms. We are not unmindful of the Queen's Mother to whom we owe such a debt for her self-effacing contribution to the welfare of our Commonwealth and Empire, as to him who symbolized that Empire for us. We will pray for the Queen's sister Margaret, for the Princess Royal, and the Dukes of Windsor and Gloucester, and not least for Queen Mary, who has borne so much with so great courage and dignity.

SB 5B p 12

30 March 1952

...Almost as you receive this letter, we shall together be entering upon Holy Week. Holy Week must ever remain meaningless unless it makes every week Holy, and Good Friday can never be really good unless it makes all Fridays Good. If we really sanctify our lives, then Easter will be for us not just an annual repetition of a perfunctory belief in the resurrection of the body but will be a living and vital personal experience. Jesus will indeed and in truth be risen, for He will have risen in us. So, may we be able to say victoriously, The Lord is risen! The Lord is risen indeed! Alleluia!

SB 5B p 9

November 1953

...When I was a little boy, my Mother used to tell me of a most thrilling occasion in her young life. Her father and mother had taken the family, as a great treat, to the seaside. The climax of the outing for my mother was a ride on a donkey... But judge of her dismay when the donkey, obviously tired of the constant trotting between two clearly defined points, suddenly exhibited great originality, and galloped straight into the sea, with Mother holding tight round its neck, and rending the air with loud shrieks. So marvellously did Mother tell this story, and so exciting did it seem to my untutored mind, that captivated by the narrative, I would say, time and again, "Tell me again about the donkey. Tell me again, tell me again." There is an old mission hymn that is outmoded, except in certain circles, upon which many look askance, "Tell me the old, old story." We are just approaching the season of Advent, which is the prologue of the greatest drama the world has known or will know. We are going to prepare ourselves, like children, so that our minds can become receptive to the great story "of Jesus and his love." *So* God loved the world, that He gave His only begotten Son."

A Likely Lad

Christmas is essentially a family time, and I want to send all the members of this Diocesan family the kindliest greetings from my wife and Elisabeth and myself, and we pray for you that the "old, old story, of Jesus and his love" may be re-enacted in your hearts. We pray that when Christ comes you may fling open the doors of your earthly mansions and make your hearts his throne. If Christmas means this to us and to the people whom God has entrusted to our care, and for whom we must answer at the day of judgment, then the new year **must** be a happy new year, for we enter it, hand in hand with God himself.

SB 6 p 17

26 January 1955

As usual the January letter includes an itinerary for the year. He adds:

...At this moment the house is simply upside down as the decorators are in complete charge and helpful as they all are, there is a necessary turmoil, and any thought of holiday is impossible. As soon as they finish their work, I hope to secure a few days' rest, but I trust that my brothers will be understanding, if I try to have a break at the first possible moment, especially after General Synod.

May I take this early opportunity to express the hope that you will find God's richest blessing resting upon your labours of love for Him, this year, and I pray for strength for you, that you may spend and be spent in His most glorious service, in this job to which we are called, so poorly paid, perhaps, but so richly rewarded, most certainly.

SB 6 p 98

14 October 1955

Referring to the service of the Laying of the Foundation Stone, he writes:

...It was a great inspiration to feel that all the Parishes in the Diocese were 'there' physically and spiritually. Like many other people, I was conscious of being surrounded by a wealth of goodwill and prayer and I was supported and encouraged amazingly by it. Of course, it was an historic moment for our Diocesan family, and we were thrilled by the act of worship which laid foundations in addition to a Stone. I believe that many hearts of stone were melted, and I earnestly pray that God will give us strength and vision to continue the good work which He in His mercy has begun. It is utterly useless for us to build a magnificent temple for God unless "living stones" that worship therein, are also founded and grounded in Him.

SB 6 p 93

Writings, Sermons & Addresses

17 November 1955

...If we do not exercise care, as someone has pointed out, the result will be that Christ-mas, the mass of Christ, becomes X-mas, the mass of the unknown quantity.

It ill behoves us to speak disparagingly of the people who worshipped the unknown god, until Christ is well-known to us.

SB 6 p 147

14 November 1956

...Every year, since you were old enough to think, you and I have had the opportunity of preparing our hearts and minds and homes for the birth of a little Son, the Son of God. It has been possible for us to avoid history's repeating itself, and the Babe having nowhere to lay His head.

...Christmas comes annually to us as a challenge to our hearts and lives, and it can be joyous fully only to those who have made due preparation. He still seeks a place to rest, and you and I can provide it! Are we going to tell him, we are sorry, but in New Zealand, as in Palestine, there is a "housing shortage" and still there is "no room in the inn?"

SB 6 p 166

December 1958

...The older I grow, the more convinced I become that the most vital part of our Ministry is the quiet, unassuming, self-effacing and humble waiting upon God, for in quietness and confidence shall be our strength. It was not in the earthquake or the fire, but in the still small voice that God spoke. Little wonder is it that in our day, when men seek Him only in the spectacular and the propaganda highlight, that so often they miss Him. A blare of trumpets and high pressure advertising is no substitute for humbly listening to God. A Christian on his knees sees more than a propagandist on a step ladder.

This has been a year of heavy endeavour for many of us. But we are always encouraged to remember the worst year always ends with a new birth and a glorious new opportunity. God grant that we may all cleanse our hearts and lives so that when He comes, the little Christ child may find in us a home and a welcome.

SB 7 p 74

A Likely Lad

23 March 1959

...Once again, the opportunity is ours to share with our Lord the valley of shadows, and it is only for those who have grown accustomed to the shadows that the blinding light of Easter is so wonderful.

Holy Week is unfortunately for so many people but a rather hectic period of endeavouring to get things 'cleaned up' so that they may enjoy to the full the holiday which follows.

For those who owe any allegiance to our Lord it is a time of peculiar opportunity. It is our privilege to follow with Him in the paths, bloody and thorny, that belong to our peace!

SB 7 p 75

28 January 1959

He encloses the itinerary for the year, and comments that he had visited the Māori parishes after the death of Bishop Bennett, but since the consecration of Bishop Panapa he has reverted to the previous practice of the Bishop of Aotearoa administering Confirmation. He goes on:

"However, I would greatly desire from time to time to have the pleasure of coming into all the Māori parishes, to meet the worshippers, and to share with them in a service. You will therefore notice that this year I have included all the parishes in the itinerary.

...and notes that this will affect length of time he can be in other places.

...When any individual priest looks at the itinerary it may appear to have little personal application but... I do try to visit each parish at least once a year. In addition to the long list of engagements there are the bi-monthly meetings of the Te Aute Trust Board, a week of Provincial meetings in Wellington, the Annual Meeting of the New Zealand Mission Trust Board, the Pension Board and the St John's College Trust Board."

SB 7 p 77

29 February 1960

Following dedication of the first part of the Cathedral 24 February 1960.

...It is my earnest hope that we shall be able to share in a similar service in about eighteen months' time and thank God that our building is externally completed. There remains the responsibility for us to engage in a corresponding and concomitant building enterprise. That God "who is rich in mercy for His great love wherewith He loved us... hath raised us up *together*. For we are His workmanship, and are built upon the foundation of the apostles and prophets, Jesus Christ Himself being the Chief Corner Stone; in whom all the building fitly framed together groweth into an holy temple in the land."

We build two temples at once. May God give us grace to be worthy of Him, so that a dedicated Temple may be entered by temples of His spirit.

SB 7 p 159

Excerpts from Last Pastoral Letter: 5 February 1971

Thanking clergy for gift and farewell:

...To say that we were deeply moved would be the understatement of the year. To anyone who considered I was too light-hearted my reply would be that I could not trust myself to be too serious as I might have broken down.

Sunday will be an imperishable memory for us and our family.

First of all, the clergy and their wives, honouring us in a meal which was in deed and in truth an agape, and followed by gracious and generous gifts, although all had contributed to the astronomic gift to follow.

Then we went straight to the cathedral for that most moving service which we will never forget. How grateful to, and how proud we were, of the "family."

...Small wonder then, that as it was said of one person, that when they died Calais would be found printed on their heart, so with us it will be Waiapu.

We do want all our friends to know how deeply we valued their presence, their sentiments and the far too generous gifts.

Although we will never obtrude on our successors, our thoughts and prayers will be constantly with you all.

Thank you for giving us this wonderful opportunity of fellowship in service, and for strengthening us by your friendship.

We hope to live at 4 Sealy Road, Napier, and we will not use the old Lancashire saying, "Next time you're passing *do* pass," but rather "Haere mai."

God bless you all.

(Signed) Norman Lesser

SB 15 p 34

Synod Addresses: Diocesan

DYB 1947

...I am not equipped to discourse on world affairs. ...But I have enough sense to know that world affairs are only family affairs magnified a million times. It would appear then, that we, as ordinary people, with ordinary gifts, have still a great part to play in helping Him Who maketh all things new, to bring a new world to birth.

During the war a train in the Old Country was wrecked by enemy action. It so happened that there was a distinguished surgeon on the train, and he was unhurt. He moved quickly and efficiently among the wounded bringing everywhere relief and comfort. But he was heard on a number of occasions to say half aloud "If only I had my instruments!"

Brethren, I believe with all my heart that that same cry of anguish goes up from God in these days. But WE are His instruments. A new world order can only be built by new men and new women, and if we are willing to pay the price of loyalty and love, He Who maketh all things new will work marvels in our lives; then shall we be fitted for His service. ...Our modern democracy, if it is to reach high levels, will need to link democracy with Theocracy and the will of God must be the only will of His people. Unless we do this the gloomy forecast of an acute student of human nature and affairs would appear amply to be justified, namely, that "a dreary and disastrous destiny faces a doomed race." J.A. Spender, in 1942, said "We have got to get back to God... unless the world gets back to God it hasn't a chance. We ought to HURRY back to God."

...Then if I may touch on a personal note towards the end of this talk, I would remind you of what the Bishop of Nelson said at the special session of Synod... "You will commence if you are wise, in recognising that you will not secure a man as your leader who has all the qualities you desire..." "But there is one aspect of his life in which you can condone no mediocrity – that is his sincerity of heart and devotion to his Lord and Master." We are aware of the parochial representative who was asked by the Bishop "What sort of man do you want?" and gave reply "We do not mind what sort of man we get, big or little, so long as when he is on his knees he reaches up to heaven."

My constant prayer for this Diocese is that we shall grow up as a family of God, with our fellowship breaking down all the smaller barriers of prejudices which we have wrongly described as convictions... that

Writings, Sermons & Addresses

young and old alike as soldiers of Christ may give our hearts to His obedience. Give Christ your all, you can do no more, and you dare do no less.

p 23

1948 DYB

…Whither Bound? It is said that in olden days this cry of 'Whither bound?' was made and answered with deepest interest. It still is of the most vital significance to Christian wayfarers.

So easy it is for us to think that because we live in a comparatively small Dominion at the ends of the earth, that our contribution is not so urgently needed. But "at the ends of the earth" depends on where you start! It would have been ever so easy for Jesus to say "Some people with malicious minds say that I am but the illegitimate child of an untutored peasant in a despised Province on the very outskirts of an Empire. Why should I exert Myself, and give My life for the world which despises me?" Men often asked in scorn "Can any good come out of Nazareth?" and the answer then, as now, is "Come and see!"

What we have, therefore, to ask ourselves is "When men do come and see, what do they see? What sort of a witness is our own life?"

…Whither bound? To set forth the Kingdom that grows men in the likeness of Christ. There is much talk about ideologies these days, and one particular form comes in for great discussion and reproof. Our only lasting answer must ever be what Glover calls the religious life that outlives and out loves. The choice between Communism and Christianity, "My kingdom come" or "Thy Kingdom come" will be resolved when men take the traits of Christianity in Communism, for instance, self-sacrifice and discipline, and integrate their lives by finding their self-expression in being "slaves" not to a system, but to Him whose service is their perfect freedom. We have so watered down the Gospel of Jesus that it is with a shock we realise afresh that if we really put it into practice it would be the most revolutionary ethic the world has known. No one has ever seen it in practice on a large scale, and therein lies our shame and our humiliation.

…"Many people take their religion today as they take a bus: they make use of it only if it is travelling in their direction." These are days of the utmost urgency, when one rifle bullet in Berlin can set the whole world in flames. It is then, with a sense of gravity we ask ourselves afresh the time-honoured question Whither bound? It is with a sense of direct responsibility that we answer it but answer we must. Pray

A Likely Lad

God that our answer may be such that with humble pride we can say to the world when it asks if Christianity works, "Come and see!" May God's unfailing presence be with us as together we seek His will and find His power!

p 26-27

1949 DYB
Evangelism

...I have asked that we should have this word engraven in our hearts and that this synod should be for us all a testing time of our faith. May I then continue my address making special reference to this vital subject which for Christian people must ever overshadow all others?

...With night descending on so much of the world it is challenging to remember that not all the darkness in the world can blot out the light of one small candle. It is against this background that I speak to you. "Ye are the light of the world" said, and still says, Jesus.

...We all recognise that evangelism, that is the preaching of the gospel or good news, is the fundamental purpose of the Church, and we would do well also to remember in this connection that "what you are speaks so loudly that I cannot hear what you say!"

To put it simply, we are ambassadors of Christ; how do we represent Him?

...When I was on my tours recently, I saw a sign outside a garage "Break down service and repairs" and appropriately enough, immediately below the sign was parked a van, on the back of which was painted "Ye must be born again."

Let us start here. We see what Christ has done for us and for the world and we realise our unworthiness, we are a "breakdown" job, and the van gives us the answer in the words of Scripture. Being born again is the beginning of evangelism.

A man who said proudly that his church had made great strides in the previous year was asked if they had added very materially to their numbers, and he replied "No, but we have got rid of quite a lot!" There are some people who are just gospel-hardened, they have been inoculated with a mild dose of Christianity, and as one has said, it makes them impervious to a real attack! These self-made Christians, like all self-made men, take an awful load off the shoulders of the Almighty. A self-made man said to his son on one occasion "See a self-made man, my son," and his son said "Well, Dad you always did take the blame for everything!" Let us then be prepared to take our

Writings, Sermons & Addresses

share of blame for the dullness and blindness of our souls and pray God to make His love new to us. It may be that there will be a B.C. and an A.D. division in the history of our own lives, marking where Christ was born in us.

Our planning for evangelism, or sharing our love for Christ with other people, will be meaningless unless Christ is fundamental in our own lives, unless we are born again. You cannot pass on what you do not possess, you cannot introduce men to Christ if you do not really know Him.

p 26

1950 DYB

My Brethren,

After typing these words, I paused long and thought hard. If only we all were to make these words come true, half our work would be done. We are brethren and must be so because God is our common father.

p 22

...It pleases me to think that Jesus recalled the occasion when as a little boy he stood in the midst of the learned men in the Temple, and later in life He called a little child and stood him in the midst. We cannot think of Jesus other than in the midst. "Where two or three are gathered together, there am I in the midst." After eight days again Jesus stood in the midst and said, "Peace be unto you." ...A little Babe yawning in a manger in the midst of the animals with little hands outstretched – a terrible omen to be fulfilled years later when His arms were nailed in the same position, but he was still in the midst! Our prayer for this synod is that he will occupy the same position for us.

P 29

1952 DYB

...Dr Samuel Shoemaker has said in a recent book "Revive Thy Church – Beginning with Me" that civilisation is going round a corner on two wheels. Men seem to have an emotion not dissimilar to that of animals as they approach the stockyard: things have an ominous smell! He suggests that part of the reason for this is, as the Church has drawn about itself its skirts of self-righteousness and exclusiveness, and the load of hangers-on have held the Church back by the lazy unconvertedness of their own hearts because the Church has not got out into the world to change it, the world has crept into the Church and ruined it. Dr Shoemaker rightly points out that until something

A Likely Lad

happens *to* us and *in* us, nothing can happen *through* us. Hence his title for his book "Oh God, Revive Thy church *beginning with me.*"

"Thy will be done" may be a sigh of utter resignation and despair, or it could be a cry of triumph and victory. If we would prevent the world from going round the next corner on two wheels, we must see to it that "Thy will be done" is not just a pretty text to be inscribed on the tables of a tombstone, but inscribed on the tables of our hearts.

It is because we desire His Will to be done that, we are here at all. If we desire less, we betray Him. We cannot desire more. The only question that remains to be answered is what is our desire worth? A Quaker who saw a coster's barrow of fruit upset and ruined by a vehicle which did not stop heard a passer-by moan, "Oh I do so feel for him." The Quaker said, "I feel ten shillings for him. How much do you?"

That God's will may be done in our Synod is my prayer. Let us see that our actions match our highest resolve.

p 27

1953 DYB

...Even now many people are thinking and working for the coming of the Queen to our shores. This historic event may well serve to give us serious warning. There will be thousands of people who desire to attend services simply because the Queen is present, completely oblivious of the simple fact that at all services a Greater Sovereign always reigns, and they have the inestimable privilege of being in the King's presence whenever they will. There will be others who clamour that great attention should be paid to fabric and grounds of places of worship for the Royal visit. Should this not be a normal desire for those who "worship the Lord in the beauty of holiness"? I give place to none in my loyalty, but we must ever recall the words of Jesus Himself "Render to Caesar the things that are Caesar's and to God, the things that are God's."

Let us by all means strain every nerve to give the Queen the most joyous visit and make it in every way memorable for her and for ourselves, but do not let us delude ourselves that we are offering something to the worship of Almighty God when we are not.

...I read recently in a parish magazine that "in conditioning the atmosphere of a home two gadgets are now essential: a thermometer and a thermostat. The words are similar in sound, spelling and rootage, but there is a vast difference in their functions. A thermometer hangs

Writings, Sermons & Addresses

alone, has no connection with anything else; it is merely affected by the hotness or coldness of a room. It has no power to change it. It reflects its environment and adjusts itself to it. A thermostat looks much like a thermometer and hangs on the wall. But instead of being alone and individual, it has powerful connections. If it is hot, it has ways of making the room cooler, and if it is cool, of making it warmer. Instead of being affected by environment, it changes it. In brief, a thermostat does something about its surroundings, while a thermometer adjusts itself to its environment. People can be classified into thermometers and thermostats. Thermometer personalities are chameleons, adjusters, compromisers. They always take on the colour, climate, morality and spirituality of the group they are with. They merely reflect environment. They do nothing to change it.

Thermostat personalities are changers, reformers, leaders, transformers. They are not satisfied with the status quo. They are not complacent, unconcerned, unburdened and indifferent. Things and conditions must improve."

For seven long years I have had one prayer in my heart, that God will use this beloved Diocese of Waiapu to the extension of His glorious kingdom. If that prayer is to come true, then you and I must be changed men – thermostats, not thermometers. We must humbly and sincerely try to raise the spiritual temperature of our age. In a small country like this, we would do well to remember that "it is not the number of square miles of a country that makes it great, but the number of square people."

p 27

1954 DYB

...This is an age of initials and it is impossible to pick up a newspaper without being assailed by hosts of organisations being called by initials: NATO, EDC, CORSO, even mistakes are covered by E&OE, and this age thinks it has started something new, but it is good to recall that B.C. and A.D. have been going on quite a fair time!

May I conclude... by reminding you of four other letters which the world has largely forgotten to its cost? These letters are INRI – Jesus of Nazareth the King of the Jews, and as you concentrate upon them, they change before your eyes and become RSVP. The whole future of the world will depend on our response to that invitation and what our reply to His incarnate love will be. "It doesn't make an *atom* of difference to me" is a saying that has taken on a new connotation,

A Likely Lad

and our reply to Christ's challenge will determine whether we enjoy an atomic era or an atomic annihilation. But let us not forget that all our power, whether we use it or misuse it, is still God's – for *Thine* is the power!"

p 23

1955 DYB

On the building of the Cathedral:

1. The effort must be great. The Cathedral must be worthy of the Diocese. No thought of cheapness, or temptation to hurry must be entertained. It must be the best of its kind. It must be a fitting expression of the heartfelt homage and gratitude of rich and poor to the great and good Father of us all for the countless blessings which we have received at His hands as a nation, a Church and as individuals.

2. The effort must be united. It must be the work of the whole Diocese, for the Cathedral must be the Central Church and the ecclesiastical heart of the vast network of towns and villages. Its doors must ever stand open to welcome the rich and the poor, the old and the young; therefore, rich and poor, old and young must help to build it, and must regard it as belonging to them. Therefore, the smallest gift of our poor, the pence of our children, the mites of our widows, must be brought for its building, as well as the princely offerings of great landowners and our kings of commerce.

3. The effort must be sustained. A Cathedral cannot be built in a day, and perhaps not in a generation… but having put our hand to the venture we cannot look back. We must exercise faith and courage, and indomitable perseverance, and having faithfully done our part, and denied ourselves in doing it, we must hand it on to our children… for completion.

4. The effort must be made with unceasing prayer. Spiritual work calls for spiritual methods. We must build to glorify GOD, not to magnify our Diocese or ourselves. Our offerings must be winged with prayer. We must face our great task on our knees. It is only as we seek God's help that those who direct the enterprise will be filled with wisdom; that the hearts of our people will be opened to give generously and continuously; and the undertaking be crowned with ultimate success.

Writings, Sermons & Addresses

The laying of the Foundation Stone is an important part of the Synod meetings, but it is more than that, for it is a pointer to the inner significance of our Christian life. Nothing that we do in the Synod has any meaning or purpose apart from its being rooted and grounded and founded in Christ.

...This Synod could be the greatest that this Diocese with nearly a hundred years of history behind it, has ever experienced, if we all were prepared to add to our contributions in Synod and at the Service, the gift that Christ desires of us most of all, 'ourselves, to be a reasonable and lively sacrifice,' our bodies and souls, marked with the Cross to show the spirit in which we make our offering. That this may be our will is my earnest prayer.

p 27

1956 DYB

Regarding the Wells programme and the BFF.

...The Bishop's Fighting Fund will automatically draw to a close at the end of the five-year period, which expires in December 1957. Frankly I do not envy the Organising Secretary his job next year when so many of the Parishes will have undertaken the Wells programme of fund raising. ...It may be opportune at this juncture to suggest that the greatest care be taken by the Parishes which adopt the Wells system to ensure that Diocesan needs are amply catered for in their appeal figures. The re-building of our Mother Church, the constant needs of our Children's Homes, the running expenses of the Diocesan needs and the equally vital work of those who go out in our name to show the Church is true to its calling, all these primary needs must be met in wholehearted fashion.

p 26

1958 DYB

...The Mission Homes, the Children's Homes, the Waiapu House for older people, the Mail Bag Sunday School, the Diocesan Office and last but by no means least, Hukarere and Te Aute. We see the balance sheets for these agencies in the work of our Lord, but I would like to see another Balance Sheet, kept by a recording angel, with all the countless hours of extra service and loving kindness, all the little unobtrusive generous deeds, the forgivenesses. I do not think we would pass a formal vote of thanks were we to see that Balance Sheet, we would just quietly kneel down and thank God.

p 25

A Likely Lad

1959 DYB

...You will have seen the tremendous strides which have been taken in building, what I hope we all shall regard as OUR Cathedral and not merely ***the*** cathedral. Our cathedral is not just another church, it is the centre of our Diocese, and an outward and visible sign of an inward and spiritual urge. The health of a Cathedral and the witness of our parish churches must go hand in hand.

An incomplete task can please no one, least of all God.

At this Synod we shall decide before God whether we are going ahead to build the last fifth of the cathedral now, at a cost estimated at £35,500, or call a halt to our efforts, and let people twenty or more years hence finish what we have so magnificently begun. No one more than I realises the importance of building in the parishes. I have been a parish priest for the best part of my life and have built in every parish, churches and halls. In every parish I have served I have never known our contributions to a cathedral diminish our own work.

...The city of Guildford is completing a new cathedral and looking for £175,000 to finish the Cathedral which has cost £300,000 so far. The West end is unfinished, and the suggested wall would cost about £5000 and would be a waste of money in the long run.

The Mormons are building a chapel to cost about £60,000 in Napier. The Racing Club is to build a new stand at the cost of about £430,000...

I know full well that £35,000 is a large sum of money but it is not a large sum of money from 70,000 people.

£35,000 will provide seven hospital beds. Is the church still to be taunted that it is only an ambulance at the bottom of the cliff?

£35,000 will provide five beds in a maternity ward to give birth to new life. Will this proud Diocese give £35,000 to provide men and women, girls and boys with life eternal?

This is a Family affair. With all the goodwill which exists, and the business acumen which Synod possesses, can we not see our way to complete this task? It could be our privilege to complete the first cathedral in New Zealand in this century.

p 26

1960 DYB

...Your Standing Committee has given very serious considerable attention to this vital project *(i.e. completing the Cathedral)* and you

Writings, Sermons & Addresses

will observe we have let the contract for the shell of the last section of the building...

It would appear that we, in common with other Dioceses, are discovering some recession in giving in this second phase of planned giving, and I sincerely urge our people, in this day of unparalleled national wealth, to make certain that He who is the Giver of all is remembered with gratitude.

p 37

On the predicted decay of the church

...In the mid-nineteenth century an eminent person said, "In fifty years your Christianity will have died out." In fact, there has never been such a worldwide expansion of the Church as there was in the second half of last century! Back in 1655, the historian Fuller writes "An ingenious gentleman some months ago since, in jest-earnest advised me to make haste with my History of the Church of England, for fear (said he) that the church of England ended before the History thereof;" and similar prognostications might be quoted from any century since St Chrysostom wrote in 395 'The church is like a banqueting room when the host's invitations have been for the most part declined and only a few guests are seated at the board." To its contemporaries the Church has always appeared to be in a state of decay. And it really is a useful thing to know that preparations for its funeral have been going on for a very long time.

As we begin our business let us remind ourselves that it is the King's business, and that it brooks no delay. Thus, with head held high, with hearts from which all fear has departed, let us go forth conquering and to conquer.

p 42

DYB 1961

...It is a truism to say that never before was there greater need for the humble exhibition of the lively Christian faith. Can we then realise the profound privilege which is ours in having been born for such a time as this? Can our prayer possibly be other than that God will make us worthy of our privileges and equal to our untold opportunities?

...In the early part of this year during the course of a service in Nelson the Bishop in Polynesia placed in my hands a primatial Cross. Since that time, I have frequently pondered when that Cross is carried before me, and I recognise my unworthiness to follow. I cannot but

A Likely Lad

recall that our Lord, for the last part of His via dolorosa had the cross carried before Him, but He was going to lie upon it, and I, merely to hold it. His cross held Him; I hold mine; what a world of difference.

It is natural, therefore, that my prayer for our Synod should be that He who reigned from the Tree shall produce through our labours the fruits of the Spirit.

p 18-19

1963 DYB

...There was recently a quotation to the effect that a Buddhist priest had said "We think there is something to Christianity, but we don't think the Christians know what it is." The best way to refute that charge is holy and humble men of heart walking in the path where Christ walks.

...Regrettably we hear from time to time of someone being lost in the deep bush or on the sea, and quickly the whole resources of sea and air rescue, of the police force, military personnel and hosts of community-minded citizens become available for a painstaking search *until they find*. No hardship is mentioned, no suffering is referred to, by those who seek. A person is lost and he or she must be found. Jesus tells us of the man who goes after the sheep which was lost *"until he find it."* There is the purposefulness of the gospel. We muster our total resources, and how rightly, to save a man's body. We now have to answer God as to what we are prepared to muster to save men's souls. The ultimate reason for Synod is to "organise" love, and to that end we give ourselves freely in these days of meeting and taking counsel together.

... It is our opportunity in these days of doubt to exhibit faith, to show by joyous, brave living that it is not true to say that one of the greatest enemies of Jesus Christ is a religion called Christianity. We will refuse to subscribe to a religion which is dull, a pale imitation of the real thing, the only effect of which is to prejudice people against it.

The disciples were called Christians first in Antioch. The disciples of our day are called many names other than Christian. ...We are known as Christians and Jesus goes further and says, "I have called you friends." Therein is at once our supreme joy and our testing.

p 19-20

1965 DYB

In his welcome he quotes Martin Luther King as saying:

"Most people, and Christians in particular, are thermometers that record or register the temperature of majority opinion, not thermostats that transform and regulate the temperature of society."

p 13

He suggests that MRI could stand for "My Regard Increases."

"If my regard for Christ and His work increases, then I will be increasingly desirous of finding ways of making my stewardship of time and brain more effective.

...It was not only at Gethsemane that Jesus was lonely. What must He feel like in our own day when He so utterly relies on us?"

...A certain sum of money is required for us to meet ordinary needs within our Diocese family, a sort of domestic housekeeping. I recall hearing of a man who said, "My wife is always asking for money, money, money." "What does she do with it?" asked a sympathetic friend. "I don't know," replied the man. "I haven't given her any yet." From experience I judge that the response from synodsmen will be adequate for our needs and that there will be no reluctance to contribute generously.

Then too we shall desire earnestly to make a worthwhile contribution beyond the confines of our own Diocese.

He lists several overseas opportunities for giving and ends:

"Money Really Indispensable."

p 17

1966 DYB

...I would remind you, as I remind myself, of the words in St John's Gospel Chapter 12, verse 9: "They came, not for Jesus' sake only, but that they might see Lazarus also, whom he had raised from the dead"... The people who came, not for Jesus' sake only, came to witness him who had been raised, and we come that we might be raised.

A mother received the following letter from her son, "Dear Mum, I joined the navy because I liked the way the ships were kept so spick and span. But I never knew till this week who keeps them spick and span. Love, Jimmy." If our Church is to be an Ark of God, it will require that we all shall regard ourselves as crew members rather than passengers. Then will our visits for worship be in deed and in truth

A Likely Lad

"for Jesus' sake only". When this happens, then the world can look out and hold on, for like the early Christians, we will by God's power be turning it upside down. The world is in no such danger at present.

p 14

…These are days of urgency and opportunity, and we can be people of destiny if we are humble and generous and live close to God. The average church member, lay or cleric, has been described as being like a deep sea diver who wears a suit designed for the ocean's depths but who spends time industriously pulling out the plug in the bathtub.

p 18

1967 DYB

At the beginning of my address I naturally referred to our Cathedral, and there is something further about it which I would wish to offer for your thought, and which I believe applies to all our Christian life. I cannot conceive of a Cathedral as a fort to be defended at all costs, to the last man. I prefer to regard it as a place of revival from which we sally forth conquering and to conquer. A church which does not go out, will "pass out."

Together we come to worship in our Cathedral, and together we receive the strength which God alone can give us. But it is given for a purpose – His, not ours.

In 1910 there was held the first World Missionary Conference at Edinburgh. …Bishop V.S. Azariah transformed the Conference from a debate into a spiritual experience. He said in poignant fashion, in his own inimitable manner, "Through ages to come the Indian people will rise up in gratitude to attest the heroism and self-denying labour of the missionary body. You have given your goods to feed the poor; you have given your bodies to be burned; Now give us *friends*."

Is there one amongst us to whom this is not heart-searching?

Jesus said, "I have called you FRIENDS." To make a friend you must be a friend. It is this quality of life which I pray with all my heart that our Cathedral may develop, for if it fails to do that it is as desolate as the first. God help us to see our task and give us the strength to undertake it.

p 17

Writings, Sermons & Addresses

1968 DYB

Referring to Garden Parties attended during the Lambeth Conference, he writes:

"Whilst enjoying the generous and gracious hospitality afforded us, my mind moved to another garden 'party,' where our Lord was very literally 'led up the garden path' to Gethsemane."

p 14

He pays tribute to Ike Robin, the wrestler:

He exemplified all that was best in the Māori race. He was a giant of a man, an undefeated champion Australasian wrestler, but he was also one of our finest lay-readers, and in this capacity in his spiritual pilgrimage, he 'wrestled not against flesh and blood, but against the principalities and powers, against the world-rulers of this darkness.'

p 16

He summarises points from the Lambeth Conference:

The message from Lambeth was addressed to the clergy and laity of the Anglican Communion. It stated that our gathering had been set against a background of grim events in Vietnam, West Africa and Czechoslovakia, and of mounting protest against social injustice. Even in the realm of theology, familiar teaching through which ordinary Christians learned their faith was being re-examined and in part rejected by some theologians. But to those bewildered by all this we say GOD IS. GOD REIGNS. GOD LOVES. God has not abdicated. Therein is our faith.

...So far as ministry is concerned the rôle of the church must be the rôle of her Lord, that of the suffering servant...

The ministry, the service of the church to the world, is and must be discharged mainly by the laity, and a prime duty of the clergy is to strengthen them for this task.

...Among the resolutions which were adopted were a strong recommendation of the reports for careful and prayerful study and a call to meaningful prayer. The Conference stated emphatically its condemnation of the use of nuclear and bacteriological warfare and held it to be the concern of the church to oppose the claim that total war or the use of weapons however ruthless and indiscriminate can be justified by results.

A Likely Lad

...Racism was a blatant denial of the Christian faith, and there was deep concern over the economic and social frustrations of developing countries.

...The controversial question of the ordination of women was raised, and it was recommended provinces study the question and discuss the matter with other communions.

p18

...The Conference made a point of disagreeing with a papal Encyclical which appeared during the Conference, on marriage and family life, permitting only the "natural" method of contraception.

p 20

1969 DYB

...On all hands we are assailed by rapid change, and those who are older frequently resist as providing an opportunity for reflection rather than making a hasty decision. Those who are young sometimes make hasty decisions revealed only by subsequent frustration.

p 19

He Pays Tribute to Stephen Waymouth:

...I am sure you will understand how difficult I find it to speak at all adequately of Stephen, for he was not archdeacon, vicar-general, provincial secretary to me, but just a dear friend, whose judgment I trusted and whose affection I valued immensely. Frequently I still find myself going to the phone to consult him and moving back saddened. There was so much that he had agreed to do at this Synod. It must suffice to say that Stephen never thought of his own advantage, he never once took advantage of a situation, nor evaded responsibility for a mistake through claiming a technicality. He was clear and incisive of mind and ever available to the newest priest to offer all that of which he was capable and that was by no means inconsiderable.

p 16

DYB 1970

On the Plan for Union:

I have been concerned recently to read that "widespread dissatisfaction with the episcopal form of government as set out in the Plan for Union is revealed in the reports of debates in presbyteries throughout the

Writings, Sermons & Addresses

country." It is also clear that there is no hope of the Plan being approved if women are not given equality of status with men in the ministry.

p 22

General Synod Addresses

PGS 1964

...We deliberate in a world where the hungry people of the world in which we live in plenty, would make a line, each person two feet apart, that would encircle the globe and return to your door some twenty-five times. If you drove a car at 50 mph it would take you one and a half years to pass those lines.

We must think of hungry people, and we must think of those who languish because they know not the Bread of Life.

p 17

On the Toronto Congress

...Emphasis was laid on the inescapable fact that the calling of the church was a calling of the whole people of God, laity as much as clergy, and also that we are called to be saints not just to be good, but holy to the uttermost. If all who attended have endeavoured to give reality to this conviction the enormous expense of the Congress has been justified.

A significant concept has emerged in recent times with some force, namely the partnership which exists between lay and clergy, and we clergy would do well to remember that in the field of penetrating the "whole of life" it is we clergy who are the laymen. A lodestar at Toronto was the conviction that we are partners and partners share what there is to share, sometimes distress and disappointment and at other times prosperity and progress.

...It may well be asked how we can find room for Mutual Responsibility in an already over-crowded programme. But we do not fit Mutual Responsibility in as an added programme "It must penetrate everything else, not rival it." It is not really a programme, but a spirit.

p 28

PGS 1968

On re-marriage of divorced persons: he quotes Garth Moore:

"The Church has always released Christians from the external obligations of every vow they can make except that of marriage. This

A Likely Lad

is not a refusal by the Church to dispense from the marriage vows. It is a belief that those are of a sacramental nature, resulted in a God-given relationship as permanent as the relationship between parent and child."

...The decision of the Canadian Anglican Church will necessarily occasion repercussions throughout our Anglican Communion and many will urge this same action be adopted in the name of compassion. It is not a lack of compassion but a different view of the nature of things as God has created them – of what marriage is, which is the heart of a contrary opinion.

p 22

On Church Union

I cannot recall where I read some words which are not altogether inappropriate in this connection. The oft-reiterated statement that it is the function of the Anglican church to die seems to me to require more careful scrutiny. You die only if your death leaves your cause more fully established. We may decide to die as a chrysalis, for a butterfly to be born, but we must not merely commit suicide and leave those depending on us impoverished.

p 27

...With some theologians declaring that God is dead, whereas it is not God but our faith that is dead, and with other theologians of more churches than one casting doubts on what some of us believe to be fundamental to our discipleship, it behoves us to clarify our own thinking so that we may better be able to share with our partners 'in the other ship' those things which for us make union possible.

p 28

...What do you think a convinced Communist would do if he were told that he would have available for his purposes some 800 paid agents as full-time workers, with no less than 1,700 buildings to seat some 120,000 people and with free entry into 1,200 schools where he and his helpers were permitted to give instructions in his faith, and that to train new workers training colleges were provided with liberal assistance to students, and that to support his work something in the vicinity of $4,000,000 per annum was available?

Yet that is approximately our position, and those roughly our physical resources. I would only add that Jesus reminded us that to those to whom much is given, of them will much be required.

p 29

Writings, Sermons & Addresses

...The dynamic of all our work here in Synod is the power of Jesus Christ. Jesus is all that God could give or man could need. Some people seem to be increasingly scared to affirm that Jesus is the Saviour of mankind and that there is power through a risen Christ. Every Christian worth his salt should be a walking advertisement of the proof of the resurrection. I believe implicitly that Jesus rose from the empty tomb, and that His power is available to us and that if we attempt His will faithfully, He meant it when He said "I go to prepare a place for you." There is little point in preparing a place if we are not to occupy it.

My prayer for our Synod is that God will not allow us to "depart in peace," but that the Holy Spirit will have so stirred our hearts and consciences that we shall know no peace until we re-dedicate ourselves to His obedience without counting the cost. In that spirit we may address ourselves to God's work and ours.

p 30

PGS 1970

...Since our last Session I have observed two definitions which I know full well to be inappropriate to this august assembly. Such work as we are to engage in was described as 'the unready who have been appointed by the unwilling to do the unnecessary.' In another place, one member is reported as having given expression to the thought 'that General Synod is the discussion of the irrelevant by the incompetent.'

p 16

On the Lambeth Conference: He expressed pride in the contributions of the other bishops:

Although they did not speak at length, they spoke deliberately and helpfully. They may have had in mind what one Bishop said at a Lambeth Conference, 'I regret to occupy the time of the regular speakers.'

p 20

On the New Liturgy

The consideration of our opportunities for worship is of vital importance, for our worship is to our souls what air is to our bodies. We must therefore insist upon the noblest forms both in order and in word. The improvement in the wording of some of the Collects is a move in this direction and was most necessary.

A Likely Lad

The ultimate in our worship will reveal a little more of the Man hanging from the cross, and a little less of the cross hanging from the man.

p 21

On Inter-communion

We alone of the negotiating churches find this a problem and some of our most devout members say that this must be so since the question is inextricably bound up with Ministry. Others of our members find no theological or practical difficulties in the whole-hearted acceptance of inter-communion. Yet others are of the opinion that if we permit inter-communion, the desire for Union will evaporate.

p 22

On Church Union

It is necessary to stress that the Plan is not just window dressing, for we are conscious, all too conscious, that window dressing might sell the goods but result in a dissatisfied customer. The Plan is an honest attempt to place before the members of the negotiating churches the plain facts of what Union will involve in terms of enrichment and loss. Of one thing we must be assured: that there is no ambiguity which is not resolved, and which would result in future recrimination and charges of "trickery" or bad faith.

There has been a purposeful endeavour to 'gather up,' that nothing be lost. We of our own communion, most certainly have much to bring with us as our dowry. As I have quoted on another occasion the words of a Hungarian, I repeat them now. 'You have a wonderful opportunity, you have the Presbyterian love of Holy Scripture, the Methodist fire of evangelism, the Congregational sense of belonging to each other, the Baptist sense of the urgency of baptism PLUS a catholic heritage.'

p 23

Miscellaneous Letters, Articles, Messages:

Letters re Bishop's Fighting Fund to Clergy, Vestries and Synodsmen 1952

After outlining the three projects of the BFF – the Cathedral, Old People's Homes and Church Extension – he writes

"All these causes are not just worthy, they are essential. Napier has just had one of its biggest buildings taken over by the Totalisator Board for betting purposes. …Is it not more fitting that the biggest and most

Writings, Sermons & Addresses

beautiful building should be erected to the glory of the worship of Almighty God, and as a central Home for all the worshippers in the Diocesan Family Life?

...There is not a parish priest or Synodsman or Vestryman who is not daily in touch with cases of old people who urgently desire to spend their remaining days in a degree of comfort without the monotony and cramping conditions of "institutionalism."

SB 5B p 3

Letter to all parishes to be read aloud on Sunday 6 July 1952

We need a Cathedral to replace that which was destroyed by fire and earthquake. Our forebears gave of their substance to erect it, shall we be less generous in our impulse than they? Is it not a tragedy for parents to have no home in which to welcome their children? We desire to have a worthy Home where the children of God in this Diocese, may, I pray most earnestly, always feel that they are coming home.

We desire also to build Old People's Homes... We want old people to spend their declining years in an atmosphere of love and care, with no undue "institutionalism" to cause them any embarrassment. ...If when you pray "OUR FATHER, you mean it, you will yourself know no rest until you have done something to ease His burden, and in so doing, you will remove your own.

SB 5B p 4

Article in *Daily Telegraph* on re-building the Cathedral 25 August 1955

Two months before the Laying of the Foundation Stone:

...Here then is an opportunity which presents itself to all people of good will, to become instruments in the hands of God and to preserve their service bright, not allowing it to become dulled through selfishness.

There is still a disparity between the tender price and the funds at our disposal, and we sincerely trust that those who have this venture of faith at heart will not be slow to show their practical interest and support. It was said of one man that "he will give till it hurts but he is mighty sensitive to pain"! My own conviction is that love never reckons, and that people will respond generously to this opportunity afforded them of placing in the heart of our city, not merely a dignified and beautiful architectural exhibit, but a living challenge to the soul of man.

SB 6 p 183

A Likely Lad

Christmas Message to the Community 1956

At Christmas time it is customary for people to be particularly forgiving and understanding, but the spirit wears off as time passes. The challenge of Christmas is to make the Christmas attitude something permanent – not merely transitory. Every year, no matter how difficult and dangerous it has been, ends with Christmas, as if God Himself were speaking to man, and reminding him of the stuff of which he is really made. …indeed, Christmas is a time when God does speak, and the Word becomes flesh and dwells among us, and we call his name Jesus.

SB 6 p 164

On Lambeth Conference in *Church and People* July 1958

The Lambeth Conference must ever recognize that it follows most truly in the Apostolic Succession when in humility it strives to know the mind of Jesus, and then prays for grace to make their dreams come true. …Now a decade has passed. …The Lambeth Conference will be strengthened by the sure knowledge that though a thousand satellites circle the earth, that one little white star over Bethlehem will do more to change the course of history than a million red moons. There will issue from these deliberations a voluminous report and certainly an Encyclical

…There will be laid upon the mind and conscience of every member of the Communion a responsibility to rededicate themselves to the service of our common Master. If it is God's will to give us a Pentecostal blessing, let us not be blind to the fact that a Pentecostal power is given only for a Pentecostal task. It is never given to those who say, "Here am I, send someone else." We may not be able to go to Lambeth, but we all can go to Calvary.

"Let us just do that very thing, and seek afresh the secret, the open secret, of our power. We may be limited as to what we can take out of the country, but we are not limited as to what we put into the country."

SB 7 p 14

NCC Christmas Appeal September 1958

Written as Senior Bishop

When we remember the salient facts of the brochure which accompanies this request. …we are forced to recognize the significance of the results of a generous appeal. Over 250,000,000 people live within 24 hours' journey of our country. …100,000 people in Hong Kong

Writings, Sermons & Addresses

have no home but the pavements. ...At Christmas, when we think of Another who had not where to lay His head, we must remember with humility and shame the countless people who are one with Him in this respect.

May I humbly and sincerely suggest that we first of all make our hearts a home for the little Christ Child, and then, in the midst of our plenty, reach out to provide for some of those of whom He said "Inasmuch as ye have done it unto one of these, ye have done it unto Me."

SB 7 p 63

NCC Christmas Appeal 1961

...Yet again it is given to me to invite the Churches of our Province to assist in the Inter-Church Aid Christmas Appeal... The Appeal is entitled "For the People next Door" and more especial emphasis is laid on the peoples of Indonesia.

To the best of my knowledge, the "people next door" did not afford succour to some who had perforce to be content with a stable in an Inn. In memory of the Babe of Bethlehem, can we show our gratitude by providing for thousands, who, like Him, have not where to lay their heads?

It is my earnest hope that together we shall accept the opportunity afforded us to exhibit our love for our Saviour by fulfilling His command to feed His lambs.

SB 5 p 119

Christmas Column *Daily Telegraph* 24 December 1961

...In a world where most countries are implicated in "wars" in varying degrees of "heat" or cold, there appears to be more need than ever to plead for the following in the steps of the little Prince of Peace.

To enlist in His "forces" does not meant the abandonment of virility and courage, but calls for an accession of strength, worthily to exhibit the eternal qualities of faith, hope, and love, with the Christmas reminder that the greatest of these is Love.

SB 5 p 122

Letter to be read in churches 1 April 1962

...Jesus gave Himself absolutely and utterly, and we are His faithful followers, (not just admirers) when we walk in those steps which lead to a throne, but only through a cross. If we desire His work to continue, we must be willing to try to match His sacrifice.

A Likely Lad

> At our last Synod, the Diocesan representatives, including your own, set a budget of £37,500 to do God's work in this Diocese. *(He outlines budget items.)* Of this sum, of just over £37,000, as I write, only £13,834 has been contributed and the financial year ends on 30 June. ... It is imperative that the most urgent attention be given to this matter. All vestries have received a letter signed by me, asking them to regard this question as one of urgency and deep significance for our whole future work.
>
> It has already been my privilege for fifteen years to serve in this Diocese and I have learned to love it and be proud of it. We have never flinched from responsibility and I believe that now that you know the nature of our difficulty, you will respond at once, and ensure that the necessary funds are forthcoming.
>
> For myself it will prove to be a miserable Easter, and much of its joy will disappear, if I have to face my risen Lord knowing that you and I together have not risen to His needs.
>
> Today is Mothering Sunday, and I appeal to you with all my love and strength, to give the word reality, and see that Mother Church is provided for her "housekeeping."
>
> May God bless you as you humbly ask God what it is He requires of you, and thank Him for what He has done for you.
>
> SB 5 p 192

"The Religion of the Plus" *Sunday Times* 25 July 1965

> ...Jesus is the Saviour of mankind and His cross is always the plus sign, there is always abundance with Him. ...Those who seek "treasure" are poverty-stricken unless he is in their treasure because their lives lack a quality.
>
> ...A man may build a most expensive house with every modern labour-saving gadget, he may have wall-to-wall carpets, washing machines, pop-up toasters, TV, radio, electric toothbrushes and a multiplicity of things to ease his physical burden or pamper his vanity, but he may still occupy only a palatial pigsty, since he has not built a HOME.
>
> ...You cannot judge a chicken by the parsley on the dish.
>
> ...The religion of Jesus Christ, the religion of the plus, will add to the material acquisitions a quality, and convert them into a veritable sacrament.
>
> SB 11 p 62

Christmas Message to the Nation *Daily Telegraph* 1968

An American Indian, having taken stock of the world situation following the last war was reported to have said: "They all smoked the pipe of peace, but I don't think any of them inhaled." We look at a world with its misery, frustration, want and fear, and as Christians we are bold to say that in deed and in truth a little Child can lead them.

Amidst the plethora of gifts which will be given from diverse motives this Christmas, there will remain one gift unalloyed: The Lord that came down at Christmas, and still comes to those who are willing to open up.

We make a gift, we give ourselves. The Christmas cult is ephemeral, the Christmas spirit is lasting and effective. In wishing readers a Happy Christmas, my prayer is that they will acknowledge gratefully the opportunity of making the spirit of the day, the opportunity of all days. May He whose love is as old as the hills, yet new every morning, give freely that peace which the world cannot give and cannot take away.

SB 13 p 53

NCC Christmas Appeal 1 October 1969

Reference to Christmas brings to the minds of the vast majority of people of most faiths and none, the idea of a child.

To the Christian, God, born in a manger and dying on a cross, gives them to think furiously and to enlarge their ideas of the nature and purpose of life. A little child is a symbol of humility, trust, purity and latent possibilities. The little Christ child knows our needs and provides resources. Never having owned a home, he bids us care for the homeless; having hungered he bids us share our food; having suffered he bids us feel deeply the agonies of a torn world. Having plied an honourable and worthy trade He bids us encourage those who would learn.

The Inter-church Aid Christmas appeal is not made primarily by the churches but by the Lord of the Churches whom they so imperfectly obey. The hungry fed, the homeless reinstated, the suffering of masses assuaged, the capacity for productive work encouraged and assisted, young people's enthusiasm God-centred, these are part-realised goals of Inter-Church Aid. The aim of the Christmas Appeal is that these efforts may be intensified through your willing help.

It is my earnest hope that all Anglicans will respond generously to what is literally a "crying" need.

SB 13 p145

A Likely Lad

Whitsunday *Daily Telegraph* 9 June 1973

Whitsunday is a reminder that God is always eager to fill our hearts and lives with abundant joy and peace. Some time ago an advertisement appeared from a widow who expressed a desire to meet a gentleman view friendship. "Has good sense of humour and enjoys drinking, not religious." Which reminded me of a servant who was sent to meet a visiting bishop at a railway station. The servant approached a tall angular man with a red nose and ascetic features and asked "Excuse me but are you the bishop of...? "No" responded the person addressed. "It's indigestion that makes me look like this." Which reminds us with force that "I am come that ye may have life and have it more abundantly." Christians should ever be responsive to the guidings of the Holy Spirit, but they must be as sure as is humanly possible that it is the Spirit to whom they are listening. All too frequently it has been known for people to claim the promptings of the Spirit to bolster up their own predilections, which are patently at variance with Divine wisdom. The Spirit will assist us to change for something better. I am of the opinion that He will not encourage us to change simply because a thing is different.

Let us hope and pray that the Spirit will be heard as discussions rage over changes which have been mooted in liturgy. Are we to hear our Lord's Prayer begin, Solo Parent, who art in heaven...' to mollify the whims of those who apparently consider that Jesus should have foreseen difficulty with the beginning of His prayer for us?

People frequently refer to New Zealand as God's Own Country, so if that be true, let us do something for its Owner and acknowledge His Spirit as our way of life.

"Today if you will hear his voice, harden not your hearts." Do not say, there's no hurry. I've heard of eleventh-hour conversions. How do you know that you will not die at 10.30? Whitsun reminding us of the outpouring of God's Holy Spirit, calls for a total offering of one's self and of all one's gifts to God, and that it should never be true that the only time we mention God is when we have a flat tyre. So live close to the Giver that others will not only hear the good news, but they will see it, in us. We are told that there are millions of Christians in the world and sometimes God must wonder where they are all hiding.

Archbishops and bookies are both alike in one respect, they are both looking for the outsider to come home!

Whitsuntide could be the main chance for you and me. Shall we take it?

SB 15 p 79

Thought for the Week *Daily Telegraph* 22 March 1975

The Cross was never meant to be so mystified and intellectualized as to be unintelligible to simple folk. Enough light always shines forth from the cross for simple folk to walk in and rejoice.

INRI Jesus of Nazareth, King of the Jews, was inscribed in Hebrew, Greek, and Latin, over the head of the Crucified, and we would do well so to fix our gaze upon those significant letters that in the intensity of our gaze they become transmogrified and our souls are seared with letters more commonly in use, RSVP.

SB 15 p 85

Dead Men Do tell Tales *Daily Telegraph* 29 March 1975

...Love is indestructible and will and must proclaim its "tale" through time and through eternity. "Dead" men do tell tales to our lasting benefit.

The first tale that love in the form of Jesus Christ tells is that, though a man may aver he could not care less, God always shows that He could not care more.

With every butterfly a living advertisement of resurrection, we are faced with the opportunity to accept the responsibility of living the resurrection life. On one occasion my dear friend Frederick Bennett was attending a conference in England, he found himself constantly referred to as "our coloured brother." When it was Bishop Bennett's turn to speak, he began his speech, "Your Grace, colourless brethren..." Easter, which should be such a time of exuberant joy, can be sad if we are content to be colourless brethren instead of vibrant followers of a risen and joyful Redeemer.

SB 15 p 89

Thought for the Week *Daily Telegraph* 23 October 1976

...There appears to be a constant obsession to change as much as possible, sometimes regardless of consequences. Why will people not remember that to change is easy, to improve is more difficult?

Change there must be, otherwise we would still be eating nothing but cold foods, and we would still be carrying everything on our backs since fire and wheels would be unknown. To change merely for the sake of change is obnoxious; change should be effected only for improvement, and I think that this is at the heart of "Behold, I make all things new."

A Likely Lad

Those of us who are older can recall many changes during our lifetimes and we regret some and welcome others. There seems to be more brashness about life than there was and a greater desire for recognition of service. No one knows the name of the Good Samaritan, but nowadays the news media carry photographs of donors holding or pointing to their gifts to the community.

…Modesty and humility (not of the Uriah Heap type) are still endearing qualities but are not calculated to ensure advancement to top executive posts with certainty. Jesus said He made all things new, in other words both changed and improved simultaneously with the end result a changed and worthier existence.

We are bombarded with advertisements that this and that gadget will make life easier. Jesus did not come to make life easier; He came to make men great. Of course, we can resemble the man who craves naught but to be left alone.

…The symbol of the Christian faith is a cross, not an electric blanket, and that is disturbing enough in all conscience.

SB 15 p 93

Thought for Every Day *Daily Telegraph* **24 December 1976**

The stench of animals and a crude manger spelt the world's danger and its hope. Its danger because the world would endeavour to use its restrictive swaddling bands of opposition or "couldn't care less" to make the little Christ child a cocoon of impotence. Its hope because He would free Himself and proclaim freedom to all captives of thought and deed.

The tiny baby hands outstretched to plead a mother's instant attention were later nailed in that outstretched position signifying His desire to embrace all men in its love.

…It was said of a great man that his entry into any company was like bringing a lighted candle into a darkened room, and He who was born in the dark and died in the dark was nevertheless the Light of the world and illumined the darkness.

Politicians are continually telling us that given good will, this and that will become possible. It would appear that good will is in short supply. It is not just peace on earth to men of good will, but also good will on earth to men of peace, and peace is not just the absence of war. There is peace, God's peace, which men can neither give nor take away.

SB 15 p 90

When the Boat Comes In *Daily Telegraph* 4 June 1977

...Will you be content when your boat comes in? What will life have meant for you and for those you have influenced?

...Trinity Sunday pronouncing the grace of our Lord Jesus Christ and the love of God and the fellowship of the Holy Spirit surely demands a significant response. But as we view the world with its frustrations we wonder if the child was essentially wrong when she prayed, "And Jesus don't come back yet, 'cos they'll do it to you again."

This season affords us the brilliant opportunity to prove that we do not regard God as a clerk in the Samaritans for us to contact on the "hot line" when we are in trouble, but as Father in its truest connotation. Yet again, will you be content when your boat comes in?

And a final word to others who like me are advancing in years – $10 notes are still of value even if they are wrinkled!

SB 15 p 93

Christmas Column *Daily Telegraph* 23 December 1978

"Cherish the Thought."

A world-wide desire is for stability, and our resolution could well be that the best way to achieve this stability is through that tiny little stable in Bethlehem where real stability was born, and the Light of the world pierced the darkness of night. Jesus was the most beautiful thought that God ever had, and we have the inestimable opportunity of cherishing the Thought and allowing the spirit of that supreme event to become our daily attitude to life.

...Christmas then is a tonic, especially for those who bemoan "what is the world coming to?" For it answers the question with the reply that the emphasis is not on what is the world coming to, but rather what is coming into the world.

To all with open minds there may come peace, the gladness of Christmas; joy, the spirit of Christmas; and love, the very heart of Christmas and God himself.

The Son of God became the Son of Man that the sons of men might become the sons of God. Christmas is an excellent time to accept the proffered opportunity and to ensure a really happy Christmas.

SB 15 p 96

A Likely Lad

Christmas: A Day to Remember *Daily Telegraph* 24 December 1979

Behold, what a gorgeous lily with its colour and exquisite form to delight the eye. But let your gaze wander down to the earth from which the lily rises and behold the dung.

We sing "In the beauty of the lilies Christ was born across the sea." But He was born in much less exotic surroundings, with animals for His spectators and their odour His incense.

God so loved the world that He gave, and Jesus is whom He gave.

> "Because the Eternal infinite,
> Was once that naked little mite,
> Because, O Love, of Christmas night,
> I thank my God."

The humility so redolent in this simple narrative is indeed remote from much of the life of our own day. Those who cling so desperately to the half-truth of so-called progress should beware that they do not hold onto the wrong half.

The prevalence of the "self-made man" is alarming, for as one has said, he is an excellent example of unskilled labour. Who was it who remarked that "despite inflation, a penny for some people's thoughts is still a fair price?"

This year there are fewer Christmas cards being exchanged, partly on account of increased postage charges and increased charges for the cards themselves, and also some people are giving to a charitable object what they would have spent on cards. But an interesting Christmas card would be a picture of the Babe of Bethlehem in all His poverty and glory, and underneath the picture the simple inscription RSVP.

As we prepare to face Christmas with its eternal challenges, we agree with the person who said that some open minds should be closed for repairs. It is so easy to be inoculated with a mild dose of Christianity that it makes us immune from the real thing.

Our response to the Gospel – yes, gospel, for it is essentially good news – should be a total commitment to the lifestyle of which it is the mould. Honest men and women frequently say with real integrity that they do not consider themselves worthy, but it would be worth their while to recall that the Church is the only fellowship in the wide world where the unworthiness of the intending member is the qualification to membership.

It is a frequent observation that the essence of the Christmas experience does not work in our world and I recall that more than 50 years ago a keen observer of human nature remarked with a degree of perspicacity that the trouble with Christianity is not that it does not work but that it has not been tried.

The prodigal son called on his father to "give me," but after his excursion with the swine and the harlots he came to his senses and asked his father to "make me."

Christmas gives us, then proceeds to make us.

We all are saddened by the growth of unemployment but there is no necessity for the scourge to attract Christians. There are already too many Christian people unemployed in the works which are the essence of Christianity.

...Even the worst year ends with a Christmas, an opportunity for the birth of new resolves, new generosity, new forgiveness, renewed humility and loving care.

The Son of God became the Son of Man so that the sons of men might become the sons of God. If we have the courage to accept this opportunity then we shall indeed have happy Christmas, for this is what we wish for our readers.

SB 15 p 98

Christmas Column 24 December 1980
"Have a Nice Day"

...An honest appraisal of our inner selves and a weighing of our true recognition of eternal values is a worthwhile exercise, but it can be disconcerting. In the early days in Africa, when a missionary died, the native people would place a chalice on his grave. I was told that when an immigrant who was well known to the local populace died, the Africans placed a bottle of whisky and a box of cigars on his grave. I presumed that this was on the principle that "where your treasure…"

Christmas affords us an opportunity for self-determination, a chance to ask ourselves with painful honesty just what the festival signifies for us; whether it is a holy day or just a holiday.

...It is right to celebrate this wonderful birthday, especially if we remember that the best spirit of Christmas does not come out of a bottle.

Well do I recall a little child in the Old Country many many years ago who was dreadfully afraid of the dark. His mother put him down to bed and put out the light as she left the room, saying, "Don't fear; the angels are with you." The child called out "But mother, I want a flesh face." That is precisely what Christmas supplies. "The Word became flesh and dwelt among us" and we can still triumphantly exclaim, "and still does so."

...Increasingly, almost to the point of being a habit, we are bidden to "Have a nice day." "Nice" according to the Oxford dictionary means "delicately sensitive" and so this journal wishes its readers a nice day, hoping they all will be delicately sensitive of the day's significance, and mindful of the millions envisaged when we say, 'OUR Father.'

SB 15 p 102

Buy Milk Without Money *Daily Telegraph* 1 August 1981

...Our kindness should come straight from the heart of Christ: "God so loved the world..." If we would know the significance of 'so' we must look hard at the Cross.

I recall passing a house many years ago when the milkman was pouring out a blue watery liquid into a jug at a front door, and hoping, I presume, to distract the attention of the purchaser from the quality of the product, said "It looks like rain Ma." The hawk-like eye of the purchaser had missed nothing and she promptly replied "Aye, an' it tastes like it too."

Let our "human kindness" be the real thing given undiluted and with true willingness, unaffected by grudging thought.

...One of the most moving incidents allied to milk that it has been my good fortune to learn, occurred many years ago in a city I know full well. Children were playing in a street and a runaway horse knocked over a child and broke her leg. An ambulance took the child to the city hospitals and after the surgeon had done his work, the nursing sister of the children's ward went to the child and took her a glass of milk. The child lived in abject poverty and in her home, there was no glass, but a cup was part-filled with milk watered down and passed from child to child. Each child knew full well exactly how far down to drink! When the sister gave the glass to the child she looked up in bewilderment and asked, "How far down can I drink?" These poignant words have lingered in my mind for over half a century and every time I think of them, they constitute a challenge to my own limited service of one whom I call Master.

I think of Him who said "Can ye drink of the cup that I shall drink of?" and I wonder how far down I can drink. Do you?

SB 15 p 103

"Make the Most of your Minute" *Daily Telegraph* 30 October 1982

He quotes from John Masefield's play The Trial of Jesus where Mary is given a minute to say goodbye to her son.

In these days of change it is of supreme importance that all of us should jealously guard our opportunities of decision.

In church notices it used to be D.V. – God willing, but this has largely been substituted by W.P. (weather permitting). Wedding rings used to be substantial because they would be in use for many years. The Holy Sabbath became Sunday and has degenerated into "the weekend."

…Jesus said, "He that hath seen me has seen the Father." Is it possible for us to say with sincerity "He that has seen me has seen something of Jesus?" Let us remember that Jesus never asked for admirers, only followers, and that he does not call those who think themselves fit but fits those whom he calls.

In our day men and women do not want just to hear the gospel, they want to see it. In a poor parish where I served, I remember calling at a home one evening and the children were doing their homework. The youngest boy aged about 3, was lying on the floor with some scrap of paper and a stub of a pencil. His mother asked him what he was drawing, and he replied, "I'm drawing God." His mother was pleased that he should add this touch of religion during my visit but said "But George, no one knows what God is like," and out of the mouth of babes came the reply "They will when I finish this."

Can we then make valiant use of our minutes and leave no doubt that many people are to have more than a vague idea of what God is like, and we must do this with modesty and strength, unlike the man who boasts that he is a self-made man and reveals obvious traces of having run out of material.

It is thought that about one billion people on earth have not heard the good news of Jesus Christ, and for us to say that we have a nice enthusiasm is totally inadequate. Let us remember that salvation is free but is bought with a price.

Two ex-servicemen were talking about old times and one said to the other "I remember knowing Monty," his friend said, "Did you know Monty?" "Yes," replied the first man. "To speak to?" queried the friend.

The gospel implies a personal relationship, and the more this is cultivated the more efficacious will be our witness.

The making of the finest use of our minutes involves us in utter sincerity … Our witness must be transparently honest, and dare we ask ourselves, "If you were the last Christian in the world, would Christianity survive?"

Please God it would.

SB 15 p 103

Fit for What? *Daily Telegraph* September 1984

...After viewing a surfeit of athletes, I recalled in a moment of reflection, an incident in which a boisterous athlete asked a quiet poet, "How do you keep fit?" The poet's response was worthy of consideration for he replied, "Fit for what?"

For a professing Christian the aim is to keep fit to be a worthy representative of a God and Father of infinite grace and love.

I use the word Father deliberately, realising that some find it objectionable. I do not. However I remember that when taking a Confirmation class 58 years ago I was talking with some feeling about God our Father and His love, and after the lesson a little girl came up to me and said "When you said God is our father, vicar, you don't mean He's like my father do you?" I knew well the condition of the home from which the child came and assured her that I certainly did not mean that, for her father was not worthy of the name; he was only a male necessity for the birth of a child.

...There is so much avarice in the world today that people ought to remember that shrouds have no pockets.

And sometimes we are despondent and wonder if our puny efforts can achieve any lasting result. At times like these it would be well to remember that if there were only one grain of wheat left in the whole world, and that were sown, and matured, and then those resulting grains were sown with full maturity, and this exercise were to be repeated and repeated with perfect success, the earth would be replenished in 15 years!

Have we ever seriously applied such a thought to the evangelization of the world? And if we have done so, have we ever committed ourselves to its implementation?

The explorer spoke in Christian terms when he said " I will go anywhere so long as it is forward." And this requires continuing dedication. It is useless to say "Our Father" on Sunday and then live the rest of the week as if you were an orphan.

...Another point about this adventure in faith is that it is a corporate adventure. I remember being told by the clerk of works building

Writings, Sermons & Addresses

Liverpool Cathedral, that vast edifice, that a labourer came into his office and requested to see the plans, saying "I'd love to know what I am trying to help build."

We are fellow labourers with God and His plans are crystal clear. Committing ourselves unreservedly to this adventure is a soul-absorbing experience, and one from which there is no return nor weakness in avowing our aim like the man in the amphitheatre with others when the lions were let loose, who looked fearfully at the lions and said "Me atheist."

…One of the humblest men I have ever known was my lay reader in our first parish. He used to walk to and from Church in all weathers for he did not approve of Sunday transport. He studied the Lessons during the week and asked me about words and names which could cause trouble. One Sunday after the evening service we were talking together and he said "I wish I had had the chance of a good education," and then came words that are engraved in my soul, "I have never been to Cambridge but I *have* been to Calvary." It is a good place to go if you can meet the challenge.

SB 15 p 104

The Spoken Word: Extracts from Sermons, Speeches, Addresses

To Hastings Rotary (Holy Week) March 1948

"We all have our own view on what is right, what is true, what is lasting and what is good, and while I have no desire to offend the feelings of any of you, I do feel that there is a comparison between the season in which we are living and the conditions of the world today – a close relationship between Lent and a crucified world. Rotary has a big part to play in the solution of the world's problems. A crucified world, if it has any sense, will turn to a crucified Lord, if it wishes to discover the secret of the Resurrection, and Rotary, if it will, can give a lead.

…We have it in our power to grasp the vision and the opportunity to recreate that men throughout the history of the world have never known before, but I am reminded of George Bernard Shaw's remark that "Rotary is a lunch." I have been a member of Rotary clubs for some years and I know there is sufficient truth in that remark to provide a sting… Here is the chance for those people who have the answer. We have the answer – let us proclaim it. What is the answer? There are some who say it is education, but education for what? Education

A Likely Lad

in itself is not the answer. I say plainly – and I make no apology for saying it – it is education for life here and hereafter."

SB 1 p 112

Prizegiving Hastings High School December 1948

…"I want to put the challenge into your hearts – the challenge that you go out and put into practice the traditions of your school, to make a tired world grow young again and bring sunshine into shady places. …Of course, you of your generation may say that people of my generation are not much good to give you advice, seeing that we have made such a mess of things, with two world wars. That is true but people of my age feel a sense of responsibility and, with a degree of hesitation, we tell you young people how to live. Yes, if you follow the ideals learned here, you can make an unparalleled contribution to a world in which so many people know the price of everything and the value of nothing."

SB 2 p 61

At George VI Memorial Service: 15 February 1952

…"Our hearts are at half-mast … A crown has been laid down, and a gift of life has been exchanged for it. The Donor wears Himself a crown of simple fashion – the precious stones are rubies, drops of blood on thorns of wood. …The King, from his home in Sandringham with its many rooms, has passed to another home of 'many mansions,' to prove again that home life is life at its best. …It is said that an ancient king was daily awakened by a servant who said, 'Master, awake, and consider why thou art set on the throne.' Our King, through his prayers had often considered well, and the life, for which today we thank God, was the result of such contemplation. In a broadcast the King quoted a hitherto little-known poem 'Put your hand into the hand of God.' He took his own advice and the King became a subject to the King of Love. So, do we give thanks to God for a great and good King, a great ruler, because he was a great servant."

SB 5B p 16

Queen Mary's Memorial Service: 27 March 1953

The Bishop recalled the times he had seen Queen Mary before continuing

…"Like another and greater Mary she has stood at the foot of the Cross and wept – in the Winter of 1928 at the King's illness, in 1936 at his death. Then as though the cup of her sorrow was not already full, she saw her eldest son abdicate, then the death of the Duke of Kent and recently the death of her son George VI. The open secret of her life was her insistence on the power of prayer. Both she and the King liked the National Anthem sung kneeling, like a prayer.

SB 5B p 68

To Napier Rotary Christmas 1953

Bishop Lesser said the emphasis of his message was on youth – "eight pounds of humanity, more dynamic, more explosive than any hydrogen bomb. The chief difference is that the little bundle of humanity, cuddled in the loving arms of His mother, was creative…"
"It is a simple story, the story of Christmas. It is a story of a despised province on the edge of a mighty empire. In a stable in a small town, a young peasant girl gave birth to a baby – that is Christmas. We call it the Incarnation. A lot of people say they don't like theology; they don't like technical words. You won't throw away your radio simply because you don't understand its technical parts; you won't throw away your car because you don't understand the working of the differential. If you are keen you will learn. I suggest you should learn what the technical words of religion mean. It is worth it. It is important.

Christmas is just this; it's God showing us what He is like, showing us how humble He is." "…We are living in a 'gimme' age – gimme this, gimme that. Christmas is not 'gimme'; it is a self-giving. …If we are living simply for what we can get out of life, we are missing the whole point of life. When someone looks at a boy and then at his father and says, 'Isn't he like his father?' what man on earth would not swell up with pride? Don't you think God wants to hear that?"

SB 6 p 25

Easter Day Sermon: Cathedral 1954

…"Easter is the constant reminder that eternal life is not just life beyond the grave but life in God here and now. …Easter competitions are going on here in Napier now; they went on on Good Friday, unfortunately. I say unfortunately because the greatest competition of all time occurred on Good Friday, and it took three days, and Jesus won. Christ is risen! Alleluia! There was abundant evidence of a dynamic, explosive Christian life. The common people of the world are gravely disturbed by the world trends with the coming of the H-bomb – the hydrogen bomb. If it were called by another name beginning with the same letter it would be a more accurate description. When the hell bomb is a relic of an underground museum in a race of troglodytes, the Christ will still shatter the tombs and rise in the hearts of men. His resurrection life in ordinary people is the only answer to the hell bomb and its like. There was much talk of the bomb and explosions and then we had the worst electrical storm in living memory in Hawke's Bay. This storm put the bomb in its true perspective – just a damp squib by comparison. God always has the last word, because He is the Word, made flesh, and the King of hearts is always the Ace of trumps, and let men remember!

…Jesus never said goodbye. You have no need to do so if you are not going away."

SB 6 p 37

Prizegiving Napier Boys' High School December 1954

…"Strive always to be like a good watch. Have an open face, busy hands, be of pure gold, well-balanced and full of good works." … Education is essentially a drawing-out process rather than a pumping in one." "It is more important to learn to live than how to earn a living; and more important to learn a trade than to learn the tricks of the trade.

"Some of our young people are thrust out into a world which must bewilder them. They find places in a highly complex social structure, in cities which resemble jungles without trees, a world of jargon where a coffin is an 'eternity casket', a rat catcher a 'rodent operator' and I suppose a Bishop an 'eternity pointer.' "…Only by the application of the principles of sound education can our young people hope to stand up to the effects of the present-day world. In addition to these difficulties, there is the heresy of the age, the cult of the high standard of living to which capitalists and communists alike join to pay allegiance. True education must teach people that the best things in the world are free, and that money cannot buy them. All God's best gifts are so constituted that avaricious men cannot corner them."

SB 6 p 80

Laying of Foundation Stone of Cathedral 15 October 1955

"The foundation stone is a promise to God; it is a promise to ourselves and to generations yet unborn. In this process of re-building a city today marks a climax. No longer is the city without promise of a cathedral, no longer is the frame to be without a picture. We hope to be able to press forward with the first section of the cathedral,

Writings, Sermons & Addresses

and it is public munificence that will determine how soon the entire structure may nobly bear witness to our common faith and heritage. Many people who leave religion till the eleventh hour die at 10.45. Be thoughtful. Be generous. It is later than you think. Don't count your days – weigh them.

When the Queen visited our country, one or two people were honoured by being allowed to place a home at her Majesty's disposal, and deeply they appreciated the signal honour conferred on them. Today this privilege is extended to all of us. We can see that a beautiful Home is prepared for the King of Kings, that it may be fitting for One whose House had many mansions."

The Bishop pointed out the significance of the stone being laid half on the new piece of land, and half on the old.

"The spiritual significance of this alignment of the stone is that we are grateful to the past and hopeful of the future. We recognize with due humility that it is given to us, not only to receive traditions, but to make them. In the same spirit we earnestly desire to build spiritually and materially."

He quoted from a US information pamphlet 'Atomic Power for Peace.'

'Power – the greatest ever known on earth – man now holds in his hands to use as he will: a force so great it can change the world…'

Bishop Lesser reminded his hearers of the danger of this power which could only be handled behind walls of lead, and continued…

"If we are humble enough and sincere enough, we shall build here a real power house, and not of this diocese alone; and no longer shall a world languish in fear and frustration because material advance and mechanics have outstripped spiritual growth and peace. Can we enlist men and women of high courage and noble resolve to give themselves utterly to the highest endeavour? Can we scale not only an Everest but a Mount of Transfiguration? The River Jordan rises in the Mount of Transfiguration and ends in the Dead Sea. May God grant that our high resolve and fixed intention may never end in a dead sea of failure, but let us say, with those who cannot come and yet are here, what David Livingstone said: "I will go anywhere so long as it is forward."

SB 6 p 119

St Paul's Wairoa, 75th Anniversary 8 December 1955

…"A common question addressed to men and women, particularly to women, at this time is, 'Are you ready for Christmas?' And this is

A Likely Lad

almost universally regarded as an enquiry as to whether we have the turkey in the 'works' or whether we have made adequate preparation for the Christmas dinner and festivities in general. It should mean for Christian people, is Advent a reality in your life, are you getting ready for His birthday? It seems a strange thing to prepare for a birthday party, and then not to have as the central figure, the Person Whose birthday it is!

We hear a great deal of talk about Iron Curtains, but we Christian people have our own make. There are plenty of Iron Curtains of suspicion and envy and hearty dislike, which we lift for one day, Christmas Day, and then restore on the following, not to be lifted again for a year. This is a tacit admission that we know what is right, but the price is too high, and we want a high living standard in all things, except those that count most!

… Let us therefore thank God for what He has enabled us to do with Him, and for Him, and pray for grace to go forward daringly, that we may echo Geoffrey Studdert Kennedy's poem and say,

> "We shall build on! We shall build on!
> On through the cynic's scorning
> On through the coward's warning
> On through the cheat's suborning
> We shall build on!
>
> Firm on the Rock of Ages
> City of saints and sages
> Laugh while the tempest rages
> We shall build on!
>
> Christ though my hands be bleeding,
> Fierce though my flesh be pleading,
> Still let me see Thee leading,
> Let me build on!
>
> Till through death's cruel dealing,
> Brain wrecked and reason reeling
> I hear Love's trumpet pealing,
> And I pass on!"

SB 6 p 80

Christmas Message to Napier Rotary 1955

"Our Carols by Candlelight can be – and have been for many – a very inspiring spiritual experience. But it could of course degenerate merely into an exhibition of sentimentalism. It need not, and I hope it will not. At our Carols by Candlelight this year, let us light two candles – one by which to read the carols and the other in our hearts to lighten the world.

...We have been told that never has our country been so rich. And yet never before has a government felt compelled to produce a series of pamphlets to tell parents and teachers how to do their own job of bringing up our children. The reason is that we have forgotten Christmas. We are poverty-stricken in those things money can't buy. We hear a good deal at present about putting Christ back into Christmas. I must confess I do not like that phrase, but Christmas without Christ is meaningless."

SB 6 p 156

Dedication of Waiapu House 4 February 1957

..."Today it has been my privilege to dedicate a building which we trust and pray may be transmuted by the alchemy of love into a home.

We intend that this shall be a home in the true sense of the word."

..."The easiest thing to do is to erect the dry bones; the most difficult is to breathe into them the breath of life."

SB 6 p 198

Funeral of Archdeacon Brocklehurst 26 July 1957

Bishop Lesser said that Brocklehurst had left instructions that this address should not be about him personally.

..."I am sure that we would all agree that fulsome recognition at a time like this would be nauseating to a degree. Nevertheless, I cannot but make some reference to a man of such worth. To him the Cross was never a burden to be borne, any more than are wings to a bird or sails to a ship."

The Archdeacon had served at times of great disability, but the legacy he handed on to his friends

"was a flaming faith in the eternity of Christian love." "...He had asked especially that this address of mine should lay a special emphasis on the surety of eternal life. When he quoted 'I know that my Redeemer liveth' it was a battle cry, and at the end he shared the wartime desire of a great statesman in exile: 'I want to go home.'"

SB 7 p 3

A Likely Lad

Thanksgiving Service for Centennial of Hawke's Bay Province 1958.
"Man cannot live by bread alone, even if it is overlaid with a thick smear of Social Security jam." "...This service is not just the parsley on the dish to garnish the real thing. This IS the real thing, and the focal point of the total observance." "...For a complete dedication we need God, for we all know in our hearts that a City Council can get a man out of a slum, but only God can get the slum out of a man."

SB 7 p 27

New Year Sermon in Cathedral 31 Dec 1959
"Before we cross the threshold of the New Year, we could with profit, emulate many of our business friends who are busily engaged in stocktaking. Humbly we face the unknown – we do not know what waits for us round the door – for He said, 'I am the Door,' and thus in confidence we go forward. As the clock nibbles at eternity, we will humbly prepare for it."

SB 7 p 147

Dedication of First Part of Cathedral 24 February 1960
..."The work and devotion of years in tangible form was destroyed in seconds. The havoc wreaked by earthquake was intensified by conflagration, but on this occasion the Lord was in the earthquake for He gave comfort and inspiration and hope. He who is always the resurrection has stirred our imagination and rocked our hearts by the cataclysmic force of love. We have felt that for too long we have allowed Him to dwell in the transit camp. The Diocese finally decided to accept the challenge to rebuild a worthy home of God's worship and praise. Ancient and modern assumed a new significance for us as we saw the sanctuary and choir, the memorial chapel in memory of Bishop Bennett and Sir Apirana Ngata dwarfed by the contemporary church building which held such precious memories."

..."We felt we must bridge the gap that separated old and new. Auckland was to pay some six and a half million pounds for a worthy bridge, and we asked ourselves what we were prepared to pay for a bridge to God.

...Let us know no rest until we dedicate our lives with our Cathedral to the Master Builder and Carpenter of Nazareth, praying the while that He may see in us a reflection of His own beauty... And as we give humble and hearty thanks for this great moment in the life of our Diocese, we offer to Him ourselves, 'our souls and bodies,' dedicated

Writings, Sermons & Addresses

anew, praying the while 'God, give us work to the end of our strength and strength to the end of our work' for we would build on."

SB 7 p 155

Consecration of Memorial Chapel at Hereworth School 5 November 1960

Bishop Lesser suggested that if less money had been spent on fireworks before the Second World War, and more on Christian missionary work, the world might have been spared the catastrophe of the war.

"£1 million a year was spent on fireworks in Britain before the War. A few years later, £15 million a day was spent on the War. £1 million was spent each year before the war on missionary endeavour. Had these figures been different, we might have been spared so much!" ...He reminded listeners it was Guy Fawkes day, and said the early Christians were accused of blowing up the world "but these early Christians were creative, not destructive. ...There were lots of people who admired Christianity, but it was the practice of it that was needed."

SB 7 p 229

Funeral of Archbishop Owen 27 February 1961

..."As one has said, some bishops are more like fathers-in-law than Fathers in God but there are many priests in the Wellington Diocese and beyond its boundaries whose spiritual life had been deepened by the Archbishop's counsel and advice.

..."One who was accustomed with vigour and skill to race on the river at Oxford, has found Christ walking on the waters in blessing. One who for so many years served as headmaster teaching by word and example now sits at the feet of the Great Teacher to learn more of the inexhaustible love of God. One who acted with such conspicuous success as a chief shepherd and pastor is now with the Good Shepherd to be guided into the paths of His peace."

SB 5 p 37

CEMS Service in Cathedral 14 March 1961

"If our life is God-centred we will seek to give freely of all that has been entrusted to us. I know that we require £75,000 to complete this cathedral and have it consecrated to the worship of Almighty God, given to Him as a gift, not as a lay-by object."

A Likely Lad

> He spoke of the turnover in football pools and gambling in England and said,
>
> "What must He who has given us all things richly to enjoy think of what we give according to our meanness instead of according to our means?"
>
> SB 5 p 23

Dedication of Memorial Windows in Cathedral 20 March 1961

> …"We live in an age of colour and one of the purposes of stained glass windows is to provide colour and warmth for all worshippers, even on the dullest day; in other words, to provide something of the beauty and light of God Himself."
>
> "Art is, in fact, man's applause to the glory of God. We must encourage men to recognize what the philosophers know to be true, namely that the spiritual life depends upon the three ultimate values: beauty, goodness and truth. The artist must understand that beauty is not the only spiritual value. The religious man must understand that goodness is not the only spiritual value. The scientist must understand that there are two other spiritual values besides truth. …Thus beauty, goodness and truth are a trinity of power.
>
> So may these windows encourage our love for beauty, inspire us to goodness and lead us to Him who as well as being the Way and the Life, is also the Truth."
>
> SB 5 p 25

Funeral of Bishop Simkin Auckland 11 July 1967

> "…The Cross for Bishop Simkin was no burden, any more than wings are to a bird, or sails are to a ship. It was his inspiration, and this did not detract from his brilliant exercises in Canon Law and administrative artistry, but on the contrary provided the spring of action.
>
> Simplicity, humility, generosity, endurance and hard work were the marks of his ministry. Like his Master, he had a deep love for children and the shyness in his nature which some who did not know him mistook for aloofness, fell away in the presence of children.
>
> You will understand that I feel this as a personal loss but when I saw the Bishop's name in the Obituary column, I felt that it was in the wrong place. It should have been in the Births for in the ancient Christian terminology, he had been "born into eternity."

He stands best who kneels best was true of William John Simkin and that was the driving power of his life. "I know that my redeemer liveth" for him was not a pious quotation. …but a vibrant battle cry and a deep reality.

All that can die, and how little that is, will be laid in the grounds that he loved and in a setting for which he made such supreme efforts. Near places hallowed by Selwyn's love with a whisper of memory that Bishop Simkin knew Mrs Selwyn when he was a student at Lichfield.

We offer to Mrs Simkin our affectionate prayerful wishes, knowing that God will support her with the same everlasting arms in which her loved one rests, for there is no separation in the realms of love.

When I was a little boy I was frequently sent on errands by my Mother and since the economy of our humble home was very delicately poised very often my Mother would say to me as she handed me a threepenny bit, "Now hold it tight in your hand all the way." The coin, because it was so precious, was firmly to be held. The soul of our brother is so precious that the everlasting arms will hold him firmly all the way.

The souls of the faithful departed are in the hands of God, and they rest in peace. So be it. Amen.

SB 12 p 116

Sermon at the Consecration of Waiapu Cathedral: 8 October 1967

Televised

"…The sole purpose of this cathedral is worship in its widest connotation, to proclaim salvation to all creation. Salvation is free but as Bishop Obadiah Kariuki has so poignantly added, it is not cheap. Salvation is free but not cheap. If you foolishly think that it is, then look into the bloodshot blackened eyes of the carpenter who reigns from a tree, and if you are not nauseated by the exposed cheekbone and the matted sweaty hair, offer yourself an invitation to hang alongside him. The meaning of this building will depend upon how we answer that RSVP.

The last thing that any of us who have had a tiny share in the erection of this lovely building desire is that people should be allowed to think of it as ONLY a place of comfort. That indeed I pray it may be, but I look at this large body of the youth of the Diocese in their pilgrimage today, having traversed thousands of miles in their journeyings, and having walked the last portion. I look at them and say, Come here and receive the inspiration and the power which God alone can provide in its plenitude, but then take it out and use it! You go out not to preach a gospel but to *be* a gospel. A creed such as we have which tells of God born in a stable and dying on a beam of wood, surely makes you look for Him in unexpected places. Then look!

SB 12 p 88

Christmas Message to Napier Rotary: December 1967

"Christmas was not only a brainwave; it should also be a permanent wave. It is time to stop worrying about what the world was coming to, and greatly rejoice in what had come to the world." ... "For some, Christmas day will be like a birthday party for a child which ignores the child completely and gives unbounded pleasure to all the participants."

Referring to the recent heart transplant in South Africa, he said Christmas was also a change of heart operation

– "not a physical surgical miracle – but a spiritual victory."

SB 12 p 60

CEMS Service in Cathedral 20 March 1969

Referring to the National Wine and Food Festival, he said,

"This could provide a pertinent reminder that there was a continuing 'International Wine and Food Festival,' recalling the One who, referring to food said, 'This is my Body' and referring to wine said, 'This is my Blood.' Thus, was privileged the holiest toast ever proposed. Men are challenged to drink to the dregs, the toast is the Kingdom and only those with no courage are content with a mere sip."

...Some regard our present days as representing a moral landslide. The abuse of drugs is one evidence, pornographic products another. Recently it was reported that a Yugoslav writer freed from prison, was seeking permission to publish abroad historical novels which he wrote on toilet paper while in prison. Some products which appear available give the impression that they were likewise composed."

He emphasized the fact that with the number of Christians becoming smaller, it was more necessary that the quality should be better. He appealed for an all-out endeavour as a Christian family.

..."Jesus, humanly speaking, risked his message with 12 men" and posed the question "Is He safe to risk it with you and me?"

SB 13 p 103

Sermon at Community Act of Worship Cook Bi-Centenary celebrations at Gisborne 13 June 1969

… "It is not without significance that Cook sailed in the *Friendship* and the *Endeavour*; they are two signal aspects of the Christian experience." "…Friendship is a language which the deaf can hear, the dumb can speak and the blind can see. It is the essence of God."

'Give us friends' and 'give others a chance' are noble sentiments expressing the highest thoughts of all thinking Māori and Pakeha people of this glorious country which we all share for our common benefit.

… A New Zealander working in Africa said that an African chief had remarked with justification, 'Europeans know how to scratch, but they don't know where we itch.' Friendship is discerning, it seeks out need and matches it with remedy. Like Cook, it frequently sails in uncharted seas but always with high hopes. Friendship is always marked by unselfishness, unlike the little girl who wrote to her aunt, after being rebuked by her mother for not having done so. The child wrote, Please forgive me for not writing for your birthday It would serve me right if you forgot mine on Friday. Friendship is love activated and therefore seeks not her own.

…Meticulous attention to the task in hand was the hallmark of Cook's service. Could it be true of us that we have the most sublime opportunity and that we neglect it and try to cloak our failure by subterfuge? In our feeble Christian endeavour are we satisfied to be mere parasites, going through the swing door of life on somebody else's push?

The old sailing ships when they passed, would have a member of the crew bellow through his megaphone, "Whither bound?" It was always the first question, and one which could with profit be addressed to each of us in our endeavour. Our response will determine whether the Church is to be regarded as a dreaded herald of the future or merely tolerated as a survival of the past. The way in which we now play God will determine whether these are the first moments of mankind's greatest hour, or the last few seconds of his ultimate tragedy.

We need a change of heart, that is endeavour, and for a change of heart we do not need Professor Christian Barnard, but Jesus Christ. A young carpenter in the prime of life, reigning on a wooden throne, with a wooden sceptre clutched in his bloody hand and a wooden crown tearing his scalp; with the spittle of a drunken soldier oozing

A Likely Lad

down his beard, and the blood and sweat matting his hair, offers us friendship and endeavour.

A Church living as its Founder died is the best way to celebrate this occasion or any other.

SB 13 p 185

Confirmation Service St George's Whakatane 24 Sep 1969

This appears to be a transcript for the local newspaper

..."How much is a man of more value than a sheep? Matthew chap 12 verse 12.

I'd always just skipped over that; I'd read it, but I hadn't stopped to think about it. And then I did. As I don't know much about sheep, I asked some of my friends who are sheep farmers what was the value of a sheep and got rather conflicting answers. I imagine it really depends on whether you are buying or selling sheep. Well, as I couldn't get a definite answer, I am going to supply an answer which is probably wrong. But I must have a figure. I'm going to say that a sheep is worth $5. Perhaps I might add that I haven't any to sell at that price.

Now as far as a man is concerned, I've a little more knowledge. He is 70% water, there is enough fat in him for seven bars of soap; enough iron in him to make a decent-sized nail; enough phosphorus for seven boxes of matches; enough lime in him to whitewash a chicken coop; enough magnesium for one dose if he got indigestion; enough potassium to explode a small firework on November 5th; enough sulphur to rid a small dog of fleas temporarily; enough sugar in him for ten cups of tea or coffee.

If you go to a shop you can buy the lot for a dollar – or if you want a man of my size, you'd probably get it for 50 cents.

How much is a man of more value than a sheep?

Well that man is worth about a dollar and a sheep is worth about five. It seems as though the text is the wrong way round.

Some of my friends may wonder what this has to do with Confirmation. I'll try to show you. I've missed out the most important ingredient – the man's soul and spirit, that by which God speaks to him and he speaks to God. And that you cannot price.

It always used to amuse or irritate me, many years ago when I read each morning in the newspaper in the Old Country that So-and So had died worth $100,000, $300,000, $200,000. You don't die worth any amount of money.

I remember in my early days of ministry getting into hot water by saying to a congregation that when they died, they couldn't take it with them. And judging by some whom I knew, if they could, it would melt. A shroud has no pockets. All you take with you is what you've absorbed of the spirit of Jesus Christ, if He has, in deed and in truth been your Master and your Saviour and your friend. It's the likeness to Him that you take-that's all. All other possessions drop away.

How much is a man of more value than a sheep?

He can know God and give himself to God, ...and I think that this is a time in our history to be honest.

I want tonight to suggest that an occasion like this could prove to be a good occasion for all of us to be honest; to ask ourselves whether those promises that we made at our Confirmation are still real to us; whether they still mean the same thing as they did that morning or afternoon or evening when we stood up boldly, like these people here tonight, and answered that we will give God ourselves, our souls, our bodies to be a reasonable, a holy, and a living sacrifice.

Some of my young friends may say, "Well that's alright. He's probably talking to his own age group. But what about young people? Can they show their faith and belief in Jesus Christ and exhibit courage?" I believe they can.

Right Ideals:

Are you going to tell me that young people can't show their love for Jesus Christ? I don't believe it.

I think if we had less news in the press, on the radio and on the television about some of those young people, the small fringe of them, who are so-called delinquents, and had a little more about those who are doing good things, it would be for the better.

I believe that we still have young people who have the right ideas and the right ideals and are prepared to pay the price for their convictions. That is something of what it means to be Confirmed – that you nail your colours to the mast and follow in the steps of Him who went to the Cross with His eyes open and His mouth shut. Most people, and I include myself, would have probably gone with our mouths wide open, crying for mercy, and our eyes shut so we wouldn't see what was coming to us.

I want to say a word to the boys in particular. Before you decide what, you are going to make of your life, ask yourself whether God wants

A Likely Lad

you to be a priest. And don't let people put you off like the man who said he had two sons living and one in the ministry.

There are people with queer ideas, but a lot of young people have got jolly good ideas and some of them are not as dumb as other people think. Like a little boy who was left alone with a visitor and the visitor said to him, "What are you going to do when you grow very big like your father?" The little boy said, "Go on a diet!"

Some of them have got the right idea. They know one thing from another; and if you ask God quite honestly to tell you whether he wants you to be a priest, He'll tell you. He may say, "Yes, I do," and if He says that, you'll know no peace till you give yourself to Him. But he may say "No, I don't. I want you as a Christian doctor," or "I want you as a Christian lawyer," or "I want you as a Christian dentist," or "I want you as a Christian behind the counter," or "I want you as a Christian farmer." He'll tell you what He wants, and you give yourself to Him. Then you'll know peace which otherwise you won't.

I hope you will carry in your hearts and in your minds the vision that Christ in God has given you power. The power of the Holy Spirit will strengthen and guide you and encourage you. But you are never given anything to keep it is always to use. And if you try to keep it, you'll lose it. And if you give it away, you'll always have it. That sounds nonsense but if you try it, you'll find it is true.

A few weeks ago, I was shocked to hear on the early morning news of the senseless and ruthless murder of Tom Mboya in Nairobi, because I knew him 25 years ago when I was there. I suppose it was thinking of those days when I served there that brought to my mind a heathen village where a missionary had been working. At last there came day when the first person was to be baptized. After the baptism he came up to the missionary and said, "I am the first Christian in this village. Go on praying for me that I may be a good one."

That's a prayer that every one of us could use.

We are constantly being told that the number of Christians is decreasing and that by the year 2000, if it goes on at the present rate, it will only be about 20%, or even less; that only 15 people out of every hundred will acknowledge Jesus Christ in any shape or form. If there are going to be fewer of us, we must be of better quality.

SB 13 p 146

Dean Monteith's Farewell. 23 November 1969

Televised.

...Most members of this congregation have come to the service by car and after the service will return home to enjoy at leisure a liberal meal. In the early Christian church people made their way by circuitous routes to the catacombs to partake of their communion, and if unfortunately, they were detected, they themselves provided a meal for the lions. On one occasion, soon after I came to make this country my home, I was invited to speak, but I was horrified when I observed at the foot of the programme, "Procession of witness – weather permitting." My mind's eye conjured up a scene of a young Man in his prime of life with rippling muscles in arms and strong legs, born of heavy manual work. This young man, a carpenter, was appropriately enough lying on a log of wood; He couldn't move for He was nailed to it. Some desired to make sport and thrust a dowel of wood in His hand as a sceptre. To add to the fun, they twisted a crown of thorny nubk with a stick and laid it on His head and pressed it down. Then they knocked it off and some of the thorns remained and blood mingled with sweat and matted His hair. Later thunder and lightning and rain broke, and I could feel those piercing eyes looking right through me and saying, "So you will have a procession of witness, if it does not rain!"

What does it mean to us to be His friends and followers? I can never sing those words "In the beauty of the lilies Christ was born across the sea." He was born in a stinking stable and died on a bloody Cross, and we are content to be fair-weather friends.

God, born in a stable and dying on a cross, surely makes us look for Him in unexpected places – the whole world is a sacrament for those with eyes to see. ...outside the city wall they crucified Jesus, we have no inhibitions now; we do it inside.

...This is my body; this is my Blood and Jesus proposed the holiest toast ever known, the Kingdom. It is left to us to say whether we will drink to the dregs and commit ourselves to His cause completely or be cowards and just take a sip. ...It is devotion and utter commitment which will impress the world and make the church a dreaded herald of the future rather than being tolerated as a mere appendix or survival of the past for which there is no present need...

SB 13 p 184

A Likely Lad

Graces and Prayers

At the State Luncheon for Lyndon Johnson 20 October 1966
God bless His gifts for our use, and our gifts to His service, that with thankful hearts we may supply the needs of the bruised and starving. Amen.

SB 12 p 5

At the Bank of New South Wales Centennial Dinner, 10 April 1966
God grant that when our final account is drawn, we may be in credit, and to that end may God bless His gifts for our use, our gifts to His service, and keep us mindful of the needs of others. Amen.

Prayers for National Elections in *Church and People* November 1960
Lord we pray Thee for the electors in our country. May we not be led away by plausible talk, party passion, or shallow sentiment, but exercise calm and wise judgment, and choose faithful and upright men to represent us, through Jesus Christ our Lord. Amen.

Almighty God our heavenly Father, bless our country that we be a blessing to the world; grant that our ideals and aspirations may be in accordance with Thy will, and help us to see ourselves as others see us. Keep us from hypocrisy in feeling or action. Grant us sound government and just laws, good education and a clean press, simplicity and justice in our relations with one another, and above all, a spirit of service which will abolish pride of place and inequality of opportunity, through Jesus Christ our Lord. Amen.

SB 7 p 231

Humour

Law Society's Conference 20 April 1954
Bishop Lesser punctuated his speech with a number of humorous anecdotes and was accorded prolonged applause. He said he had noticed on the programme that there were two matters exercising the minds of the members of the legal profession at the conference. They occupied some 20 items on the programme and concerned food and/or fun. Eight items referred to work.

"This seems to me to be a fair division of labour and has some merit for my consideration at my forthcoming Synod." One of the stories he told concerned a cleric who for several weeks had been preparing examination papers. The following Sunday he read out the Ten

Commandments to his congregation and then unthinkingly added "Only four of these need be attempted."

He also raised laughter when he commented that he understood that this was the first time that the conference had been held "outside what is known to the four main centres as the four main centres."

SB 6 p 71

Rotorua Post column "This and That" 15 April 1967
"This is one of the few occasions when my wife and I both share the same fear. We are both scared of getting a ladder." Sa SB 6 p 23 Wairoa Debutante Ball: "Bishop Lesser, who was in full ecclesiastical dress, delighted his audience with a number of humorous asides during a brief address – in particular his remark that "this is one of the few nights of the year when my wife and I share a common fear… that we will get a ladder in our stockings."

SB 12 p 45

General Synod Address 1968
"Recently I read in the columns of "Church and People" that a pulpit was offered as a gift. It was mentioned that it was in good order and had been treated against borer. That seemed to me to be a very wise precaution, and before I finish you may well wish that this table had enjoyed similar treatment, but if you suffer frustration and boredom I can comfort you with the thought of another, that in a few years, these trying times will be the good old days."

Confirmation Tour: First year in New Zealand

He left Napier on Friday 31 October in order to preside at a celebration of Holy Communion at 7 a.m. on All Saints' Day – 1 November, a Saturday in 1947 – at Waerenga-a-Hika – a parish near Gisborne, with a few 'daughter' churches. A Rose Show and a welcoming reception for him filled the afternoon. At 7.30 p.m. on that Saturday evening he took Evensong at one of the 'daughter' churches, Makaraka, and celebrated Communion the next day at 8 a.m. at Ormond, another daughter church; took the Family Service at 9.30 a.m. at Waerenga-a Hika, administered Confirmation at 11 a.m. at Makaraka, took Evening Prayer at 2 p.m. at Waimata and had a Confirmation at Patutahi at 7.30 p.m!

The next day – Monday – was comparatively quiet: a reception and welcome in the afternoon at Patutahi, then it was off to Te Karaka, about 20 kms away, where he held a Confirmation service at 7.30 p.m. on Tuesday in their church of St John, followed by a formal welcome.

On Wednesday after a 7 a.m. Holy Communion service there was "Wednesday school" at 12.25 p.m., and a Garden Party at Matawai – about 40 minutes away in those days. He was back at Te Karaka for a Young People's Service at 7 p.m. followed by a speech to the Anglican Men's Association.

The next day the vicar "took him to Gisborne on his way to Tolaga Bay" where he had a 7.30 pm Confirmation.

On Friday he was in Ruatoria for a 2.30 p.m. Confirmation, followed by Evensong at Tokomaru Bay at 7 p.m. and a reception at 8 p.m.

Saturday 8th found him at Waipiro Bay in time for a 7.30 a.m. celebration of Holy Communion. He then returned to Gisborne where on Sunday he would speak at a special service for children at 9.45 a.m., and take Confirmation services at 3 p.m. and 7 p.m. There were also "normal" services at 8 a.m. and 11 a.m.

Somehow, he got to Opotiki, presumably by bus through the Waiwoeka Gorge on Monday 10 for a Confirmation on Tuesday 11.

From there he went on to Whakatane for a Confirmation Service on Thursday 13, preceded by a combined churches and Civic welcome for him, coinciding with the Church Bazaar in the Parish Hall.

On Friday morning there was a MU Re-Dedication service in the morning, a garden party in the afternoon at Edgecombe and a service at Taneatua in the evening – both these places being part of the Whakatane parish at the time.

Saturday began with a First Communion service for the newly-confirmed, after which he left for Te Puke "accompanied by the vicar" according to a Bay of Plenty Times" report. SB 1 p 67

While at Te Puke, he showed a friendly ecumenical spirit by attending the dedication of the new Catholic Presbytery – a gesture noted and appreciated by those present – and did well with some of the games at yet another church Bazaar.

On Sunday morning he administered the rite of Confirmation in Te Puke and went on to Tauranga in time for a Festal Evensong to mark the Annual Parish Festival.

He preached at a MU Festival on Monday 17 followed by a Confirmation service in the evening.

Writings, Sermons & Addresses

From Tauranga on Tuesday 18, "very reluctantly I drove him to Te Puke and there took leave of him, but with a very grateful heart for all he did and said to us," wrote the vicar.

From Te Puke he travelled to Rotorua where he socialised at a Garden Party in the afternoon and confirmed 16 people at 7.30 p.m. in the evening.

He left on Friday for Wairoa, presumably by bus, arriving on Friday evening. The Wairoa visit included another garden party, and a civic welcome at the Vicarage on Saturday, followed by a very busy Sunday schedule: services at 7.30 a.m. and 9 a.m. in Wairoa, Nuhaka at 11 a.m., Tuai at 3 p.m. and a confirmation at St Paul's Wairoa at 7 p.m.

He finally returned to Napier on 24 November.

Endnotes

Chapter 1: England

1. NAL
2. Ibid
3. Ibid
4. Demolished in the 1980s according the website of Liverpool Diocese.
5. NAL
6. MP "A Brief History of Victorian England" p 173.
7. NAL
8. SB 6 p 159 Article by John Rosbotham in a parish magazine 1956.
9. SB 13 p47
10. NAL
11. Fitzwilliam Hall, later Fitzwilliam College, was established for students who could not afford to belong to a Cambridge College at that time.
12. Oxford, Cambridge and Dublin Universities automatically award an M.A. on application after four or more years following graduation.
13. NAL
14. Ibid
15. Used by his daughter EP in her lay ministry.
16. SB 6 p 142
17. SB 4 p 33 Where a history of the Brigade is found.
18. NAL
19. SB 13 pp 2, 27, 47, 51 and SB 14 p 59
20. NAL
21. SB 2 pp 3-46
22. In his preface to "The Creator Spirit" he thanks "his colleagues of the Liverpool Chapter especially Dean Dwelly and my Bishop."
23. SB 2 p 42
24. NAL It seems he took his collection of services with him to Kenya.
25. NAL
26. Pers. Comm. EP
27. SB 5 p 79
28. LC Vol 1 has 46 pages of the Form and Order of the service and ceremonies to be observed on the occasion of the Hallowing of the 50th year commonly called the Jubilee Year.

Notes

29. DIO 5/9/281
30. LC Vol.3 This may be "Kinship with the Sea"; the poem "Liverpool" by Masefield with music by Shaw performed in 1930 celebrating the kinship of Liverpool with the sea.
31. Dwelly wrote the service of Consecration for the first part of the Cathedral in 1924, when he was vicar of Southport. Its success led to his 1928 appointment to a position at the Cathedral.
32. These have only recently been found by the Waiapu Diocesan archivist.
33. "A Brief History of St John the Evangelist, Barrow Island." 2010 p 4
34. NAL
35. NAL
36. SB 5 p 99
37. Pers. Comm. EP.
38. SB 15 p 18
39. BH p 3-4
40. SB 15 p 18. And the "Brief History" p 2 describes it as "Byzantine in design and constructed in ferro-concrete."
41. SB 12 p 43
42. Rev Bill Bennett's observation.
43. SB 15 p 14 This may also have been why he once suggested to Rotary that they should open their membership to manual workers. SB 6 p 156
44. SB 6 p 158 and 159
45. SB 6 p 142
46. SB 9 p 202
47. SB 4 p 17 All Saints' Taradale parish.
48. SB 4 p 17
49. SB 5 B p 41
50. SB 5B p 8 sa SB 9 p 91 for a long article on this parish in the "West Derby Report" 1962 describing the "Hut" as the "House of God and the gateway to Heaven" for those who worshipped there.
51. For 1963 SB 9 pp 141,145, 181; for 1968 SB 13 pp 1, 2, 7, 27 ,47, 51, 54, 91, 196
52. Minutes of Furnishing Sub-committee 29/5/57 p 128 "at the instance of the Bishop, the secretary was asked to communicate with Powell and Sons (Whitefriars), the manufacturers of the stained glass windows in Liverpool Cathedral."
53. Ibid 8/10/57 p 134
54. Ibid 20/11/57 p 136

A Likely Lad

55. SB 12 p 96 The block of sandstone was sent to NZ by the architect of Liverpool Cathedral as gift to a relative who in turn gave the stone to Dr Lesser to place in the Waiapu Cathedral.
56. DIO 5/9/281
57. SB 13 p 57 The Dedication at the Synod Evensong includes the words "The Dean and Chapter of Canterbury Cathedral have most generously presented to Waiapu Cathedral a white stone from the fabric of our Mother Cathedral, bearing the ancient Cross of Canterbury, wrought by the mason's skill." This stone will serve as a constant reminder of our joy on the occasion of the Dedication of our completed Cathedral on 9th March 1965 when the Archbishop of Canterbury (the Most Reverend and Right Honourable A.M. Ramsey) preached the sermon and gave the final blessing."
58. DYB 1970 p 24
59. DIO 5/9/281
60. Pers. Comm. Bishop Peter Atkins mentions him being "anxious about his Englishness."

Chapter 2: Kenya

61. NAL
62. SB 9 p 96 and in welcoming him to the 1949 General Synod, Archbishop West-Watson described him as "a missionary leader in Africa where he became Dean of Nairobi."
63. NAL
64. SB 1 p 102 Article for *The Young Churchman* a parish magazine.
65. Diocesan archives, Nairobi.
66. Pers. Comm. EP
67. NAL
68. NAL
69. Mombasa Synod Sep 1944
70. Pers. Comm. EP
71. Pers. Comm. EP who said she and her friends were terrified of being the first to fail!
72. NAL
73. NAL for the above information. sa SB 1 P 90 for reference to the Liverpool men who had served in East Africa who would have memories from the war of Bishop Lesser.
74. SB 1 p 5
75. NAL
76. Ibid
77. Ibid

Notes

78. In March 1940, sometime between this date and September 1943, and in November 1945. It may be that these are the only ones recorded.
79. Finance Committee Mombasa Dio archives.
80. All Saints' Cathedral Nairobi Chapter meeting 22/11/1945, Mombasa Dio Archives.
81. Mombasa Synod 1944.
82. TGE p 140
83. Pers. Comm. EP
84. SB 1 p 4 dated in Lesser's hand 28/3/47.
85. SB 1 p 8
86. SB 1 p 41
87. SB 1 pp 7-8
88. SB1 p 102 op cit
89. SB 2 p 128

Chapter 3: New Zealand

90. SB 1 p 11
91. DYB 1947 pp 62-64
92. Pers. Comm. Gronda Avery, Brocklehurst's granddaughter 25 February 2013.
93. WPM p 188 He had been Suffragan Bishop of Barrow-in-Furness, a position now in recess.
94. SB 1 p 111
95. WR p 131 The damage was estimated to be worth £100,000.
96. Ibid p 138
97. Ibid. p 141 It seems he had never driven a car before which must have made his position very difficult.
98. DYB 1946 p 56 "It is most important that every member of Synod observe the strictest secrecy about the results of our deliberations."
99. WR pp 141-142
100. Ibid p 142
101. SB1 p 23
102. SB 1 p 17
103. SB1 p 16
104. SB1 p 32
105. SB1 p 30
106. SB 1 pp 28, 30-31, 35, 37
107. SB 1 p 34 Vicar's letter.
108. SB1 pp 37, 49

A Likely Lad

109. SB1 p 49
110. SB 1 pp 56-57
111. SB 1 p 92
112. SB 1 p 48
113. SB1 p 49 Bishop Bennett, as Suffragan Bishop in Waiapu, had to ask permission of each Diocesan Bishop in order to minister to Māori people in other parts of New Zealand.
114. SB 1 p 53
115. SB 1 pp 35, 39, 42, 43
116. SB1 p 40
117. SB1 p 44 Vicar's newsletter.
118. The Synod Order papers are pasted into Scrapbook 1, pp 45-47 with many annotations, including alterations to motions, cross-references and ticks.
119. DYB 1947 p 57 General Synod was the only body able to change the ruling.
120. SB 1 pp 49, 85 and DYB 1947 p 57
121. DYB 1947 p 39
122. SB 1 p 56
123. Ibid p 40
124. Ibid p 41
125. Ibid p 56
126. Ibid p 50
127. DYB 1948 App 2 pp 48-50
128. SB 1 p 59
129. SB 1 p 58
130. SB 2 p 13
131. SB 2 p 2
132. SB1 pp 41, 42, 43, 44, 46, 47 61, 62, 64, 65, 66 67, 74, 80
133. SB 1 p 80
134. SB 1 pp 63 and 85
135. SB 1 p 74
136. SB 1 pp 80, 86, 88
137. SB 1 pp 86, 89
138. SB 1 p 83
139. SB 2 p 48
140. Pers. Comm. Shirley Hosking.
141. TGE p144 Hickman and Eagles say he "normally travelled to his parishes by bus preferring to arrive fresh and often composing an appropriate sermon

Notes

or two on the way." and Shirley Caudwell as a Teachers' College student in Auckland recalls seeing him regularly on the bus as far as Taupo.

142. SB 4 p 30
143. Archdeacon of Waiapu 22 June 1970 to NAL with suggested travel arrangements. He writes "There is now no early railcar from Napier" … " but Hawke's Bay Motor Co runs a bus at 8.30 a.m. arriving Gisborne 12.45 p.m. There is also a railcar leaving Napier at 1.45 p.m." Once in Gisborne, as usual he was to be ferried around by members of the clergy to his various appointments. "July 4 Oxenbridge will meet and will drive you to Te Hapara on July 5. July 6th the Rev H. Poole… will call for you at Te Hapara and take you to Ruatoria and bring you back to Waerenga-a-Hika on July 8th. July 10 Rev Fussell will take you to Gisborne for your train or bus to Napier."
144. SB 1 p 87
145. SB 1 p 86
146. SB 1 pp 79, 89 and ff
147. SB 1 p 119
148. SB 2 p 21
149. DYB 1948 p 43
150. SB 3 pp 13,17
151. SB 3 pp 9,12 reports the Bishop's visit to an Australian city was cancelled.
152. It was actually four years short of a centenary but celebrations were brought forward as it was feared Sir Apirana Ngata would not live much longer. In fact, Ngata sadly died a few months before the celebrations.
153. SB 2 pp 11, 52 and SB 3 p 16 ff and 13, 18, 22
154. SB 3 p 43
155. Pers. Comm. E.P. Others also mention the occasional Wellington visit.
156. SB 7 p 91

Chapter 4: Māori Matters

157. Pers. Comm, Archbishop Brown.
158. Ibid
159. SB1 p 49
160. Pers. Comm Archbishop Brown. Rev Bill Bennett also remarks on this.
161. Ibid
162. Ibid
163. SB 6 p152
164. SB 1 and TGE p 142. It was Canon Poihipi Kohere, to whom Lesser paid tribute in his 1962 Synod address. sa SB 9 p 70
165. SB 5 p137
166. TGE p142

A Likely Lad

167. Ibid p 140
168. SB 1 p 49
169. SB 1 p 29 Bishop Bennett pointed out that the Diocese had the highest Māori Anglican population of any diocese.
170. Pers. Comm. Archbishop Brown.
171. Pers. Comm. Colin Baker.
172. SB 2 pp 43 and 58, SB 3 p 28, SB 5B pp 33, 35
173. SB 1 p 49
174. DYB 1947 p 57 Unfortunately Bishop Simkin of Auckland who was most opposed to free entry to his Diocese, was absent from the meeting through illness.
175. DYB 1947 p 41
176. SB 3 p 25
177. SB 3 p 33
178. Pers. Comm. Faith and Nancye Panapa.
179. SB 1 pp 58, 112
180. See obituaries for two other Māori clergy Pahewa and Hutana in SB 2, pp 16, 42 and 70
181. SB 6 p 23 (sa SB1 p 89) "The Diocese of Waiapu is divided into three Native Church Board Districts with approximately the same boundaries as the Archdeaconries. A church conference or Hinota is held in each of these areas once a year. Every three years a Hui Topu or combined conference is held and the archdeaconries conference is then dispelled with." (Report from *Church and People*).
182. Hinota reports are in SB1 pp103, 104, 116
183. SB1 pp 103, 106
184. SB 1 p 108
185. SB 1 p 110 from *New Zealand Herald* 13 April.
186. SB 1 p 109
187. SB 1 p 116
188. SC had requested this in 1945,1946 and wrote again in 1947 and 1948. Each time it was refused. SC 3102;3170;3303
189. It was actually four years short of a centenary, but it had been brought forward as Ngata did not think he would last that much longer.
190. SB 3 p 20
191. SB 3 p 23 for the service book. In 1952 he consecrated the Chapel. The order of service with much marking in his hand is in SB 5 B p 36. Only one hymn uses te reo and is sung by the pupils. Panapa preached.
192. DYB 1952 p 52

Notes

193. DYB 1952 p 46
194. SB 6 p 23
195. SB6 p 35
196. SB 6 p 21
197. SB 6 p 177
198. Ibid All hymns come from *Hymns Ancient and Modern* though there is scope for Māori translations of them. Test pieces are:

For Junior choirs: *The White Paternoster* by Walford Davies.
- For Senior Choirs: *Comfort O Lord* by Crotch or *Hymn of the Cherubin* by Tchaikovsky.
- Test Hymn for Junior Choir: Hymn 328 *A and M* 164 in Māori.
- Test hymn for Senior Choirs: *The God of Abram Praise* 601 *A and M* to the first tune. (To be sung in English, Māori translation to be made for the Festival) Own Selection Hymn Own Translation Hymn from *Hymns A and M*.

199. Ibid
200. SB 7 p 188 The one in 1959 at Omahu attracted up to 3,000 people (Photo in SB 7 p 95).
201. Pers. Comm Rev Iritani Hankins.
202. SB 5B p 203; SB 9 pp 2, 22
203. SB 9 p 131 According to this report Bishop Panapa presided over each session of this Hui Topu.
204. SC Minute 5389 (4/02/60) The Finance Committee noted that "the costs of the Hui Topu were affecting the ability of the host pastorate to meet their commitment to the Diocesan programme."
205. SB 5 pp 36 37
206. DYB 1964 p 33; sa SB 10 p 97
207. Pers. Comm. Archbishop Brown Turei.
208. DIO 5/9/45
209. DIO 5/9/34 letter to Dean Childs re visit of Bishop Baker from Hong Kong
210. Finance Committee Minutes 28 August 1947 and 1947 DYB p 56 records that Standing Committee had agreed in addition to raising all Māori stipends to £300 but it was all to come from the pastorates: there would not be the usual subsidy.
211. WR p 149
212. DYB 1952 p 46
213. PGS 1949 pp 191ff
214. Ibid
215. PGS 1952 p 155. In April 1951 the Council had met to consider a report of the Native Schools Trust referred to it by the Standing Committee of General

A Likely Lad

Synod which recommended drastic action such as closing St Stephen's school. "The Council views with alarm the financial position of some of the Church Māori schools."

216. SB 11 pp 88-89 and other references, e.g. Archbishop Fisher addressed the girls who "at Dr Fisher's request" presented action songs and hakas (SB 4 p1) and on his way to Wellington stopped at Te Aute where he was welcomed by the students.
217. SB 7 p 80
218. SB 12 pp 30, 39
219. DYB 1963 p 84 Te Aute Trust Board report.
220. DYB 1964 pp 35-42
221. 1964 PGS p 25 He "trusts that Synod will be willing to assist the Trust Boards of the schools to undertake their responsibilities with some relief from the brake occasioned by financial stringency."
222. SB 10 p 94
223. PGS 1970 p 25
224. DYB 1945 p 63 Bishop Fred Bennett told Synod it was "only by the courtesy of a pākehā vicar that part of a Māori service could be broadcast."
225. SB 4 p 3
226. SB 2 p 118b; SB 4 p 3, SB 7 p 19
227. SB7 p 157
228. SC 3633 and 3689
229. DIO 5/9/34 Lesser 12/12 1956 Harry's wife had also written to Lesser asking for a transfer nearer home because of this.
230. See SB 10 pp 127, 135, 152, 157, 158, 159, 163, 164, 166, 175, 193, 198. Preaching engagements included Westminster Abbey, St Paul's, St Martin-in-the-Fields and Coventry. The complete service from St Martin-in-the-Fields is found in SB 11 p 48
231. SB 10 p 198
232. DYB 1947 p 55
233. SB 10 p 116
234. SB 4 p 13
235. SB 2 p 80
236. SB 9 p 86
237. SB 6 pp 31, 47 though the Robin family had close associations with the church.
238. PGS 1964 p 25 A similar statement was made at the All Aotearoa Hui Topu in 1962.
239. PGS 1968 p 25
240. SB 6 p 8

Notes

241. DIO 5/9/29
242. Pers. Comm. Archbishop Brown; Faith Panapa.
243. Pers. Comm. Rev C.W Bennett.
244. SB 14 pp 42 ff
245. DIO 5/9/56

Chapter 5: Faith and Finance

246. DYB 1947 p 50
247. DYB 1948 p 50
248. SC Minutes of March 1949.
249. SB 1 p 59
250. SB 2 p 60 22 November 1948.
251. SB 4 p 52; SB 5B p 74
252. SB 2 p 34 18 October 1948.
253. Morris had been to a Conference on Evangelism and was possibly reporting on it to the Clerical Conference of Synod. The words do not appear in any of the records.
254. SB 2 p 49
255. SB 2 p 85, 86 sa SB 6 p 147 for his Christmas 1955 message to parishes asking: "Do you know the Babe of Bethlehem to speak to?"
256. SB 2 pp 124, 125
257. SB 2 p 117
258. DYB 1949 p 49
259. SB 2 p 138
260. SB 2 p 146
261. SB 3 p 30. Pastoral Letter 27 September 1950.
262. DYB 1950 p 41
263. DYB 1951 App 3, p 37.
264. DYB 1951 p 27 The Committee on Evangelism continued to meet for some years. Its 1963 report suggested an annual school for clergy and pointed out that in most other dioceses evangelism was now included in the work of Christian Education committees. DYB 1963 p 72
265. DYB 1951 pp 27-8
266. SB 5B p 67
267. A combined appeal was suggested at the 1950 Synod (DYB p43) and was approved in 1951 (DYB p33). The coordinator was appointed in 1952.
268. SB 5B pp 3 and 4
269. SB 6 p 19 Nov 1953

A Likely Lad

270. SB 6 p 82 Vicar's letter.
271. SB 6 p 8
272. SC Minutes June 1952 "The bishop had prepared a list of questions for the Coordinator."
273. SB 6 p 36
274. SB 6 p 36
275. SB 6 p 96
276. SB 6 p 176
277. SB 6 p 189
278. DYB 1956 p 42
279. Ibid p 26
280. Ibid p 27
281. DYB 1957 p28
282. Ibid p 30
283. SB 6 p 191
284. Waiapu Diocesan Survey brochure 1957.
285. DYB 1960 p 40
286. SB 7 p 160
287. DYB 1962 p 18
288. SB 5 p 192
289. DYB 1962 pp 18-21
290. SB 9 pp 98-99 22 June 1962.
291. PGS 1964 p 29
292. DYB 1963 p 19
293. DYB 1959 p 26
294. DYB 1963 p 53
295. SB 9 p 169
296. SB 12 p 7 Matata 1966.
297. SB 13 p 124
298. DYB 1967 p 21
299. DYB 1969 p 20

Chapter 6: Cathedral Re-building

300. SB1 p 13
301. WR P 133 "With that in mind, Dean Brocklehurst travelled to England in 1935-6, but came home disappointed."
302. Ibid and Gibson's "Behind the Scenes" p 2 account of the Re-building of the Cathedral.

Notes

303. DYB 1947 App 3 p 38
304. DYB 1948 App 3 pp 31-32.
305. SB 2 p 22 mentions £40,000 for rebuild, more than 100 times the annual stipend of a vicar.
306. DYB 1948 p 39
307. SB 2 p 13
308. See pamphlet.
309. DIO 5/9/48
310. Pers. Comm. Archbp. Turei 2010.
311. DIO 5/9/34
312. SB 2 p 152 and p 160 for photos.
313. DIO 5/9/71
314. SC 3660
315. DIO 5/9/277
316. DIO 5/9/71
317. DIO 5/9/71 June 1951 letter bears his particular style on the first page. It outlines the important place of a Cathedral in a city and a nation, and includes the paragraph "Any artist knows that a brilliant picture can easily be spoiled by a frame that is too small or unworthy in some other particular. That is what will happen in our own case if we are compelled to build a worthy Shrine on the existing Diocesan site only." …"It would be a great pity to spoil a gem by hiding it."
318. DIO 5/9/71
319. DIO 5/9/71
320. SB 5b 56
321. 22 SB 5b p 64
322. DIO 5/9/71 and SC Minute 5249
323. Pers. Comm. Rev. Bruce White. St James' Church has buttresses.
324. DIO 5/9/34 Nov 1 1954 Middlebrook indicates that he has seen the plans of the Cathedral and he wonders if an alternative design with the altar and chair differently placed would be possible. "This would, of course, mean a great deal of careful thought and extra architects' fees."
325. DYB 1968 p15
326. DYB 1962 p18
327. DIO 5/9/71
328. SB 6 p 119
329. SB 6 p 131
330. SB 6 p 135

A Likely Lad

331. SB 6 p119
332. DYB 1955 p 27
333. "The Cathedral" DIO 281"It had been my privilege to meet the poet laureate Mr (sic) John Masefield at Liverpool Cathedral when he wrote a Ballad of the Sea and Martin Shaw, who was the pianist for the Liverpool Philharmonic Orchestra supplemented the great Liverpool Cathedral Organs... I presumed to write to the Poet Laureate and ask him whether he could find time and was willing to write a hymn for the Laying of the Foundation Stone of the Cathedral."
334. SB 10 p 166. Lesser has noted on the article "Poet Laureate wrote three hymns for Waiapu Cathedral the first time a Poet Laureate had written for NZ." and also SB 12 p 27 and p 44.
335. DIO 5/9/67 for this correspondence.
336. SWG p 36
337. SB 6 p 183
338. DYB 1957 p 31
339. DIO 5/9/71
340. DYB 1959 p 26
341. SB 10 p21
342. SB 7 p164
343. DIO 5/9/71 Although Lesser was very emphatic that the money had come from many small donations rather than a few large givers, Henry Charles' generosity was at times crucial to the progress of the building.
344. Ibid
345. SB 2 p 118
346. SB 11 p 135, 195
347. SB 9 p 22
348. SB 10 pp 94, 122
349. SB 10 p 201
350. SB 11 p 6
351. SB 10 p 100 for poster. Also for article by Dean in DT headed "Attempt to make Cathedral debt-free by March Next" (Jan 30 1965) Alongside the article is list of donors and amounts given.
352. SB 11 p 12
353. SB 12 p 46
354. SB 12 p 99

Notes

Chapter 7: Church Union

355. AKD p 125
356. SB 5B p 79
357. PGS 1949 p 27 Although Archbishop West-Watson was an enthusiast for a united church and the Archbishop of Canterbury was one of the six presidents of the WCC. Lambeth 1948 had also been forced to consider the implications of the United Church of South India, formed in 1947.
358. SB 1 p 18
359. DYB 1953 pp 36-37
360. PGS 1955 p 40 The motion was moved by Lesser and read: the duty of the Commission would be 1. to examine what so far has been achieved by the Joint Standing Committee of the three churches; 2. To secure through the Archbishop of Canterbury's Assistant for Ecumenical Relations and his committee at Lambeth information on what has been done or is being planned in other branches of the Anglican Communion; and 3. in light of these findings to report to General Synod which will meet in 1958 what action it recommends should be undertaken."
361. PGS 1955 p 112
362. PGS 1958 p 67
363. He used a similar phrase in his address to GS 1964 but changed it to "fraternising jellyfish." PGS 1964 p 27 It may be a quote from Archbishop Carrington of Canada, with whom he had corresponded on Church Union.
364. SB 7 p 63 *Church and People* January 1959.
365. SB 7 p 77
366. PGS 1961 p 55 DIO 5/9/45.
367. Ibid
368. DYB 1964 p 44
369. DYB 1966 pp 22,23
370. SB 9 p 54
371. DIO 5/9/5 Other statements indicating a lack of enthusiasm for Union have been similarly marked: lack of time for study of material; undesirable haste, "we were trying to codify our beliefs too soon"; concern that action might damage relations with Rome or the Orthodox church; heavy theological language for laymen to cope with, and nervousness "as to what they were committing themselves and the church to at this stage." SA DIO 5/9/5 10 March 1966 to the Convenor of the Tauranga meeting Rev E C Barber, "I am so glad to notice that your main concern is also my own, that we should not move so quickly that ordinary members of the congregation are baffled either by the content of our resolutions or by the speed at which they are passed."
372. PGS 1966 p 27

A Likely Lad

373. DIO 5/9/4 15 Dec 1966 Lesser wrote to Terence Loten, vicar of All Saints Taradale thanking him *"for the report of initial moves for Dialogue between the Diocese and Fathers of Mt St Mary's Seminary Greenmeadows. The report makes extremely interesting reading and I am pleased to think that such an auspicious beginning has been made."*
374. DYB 1966 p 19
375. SB 12 p 35 for full coverage including copy of service, study programme May 10-11 which accompanied it and list of churches' representatives at it.
376. DYB 1967 p 17
377. PGS 1968 p 27
378 DYB 1968 p 25 and SB 13 p 45 Lambeth also recommended that under the general direction of the Bishop, to meet special pastoral needs, non-Anglicans duly baptized and qualified to receive Holy Communion in their own churches could receive it in an Anglican church, and likewise Anglicans might attend Eucharistic services in other churches holding the Apostolic faith, and receive it as conscience dictates.
379. SB 13 p127
380. DYB 1969 p 22
381. SB 14 p 45 6 June was the date set.
382. DYB 1968 p 106 Hubert Eames, Director of Christian Education for the Diocese, had asked him to commend it.
383. DIO 5/9/21 5 April 1970
384. DIO 5/9/40 3 November 1969.
385. DIO 5/9/49 30 May 1970
386. DYB 1970 p 22
387. DIO 5/9/22
388. SB 12 p 51 *Church and People* 27/01/1967.
389. PGS 1968 pp 46-47 The report from the Commission set up in 1966 caused a lengthy debate and some division.
390. SB 12 pp 104-7
391. DYB 1967 p 24
392. SB 12 p 106
393. Ibid
394. DIO 5/9/27
395. DIO 5/9/36
396. Vicar of Dannevirke. As Dean he made changes to the Cathedral which so upset Lesser; later still he was Archbishop.
397. DIO 5/9/18
398. DIO 5/9/29 25/11/ 1969

Notes

399. DIO 5/9/14 15 July 1969
400. PGS 1970 p 24
401. DYB 1970 p 23

Chapter 8: Change in Church and Society

402. Pers. Comm Synodsman Sam Donald; Archbishop Brown Turei, Rev Bob Foster.
403. SB 15 p 93
404. PGS 1966 presidential address p. 24
405. DIO 5/9/25 15 October 1968
406. PGS 1970 p 26 He reiterated that opinion in a *Herald* interview on his retirement when he commented that "too many were seeking specialist ministries."
407. DYB 1970 address.
408. PGS 1964 p 25
409. DYB 1969 p 19
410. DIO 5/9/25
411. Ibid.
412. DYB 1966 p 19 i.e. the alternative prayer at the end of the existing service would become obligatory instead of optional.
413. Ibid
414. PGS 1970 p 21
415. DYB 1970 p 22
416. Ibid
417. PGS 1968 p 28
418. ANG101/1/70.
419. Ibid.
420. PGS 1968 pp 21, 23
421. DIO 5/9/46
422. DIO 5/9/08 9 July 1970
423. DYB 1969 p 29
424. DIO 5/9/27
425. DIO 5/9/25 19 May 1970
426. DYB 1952 p 26
427. SB 5B p 57
428. DYB 1959 p 8
429. DIO 5/9/41

430. Deaconesses Sanders, Brand, Holmes and Henn all gave dedicated service in different places.
431. PGS 1964 pp 96-100
432. SB 9 p 168
433. SB 13 p 45
434. DYB 1970 p 32
435. DYB 1970 p 21
436. SB 5B p 30
437. DYB 1954 pp 40-42
438. DYB 1958 p 38
439. SB 7 p 76
440. SB 7 p 144 sa SC Minute 4865 21/8/1958 regarding Dr Woodard in NZ.
441. DYB 1969 p 50 and DYB 1970 p 109 and 5/9/55 to committee.
442. DYB 1970 p 31
443. PGS 1966 p 23
444. SB 1 p 56
445. DIO 5/9/60
446. DIO 5/9/18 20 November 1969
447. DIO 5/9/54
448. SB 15 p 14 Interview with *New Zealand Herald.*
449. PGS 1955 SC minutes p 103; PGS 1961 p 171
450. SB 15 p 17 Editorial tribute DT
451. SB 1 p 79
452. DIO 5/9/24
453. SB 5 p 131
454. SB 5 p 95
455. SB 6 p36
456. SB 5 p100
457. SB 9.p21
458. SB 10 p172
459. SB 14 p 47
460. DYB 1958 p 44
461. SB 7 p 180
462. SB 7 p 205
463. SB 13 p 104
464. SB 11 p 62 Some writers to the paper said they hoped for a stronger response
465. SB 11 p 76

Notes

466. ANG 101/1/29
467. Ibid
468. SB 7 p 100
469. SB 10 pp 121, 124, 125
470. DIO 5/9/54
471. For other items supporting CORSO appeal see SB 9 pp 35, 36, 103; SB 10 pp 76, 85, 180; SB 11 p76; SB 12 pp 8, SB 14 p 42
472. DIO 5/9/24

Chapter 9: The Province and Beyond

473. PGS 1961 p96
474. SB7 p183
475. SC Minute 4726 19/6/58 and PGS 1958 p20
476. PGS 1961 p 38; SB 5 p 43
477. SB5 p137 and 136
478. SB 5 p 11
479. SB 5 p 10
480. SB 5 p2
481. SB 5 p 28
482. PGS 1949 p 155 For further information (7 pages report) on this see the Māori Matters section.
483. PGS 1955 SC minutes p103; PGS 1961 pp 90 and 171. There was some dissatisfaction within the membership because of the framework within which it had to work, so Lesser got members to write memos about their concerns which form part of the report to General Synod in 1961.The report concludes "It may be that the spirit of Diocesan independence is yet too strong for such a committee to exist," and it was too difficult to get agreement on any subject. "Sweeping changes would be required to achieve the freedom which some members believe to be essential to adequate prosecution of their task." Synod itself had to decide the precise functions of the Committee.
484. Ibid
485. PGS 1964 p 130
486. SB 10 p 25
487. SB 9 p 65
488. PGS 1964 p 21
489. SB11 p124
490. SB 12 p 37
491. He was appointed an "alternate" Anglican representative at the 1949 GS and again at the 1952 GS

A Likely Lad

492. SB 9 pp 37, 67 He was later President of this organisation.
493. SB 5 p P88-90 His participation was perhaps not anticipated as the service shows the name of the first reader changed from "Minor Canon M R Parani" to "Archbishop of NZ."
494. SB 12 pp 4,5,6 1966 A small card on which he has noted "Grace said at State Luncheon 20 Oct 1966" The grace was "God bless His gifts to our use, and our gifts to his service that with thankful Hearts we may supply the needs of the bruised and the starving."
495. SB 9 p 96
496. SB 9 pp 122 and many others for invitations to lunch on the "Britannia", the state banquet in Christchurch with seating plan, telegrams sent to the Queen on her arrival and departure.
497. SB 14 p 9
498. SB 12 p 8 and other refs for his consistent support of CORSO's "Freedom from Hunger" campaign.
499. On his retirement in 1970, the Convenor wrote: "Your interest in the Board is apparent and will be missed."ANG 101/1/99
500. PGS 1966 p 23 and also "prays for the day when the Province will look at our common needs and meet them from our common resources."
501. PGS 1972 p 2 and SB 15 p 70
502. PGS 1961 p 17
503. PGS 1961 p 25; SB5 p34
504. PGS 1964 p 30
505. PGS 1966 p 27
506. ANG 101/1/1
507. SB 12 p 146 Brief letter accompanying an article in *Church and People* in 1967 on alcoholism and addiction.
508. DIO 5/9/42 5 July 1966
509. ANG 101/1/29
510. ANG 101/1/69
511. DIO 5/9/42
512. Ibid August 1965 See also PGS 1964 p 21 when he thanks his "brother bishops" and says how much he values their kindness.
513. SB 9 p 98-99
514. PGS 1964 p 116
515. PGS 1964 p 21
516. SB 5 p 41
517. DYB 1962 p 17

Notes

518. SB 5 p 103
519. ANG 101/1/84
520. SB 9 p 54
521. SB 5 p 116
522. SB 9 p184 letter from Archbishop, apology for missing Lesser the previous day and saying "It will give me great pleasure if you would allow me to confer upon you the Degree of Doctor of Divinity."
523. SB 9 pp 96, 141, 145, 172, 174, 181
524. SB 9 pp 186, ff; 190-192
525. SB 9 pp 188,200
526. SB 9 p 145,168
527. SB 9 p 168
528. SB 9 p 174
529. Ibid
530. PGS 1964 p 28
531. DYB 1963 p 19
532. PGS 1964 p 30
533. SB 10 p 9
534. DYB 1964 p19
535. TGE p 147
536. PGS 1966 p 23
537. SB 6 pp 49, 56-57, 60,70 for hospital clothes tag dated 11:8: 54 Ward 3. A report of the accident in the Rotorua paper "Evening Post" Wed Aug11 1954 says the Bishop "received cuts to face and other slight injuries when the car he was in was involved in a collision in the early hours of the morning. The Bishop, who was not driving, was said to be returning to Rotorua from an evening ordination service in Opotiki. There was heavy fog at the time and an oncoming car crossed the median line." The Tauranga parish magazine reported in September that the "accident could easily have proved fatal" and although the Bishop was on the mend, he was "far from well." He was due for Confirmation there on 5 Sep but "that remains to be seen." The doctor advised the Bishop not to undertake any extra work until after his return from his annual visit to the Tauranga Archdeaconry which was to be Sep 5 to 20th The Whakatane and Edgecombe district parish newsletter reports a Confirmation on 9 Sep but says "few realized how ill our bishop felt after his recent car accident."
538. SB 13 p 4, 53
539. DYB 1968 pp 18-21
540. Ibid p 19
541. Ibid p 21

A Likely Lad

542. SB 12 pp 112, 165; SB 13 pp 8,20,27, 36,51, 55, 91
543. SB 13, pp 2,27,42,51,54, and SB 14 p 59
544. SB 13 p 91
545. SB 13 P 29
546. PGS 1970 p 20 He has with typical thoroughness corrected a newspaper report on the event "'to present a gift on behalf of Māori Anglicans... .." to "*be present* on behalf of Māori Anglicans to present ...
547. ANG 101/1/93
548. TGE p 155-6

Chapter 10: Bishop and Man of Many Parts

549. SB 1 p25
550. Pers. Comm. Wilma Raumati.
551. DIO 5/9/45 July 15 1959
552. DYB 1966 p 43
553. SB 6 p 98
554. SB 1 p 91
555. DYB 1952 pp 39-40 Synod recommended a "review in light of the increased cost of living."
556. SB 5B p 55 Pastoral letter. He asks clergy to advise him if they are not able to get away.
557. DIO 5/9/54 April 1967
558. DIO 5/9/21 and DIO 5/9/46
559. DYB 1963 p 29
560. DIO 5/9/22 and DIO 5/14/145 s.a. "Letter from America" in SB 13 p 114
561. SB 5b p 40 Pastoral Aug 29 1952 and address to 1947 Synod "My constant prayer for this Diocese is that we shall grow up as a family of God" and many other similar references.
562. Pers. Comm. EP
563. Pers. Comm. Rev B Allom 2010
564. Pers. Comm. Liz Cooney, daughter of Rev John Wilson. 2008.
565. Pers. Comm. Shirley Caudwell 2011.
566. Pers. Comm. Rev A. Gardiner.
567. Pers. Comm. Rev Bill Bennett 2010.
568. Pers. Comm. Rev Bruce White 2017.
569. DYB 1954 p 24
570. SB 15 p 3
571. DIO 5/9/27

Notes

572. DIO 5/9/46
573. DIO 5/9/27 See "Change in Church and Society"
574. She wrote a second letter, saying she had been "very nervous" about complaining but said she "had to let it all out."
575. DIO 5/9/34
576. DIO 5/9/24
577. DIO 5/9/29
578. DIO 5/9/36 and SC Minute 71:06:64
579. DIO 5/9/26 A neighbouring vicar wrote to this effect.
580. DIO 5/9/40
581. SC Minute 4538 for fares and 4644 for car. New cars were rarely available at that time. He appears to have also had a £500 loan from the Diocese of which he eventually repaid only £34 in spite of efforts to retrieve more. SC Minute 5524; 5759; 6119; 6200.
582. SB 7 p 193
583. SB 9 pp 84, 178-9
584. SB 13 p 103
585. SB 15 p 80
586. Found among A.M. Anderson's papers in Parish Archives.
587. Pers. Comm. Rev Bob Foster
588. SB1 p 63
589. Pers. Comm. Rev Bill Bennett
590. SB 11 p 204
591. Rev Bill Bennett, Archbishop Brown Turei re going into committee; Robin Nairn: People joked that to find Lesser you looked for a "cloud of smoke" and Tony Gardiner: "He always had a cigarette in his mouth when many clergy smoked pipes."
592. Pers. Comm. Yvonne Mawson 2010
593. Pers. Comm. Rev Bill Bennett
594. TGE p 142
595. Pers Comm. EP
596. Corrections to newspaper reports, parish newsletters
597. DIO 5/9/27
598. DIO 5/9/22 to John McLean 20th February 1968 " *Please excuse three items in one letter but I returned home in the early hours of this morning having driven straight back from Kaitaia and found a volume of mail waiting urgent answer and I have to be away again at the weekend.*" and DIO 5/9/6 to Talbot.
599. Pers. Comm. Denis Coon.

A Likely Lad

600. Pers. Comm. Rev A. Gardiner.
601. DIO 5/9/41
602. Pers. Comm. Rt Rev Peter Atkins sa SB 12 p 97
603. Pers. Comm. Rev B Allom 2010.
604. Pers. Comm. EP and SB 12 p45
605. Pers. Comm. Kingwell Malcolm.
606. Pers. Comm. Shirley Hosking.
607. Pers. Comm. Rev A. Gardiner.
608. Pers. Comm. Shirley Hosking.
609. Pers. Comm. Rev Bob Foster.
610. Pers. Comm. Rev Barrie Allom.
611. Pers. Comm. Shirley Hosking.
612. Pers. Comm. EP. Rev Bill Bennett and Archbishop Brown Turei also mention this. Brown Turei thinks he just liked to be among a lot of people.
613. Pers. Comm. Rt Rev John Bluck 2016.
614. Pers. Comm. Rt Rev Peter Atkins 2010.
615. Ibid.
616. Pers. Comm. Rev B Allom June 2010.
617. Pers. Comm. Rev Bill Bennett 2010.
618. SB 6 p 158
619. SB 7 p 7
620. SB 7 p 51
621. SB 9 p 95
622. SB 6 p 79
623. DYB 1962 p 18
624. Pers. Comm. Shirley Hosking 2010 and also Rev Bill Bennett who says the "social, political or theological issues of the day rarely featured in his sermons or addresses."
625. Pers. Comm. Rev Bill Bennett.
626. Pers. Comm. Shirley Hosking.
627. Pers. Comm. Rev Bill Bennett.
628. Pers. Comm. Rev A. Gardiner 19/06/2010
629. SB 9 p 90
630. SB 11 p 187
631. SB 2 p 134
632. SB 6 p 73 Pastoral letter to clergy 22 September 1954.
633. SB 11 p 161

Notes

634. SB 5b p 74 and other refs.
635. SB 14 p 27 Sermon at Centenary of HB Province.
636. SB 9 p 20 and other refs.
637. SB 9 p 201
638. SB 9 p 90
639. SB 9 p 81 1962
640. SB 10 p 108
641. Pers. Comm. Rev B Allom 2010.
642. Pers. Comm. Rt Rev John Bluck 28/10/16.
643. Pers. Comm. Rev Bill Bennett.
644. Pers. Comm. Rev Bob Foster.
645. SB 10 p 43
646. SB 1 p 59
647. PGS 1964 p 30
648. SB 6 p 134 and other refs.
649. DYB 1962 Synod address p 18
650. SB 6 p 165
651. DYB 1962 p 19
652. DYB 1954 p 27
653. DYB 1960 p 41
654. Pers. Comm. Rev Bob Foster.
655. PGS 1968 p 17
656. SB 9 p 69
657. SB 10 p 63
658. SB 6 p 158
659. LC
660. SB 1 p 93 The actual service is p 95
661. DYB 1948 p 26 In his Charge to Synod in 1948, Lesser says he sent a copy of the service with a letter of Loyalty to Their Majesties. "Their Majesties sent a gracious reply in which I was told that Their Majesties were much interested to read the form of the service that we were going to hold in the Diocese."
662. SB 1 p 93
663. SB 5B p 76
664. SB 7 p 48
665. SB 4 pp 12, 13
666. SB 6 p 115
667. SB 6 p 45

A Likely Lad

668. DIO 5/9/18 And also 1st March 1969 "Enclosed is a copy of a service which I drew up a long time ago for the dedication or blessing of palm crosses."
669. SB 12 p 24 1967 "The form this year will not be based on Evensong but ...in the idiom of the Experimental Liturgy,"
670. SB 13 p 135 1969 They accepted one hymn.
671. DIO 5/9/56 September 1958 and January 1966.
672. Pers. Comm. Rev B Allom.
673. SB 6 p 101.
674. SB 2 p 143
675. SB 6 pp 100, 101
676. SB 6 p 190
677. SB 12 pp 1, 3

Chapter 11: Retirement

678. DIO 5/9/26
679. DIO 5/9/29
680. Pers. Comm. Rev Bill Bennett.
681. SB 15 p 3
682. Ibid p 4
683. DYB 1970 p 23 and SB 15 p 17
684. SB 15 p 17
685. Ibid
686. Ibid pp 18,20 The cutting is unlabelled – a very rare occurrence – but an advertisement on the reverse indicates it comes from Dunedin.
687. Ibid p 14
688. Ibid p 16
689. Ibid p 12
690. Ibid p 10
691. Ibid pp 10, 37
692. Ibid pp 31,32
693. Ibid p 32
694. Ibid
695. Ibid pp 26,27,33
696. Ibid p 43
697. Ibid p 49 for telegram regarding this. pp 61-64 for mementoes of the event.
698. Ibid p 52
699. Ibid p 72
700. Ibid p 14

Notes

701. Ibid p 13
702. Ibid p 37
703. PGS 1972 p 2
704. DIO 5/9/48
705. For the Archbishop of Canterbury's visit in April 1983 (pers. comm Robin Nairn).
706. Pers. Comm Yvonne Mawson.
707. Pers. Comm. Rev Bob Foster.
708. SB 15 p 75
709. Ibid p 14, from "Herald" interview.
710. Ibid p 59
711. Ibid p 55 Sermon at Mt Albert.
712. Ibid p 60
713. Ibid p 66 to Taradale Rotarians 1971.
714. Ibid p 74
715. Ibid p 91
716. Ibid p 95
717. Pers. Comm. Rev Bob Foster.
718. Pers. Comm E.P.
719. SB 13 p 169
720. DIO 5/9/74
721. SB 15 p 90
722. Ibid p 68. DT 1972
723. Ibid p 90
724. Ibid p 14
725. Ibid p 90 column headed "Hinge of History"
726. Ibid p 14 Interview with *New Zealand Herald* reporter.
727. DYB 1947 p 60

Index

A

Accident 1954 167, 303
Africa 27, 28, 33, 36, 37, 162, 208, 275
  South Africa 27, 132, 143, 144, 145, 157, 274
Allom, Rev Barrie 182, 183, 304, 306, 307, 308
Alufurai, Bishop Leonard 154
Anglican Communion 27, 33, 46, 113, 127, 134, 137, 151, 164, 166, 169, 170, 243, 246, 250, 297
Anglican Consultative Council 164, 168
Aotearoa, Bishop of 40, 44-46, 53, 55, 57-60, 65, 68, 152, 154, 167, 228
Archbishops
  Allen Johnston 125, 154, 158, 206
  Brown Turei 51, 55, 58, 65, 68, 93, 178, 181, 185, 291, 299, 305, 306
  Lesser 107, 109, 111, 125, 126, 138, 142, 151, 164, 169, 199, 201
  of Canterbury 24, 33, 34, 68, 69, 108, 109, 113, 115, 118, 139, 151, 160, 161, 164, 165, 286, 297, 309
  of New Zealand 6, 23, 33
  of York 161
  Owen 150, 271
  West-Watson 33, 39, 66, 286, 297
Archdeacons 34, 38, 49, 51, 59, 67, 72, 76, 79, 92, 117, 152, 169, 179, 198, 269, 289
Atkins, Bishop Peter 213, 286, 306
Auckland 36, 38, 46, 50, 51, 62, 140, 154, 156, 160, 179, 199, 200, 207, 216, 270, 272, 289, 290
Australia 36, 64, 78, 133, 169

B

Baden-Powell, "B.P." 18, 30, 191
Baker, Colin 58, 290
Baptism 43, 50, 55, 134, 135, 136, 141, 157
Barrow-in-Furness 19, 20, 22, 39, 75, 97, 168, 191, 194, 210, 287
Bennett, Bishop Frederick - See also
  Bishop of Aotearoa 35, 55, 57, 255
Bennett, Bishop Manu 68, 154, 168, 169, 199
Bennett, Rev C.W. (Bill) 181, 285, 289, 304-308
Bible 24, 130
Bishop's Court 45, 48, 55, 202, 208
Bishop's Fighting Fund 80, 81, 82, 83, 143, 237, 248
Bishops' meetings 51, 156, 159
Bluck, Bishop John 5, 173, 188, 202, 215, 306, 307
Broadcasts
  Radio 68, 109, 148, 200
  Television 111
Brocklehurst, Archdeacon J.B. 34, 38, 59, 67, 91, 92, 269, 287, 294

C

Capital Punishment 142
Cathedral:
  Liverpool 13, 16, 18, 19, 23, 24, 30, 83, 92, 94, 98, 100-102, 104, 164, 168, 191, 215, 263, 285, 286, 296
  Nairobi 24, 26, 27, 29-32, 35, 162, 194, 286, 287
  Waiapu
    Changes to 209
    Completion of 108, 152
    Consecration 109, 273, 286
    Televising of 111

Index

Dedication 103, 104, 107-109, 183, 228, 270, 286
Design 46, 91, 92, 95, 97, 98
Foundation Stone 19, 82, 83, 100, 102-104, 111, 143, 226, 237, 249, 266, 296
Fundraising 23, 32, 38, 52, 80, 92, 94, 95, 98, 106, 107
Hymns from Poet Laureate 19, 92, 102-104, 296
Windows 23, 94, 105, 213, 272
Chaplains
  Hospital 29, 139, 157, 160
  Prison 29, 31, 142, 160
  To Liverpool Cathedral 18
  Workplace 130, 157
Charles, Henry A. 96, 100, 107, 111, 296
Chavasse, Bishop Francis 13, 15, 16, 19, 25, 82, 93, 101
Children's Homes 177, 179, 237
Christchurch 97, 113, 117, 154-156, 160, 302
Christmas:
  Christmas Day celebrations Oihi 70
  Columns in Daily Telegraph 211, 212, 251, 257, 259
  Messages to Community and Nation 250, 253
  Messages to Rotary 49, 207, 263, 265, 274
  National Council of Churches Appeal 148, 250, 251, 253
  Pastoral Letters 224, 225, 227
Church and People 35, 42, 77, 81, 106, 115, 118, 122, 144, 152, 163, 166, 175, 250, 280, 281, 290, 297, 298, 302
Church Missionary Society (CMS) 32, 36, 81
Church of England 11, 13, 25, 36, 40, 42, 50, 87, 95, 134, 138, 140, 142, 143, 153, 162, 165, 183, 239
Church of England Men's Society 36, 42, 50, 143, 165, 183
Church Union
  Apostolic Succession 114, 116, 250
  Basis for 115
  Intercommunion 121, 122, 126, 127, 157, 174
  Joint Committee on Church Union (JCCU) 154, 155
  Joint Standing Committee (JSC) 113-115, 127, 150, 297
  Negotiating Churches 112, 113, 115, 118, 120, 123, 248
  Plan for Union 112, 121, 122, 126, 127, 201, 244
  Referendum 127
  Women in ministry 157
Civic
  Celebrations 48, 100, 110, 156, 185, 282
  Farewell 203
  Reception 41, 283
  Services 48, 186, 192, 270
Commission
  Church Union 53, 113, 115-117, 125, 152
  Māori Education 51, 67
  Needs of the Church 90
  Prayer Book Revision 131
  Trends in Māori Work 72
Conferences
  Lambeth 12, 15, 21, 46, 50, 53, 58, 61, 120, 121, 133, 138, 150, 160, 167, 243, 247, 250
  Pacific Council of Churches 153
  Toronto Congress 88, 137, 163, 165, 166, 245
  World Council of Churches Assembly 46, 50, 117, 153, 162, 190
Confirmation 42, 45, 47, 48, 52, 53, 134-136, 157, 171, 181, 228, 262, 276, 277, 281, 282, 303

A Likely Lad

Consecration
  Lesser as Bishop 38, 40, 41, 112, 179, 183, 207
  Of Cathedral 24, 104, 109, 111, 187, 210, 217, 273, 285
  Of other Bishops 33, 50, 63, 153, 154, 155, 228
  Of other buildings 71, 72, 98, 194, 271
Cook, Captain 68, 156, 275
CORSO 148, 235, 301
Council of Churches
  Kenya 32, 112
  Napier 41
  National 61, 112, 113, 117, 146, 160
Coventry, Bishop of 95, 161
Cruickshank, Bishop G.C. 39, 75, 91
Curacy 14, 15, 18, 20, 22, 23, 180, 207, 211

D
Daily Telegraph 24, 104, 106, 107, 109, 141, 148, 151, 199, 200, 205, 211, 249, 251, 253-258, 260-262
Dannevirke 45, 124, 125, 126
Davis, Rev Brian (later Dean and Archbishop) 126
Deaconesses 137, 300
Deans and Sub-Deans
  Childs 213, 291
  Gibson 91-93, 108, 109, 179, 294
  Lesser 26, 30, 33, 35, 38, 286
Debutante Balls 52, 155, 281
Dedications other than Cathedral 71, 104, 109, 155, 191, 202, 228, 286
Divorce 133
  Re-marriage of divorced people 134, 157, 175, 201, 245
Doctorates 162, 164, 303
Dunedin 39, 154, 155, 159, 177, 187, 207, 216, 308
Dwelly, Dean 18, 19, 25, 191, 284, 285
Dwelly, Mrs 16

E
Easter and Holy Week 16, 44, 50, 84, 86, 143, 155, 172, 178, 211, 221, 225, 228, 252, 255, 263, 265
Ecumenism
  Christian Life Curriculum 121
  East Asia Christian Conference 117
  Ecumenical Youth Conference 122
  Intercommunion 121, 122, 126, 127, 157, 174
  Joint Board of Theological Studies 121
  National Council of Churches (NCC) 146
  Pacific Conference of Churches 117, 153, 162
  World Council of Churches 46, 50, 117, 153, 162, 190
Education
  African 28, 36, 37
  Of Māori 51, 53, 63, 66, 71, 152
Election process New Zealand 40, 152
Electoral Synods 25, 38, 39, 213
  Election as Archbishop 150, 151, 171
  Election as Bishop 25, 38, 39
Euthanasia 146, 147
Evangelism
  Diocesan Plans 76, 78, 293
  Pastoral Letters 76-79, 223
  Synod Addresses 77, 165, 232, 248

F
Foster, Rev Bob 133, 177, 181, 188, 207, 209, 299, 305-307, 309

Index

G
Gambling 147
Garden Party
  Lambeth 243
  Synod 55, 173, 188
Gardiner, Canon Sydney 179
Gardiner, Rev A. 65, 304, 305
General Diocesan Fund (GDF) 47, 74, 80, 188
General Synod 51, 56, 64-68, 72, 88, 113, 115-118, 120, 121, 123-127, 129-138, 145, 148, 150, 153-157, 159, 162, 165-169, 179, 190, 206, 215, 226, 245, 247, 281, 286, 288, 291, 297, 301
  Addresses - Synod Addresses (Extracts) 72, 118, 130, 133, 150, 165, 190, 245
Gerard, Bishop G.V. 39, 57
Gisborne 42, 43, 49, 50, 60, 61, 62, 64, 68, 69, 81, 122, 155, 156, 173, 177, 183, 275, 281, 282, 289
Golden Wedding 209
Governors-general
  Fergusson, Sir Bernard 67, 69, 70
  Norrie, Sir Willoughby 67, 99

H
Hastings 42, 43, 45, 49, 50, 62, 64, 92, 163, 185, 219, 263, 264
Havelock North 43, 82
Hinota 43, 44, 290
Hobbies 20, 182, 194-197, 201, 208, 209
Holland, Sidney PM 96, 98, 156
Holy Communion - See also Intercommunion 43, 45, 47, 55, 68, 70, 122-127, 132, 133, 135, 159, 160, 168, 201, 220, 281, 282, 298
Homes for the Aged 80, 82, 237, 269
Hong Kong
  Bishop of 65, 161
Honours 30, 203

Hospital
  Admission 167, 213
  Chaplaincy 14, 29, 139, 157, 160
Hukarere Girls' School - See also Schools 42, 45, 52, 53, 58, 63, 64, 66-68, 71, 177, 237
Hydrogen bomb 265

I
Intercommunion 121, 122, 126, 127, 157, 174
International Missionary Council 162

J
Johnston, Archbishop Allen 125, 154, 158, 206

K
Kenya 18, 22, 26-40, 42, 57, 75, 105, 191, 284, 286
Kohere, Canon Poihipi 289

L
Laity 87, 115, 126, 135, 162, 165, 168, 174, 201, 243, 245
Lambeth Conference
  1948 46, 53, 58, 167, 297
  1958 133, 250
  1968 167, 243
  On Church Union 120, 121, 298
  On Ordination of Women 138
Lesser, Beatrice 18, 19, 28, 49, 53, 137, 138, 168, 173, 176, 177, 180, 182, 188, 207, 209
Liturgy
  Revised 131-133, 139, 212, 247, 254
  Writing 19, 182, 191-193
Liverpool
  City 9, 10, 12, 14, 15, 21, 24, 285
  Collegiate School 12
  Cross 24
Lord's Prayer 43, 129, 131, 132, 254

M

Malcolm, Kingwell 91, 98, 181, 306
Māori
  Choirs 63, 71
  Conference at Synod 45, 46, 58, 64, 71
  Education 51, 53, 62, 63, 66, 71, 152
  He Karakia Mihana - booklet 71
  Hui Topu 50, 53, 60, 62-65, 68, 70, 73, 155, 160, 168, 290, 291, 292
  Language 40, 66, 70, 71
  Māori Prayer & Hymns book 160
  Pastorates 46, 50, 55, 58, 61, 62, 228
  Schools 42, 66, 67, 68, 292
  Stipends 46, 65
  Tangi 60, 71
  Urban drift 62, 71
Marriage 19, 44, 134, 139, 141, 157, 159, 201, 209, 244-246
Marsden, Rev Samuel
  Celebrations 69, 70, 161, 169
  Parramatta 169
Masefield, John 19, 92, 102, 103, 261, 296
Melanesia 50, 153-155
Ministries
  Specialised 157, 299
Ministry of Healing 139
Missions, Anglican Board of 45, 59, 150, 155, 206
Mothers' Union 44, 48, 138, 282

N

Nairobi 24, 26, 27, 29-36, 38, 51, 98, 112, 142, 162, 194-196, 278, 286, 287
Napier 19, 34, 37, 38, 42-45, 48-52, 56, 58, 68, 71, 92, 94-96, 98, 102, 106, 107, 109, 112, 137, 148, 151, 155, 156, 159, 177, 181, 183, 185, 186, 199, 203, 205-207, 209, 213, 215, 219, 229, 238, 248, 265, 281, 283, 289
Nash, Les 96, 180
Nash, Sir Walter PM 96, 110
National Council of Churches
  Christmas Appeal 250, 251, 253
  Church Union 112, 113, 117, 160
  Vietnam War 146
Nelson 40, 150, 154, 155, 230, 239
Ngata, Sir Apirana 43, 52, 53, 60-62, 270, 289
Norrie, Sir Willoughby, Governor-general 67, 99, 100
Norris Green Mission District 15, 16, 18, 23, 32, 44, 75, 129, 191
Nuclear War 143

O

Ohinemutu 60
Opotiki 49, 51, 178, 190, 282, 303
Ordination 11, 13, 36, 114, 126, 127
  As ordaining Bishop 5, 49, 173, 174, 202
  Of Lesser as priest 13, 14
  Of Women 136, 138, 157, 165, 168, 244

P

Panapa, Bishop Wiremu 53, 56, 60, 63, 64, 72, 111, 150, 151, 168, 191, 228, 290, 291, 293
Pastoral Care 62, 124, 133, 177, 199
Paterson, Elisabeth 28, 207, 215, 226
Poems and Hymns 217-221
Polynesia 153, 154, 159, 160, 239
Prayer
  Book of Common Prayer 40, 129, 131
  Cycle of Prayer 191
  Litany for Clergy 192
Preaching
  Popularity 22, 181, 182
  Style 9, 55, 101, 154, 182, 185, 186, 207, 232

Index

Primate of New Zealand - See also Archbishops 38, 113, 139, 145, 147, 148, 150, 152-154, 161, 162, 169, 205, 206, 209

Q
Queen Elizabeth 24, 69, 98, 99, 107, 156, 183, 203, 225, 234, 267, 302

R
Race Relations
  In Kenya 27, 33, 36
  In South Africa 27, 143, 144
  In sport 143, 144
  In the USA 186
Rangiihu, Canon Sam 64, 68, 69, 71, 161
Reeves, Bishop Paul 138, 206, 213
Robin, Ike 71, 243
Rosbotham, Rev John 12-14, 16, 22, 284
Roseveare, Rev Watson 39, 144
Rotary 184
  Hastings 263
  International Conference 155, 185
  Kenya 28, 105
  Napier 49, 189, 265, 268, 274
Rotorua 42, 49, 53, 63, 64, 68, 72, 167, 192, 281, 283, 303
Rowe, Archdeacon 198
Ruatoria 43, 60, 282, 289

S
Schools
  Addresses to 264, 266, 271
  Kenya 28, 36
  Māori 66-68, 71, 177, 292
  Napier Boys' High School 182, 186, 266
  Napier Girls' High School 137
  Prizegivings 186, 264, 266
Sedgewick, Bishop W.W. 40, 91
Selwyn, Bishop George Augustus 40, 168, 273

Senior Bishop 64, 144, 150, 152, 250
Sermons 6, 27, 28, 31, 34, 43, 50, 72, 174, 180, 185, 208, 210, 222, 263-275, 306
Simkin, Bishop W.J. 38, 50, 272, 273, 290
Southport 18, 33, 168, 285
Sport
  Cricket 12, 56
  Football 12, 209, 272
  Playing with South Africa 132, 143, 144, 145, 157
Standing Committee
  of General Synod 113, 153, 156, 291
  of the Diocese 46, 47, 62, 65, 67, 69, 108, 172, 215, 238, 291
St Barnabas, Roseneath 51
Stephenson, Bishop P.W. 40, 213
Stewardship 83, 88, 89, 152, 155, 167, 241
Stipends 46, 65, 172, 291
St John the Evangelist, Barrow Island 168, 215
St Matthew's, Hastings 45, 50, 92, 202
St Simon and St Jude 12, 14, 22, 23, 168
Suffragan Bishops 53, 57, 287, 288
Sunday School 9, 12, 16, 20, 29, 191, 194, 237
Synod Addresses (Extracts)
  Diocesan 43, 51, 58, 76, 78, 86, 93, 106, 132, 140, 178, 230, 267, 276, 306
  General Synod 140, 158, 190, 245, 281

T
Tangohau, Rev Harry 69
Tangohau, Rev Wi 47, 60
Taupo 38, 42, 58, 69, 117, 177, 289
Tauranga 42, 47, 49, 53, 59, 121, 135, 155, 183, 282, 283, 297, 303

Te Aute
  Centennial 52, 62
  Trust Board 67, 68, 154, 155, 228, 292
Te Karaka 281, 282
Te Puke 49, 59, 121, 282, 283
Theological Colleges
  Australian 162
  Ridley Hall 13
  Siota 154
  St John's 69, 179
  Te Rau 62
Theology 114, 129, 133, 168, 212
Toronto Congress 88, 137, 163, 165, 166, 245
Tuti, Bishop Dudley 154

V
Vicarages 85, 137, 172, 193, 207
Vietnam War 143, 145, 160

W
Waerenga-a-Hika 281, 289
Waipawa 51, 191, 192
Waipukurau 40, 45
Wairoa 48, 49, 63, 64, 71, 73, 155, 186, 193, 267, 281, 283
Waymouth, Archdeacon Stephen 117, 126, 152, 153, 169, 179, 244
Weddings 43, 44, 140, 141
Wellington 2, 43, 45, 51, 53, 59, 62, 98, 99, 120, 150, 153-156, 159, 182, 215, 228, 271, 289, 292
Wells programme 83, 84, 85, 237
Westley, Rev Arthur 176, 177
Whakatane 49, 51, 63, 147, 184, 276, 282, 303
White, Rev Bruce 174, 180, 295, 304
Williams, Bishop Herbert 39, 91
Woodard, Dr Christopher 139, 300

Y
Youth Conferences 122, 155
Youth Services 131, 155, 183, 187, 193, 210, 218, 282